Advance Praise for *Job in Exile*

"Writing as a postevangelical ethicist, Gushee enters his Joban protest, not against God but against the abuses of theology and Christian community through bombastic God-talk. His close reading of the text is deeply dialogical, engaging translators, interpreters, and theologians ancient and modern, Jewish and Christian. Thus he equips 'everyday readers' to accept the book's critical challenge to live honestly, faithfully, and with compassion in the midst of our most acute suffering."

—Ellen F. Davis, Amos Ragan Kearns Distinguished Professor of Bible and Practical Theology, Duke Divinity School

"In his groundbreaking book, *Job in Exile,* David Gushee explores what happens when our experiences of God don't align with the theology held by our community—something most American Christians have experienced at least once in their lives. Gushee is one of the most accessible theologians and ethicists of our time, and this book is a must-read for anyone navigating the deconstruction and reconstruction of their faith!"

—Zach W. Lambert, author, *Better Ways to Read the Bible;* pastor, Restore (Austin)

"In *Job in Exile,* David Gushee offers a searching, pastorally attuned, and theologically rich interpretation of Job. At once a work of biblical exegesis, moral theology, and spiritual accompaniment, it unfolds not as a conventional commentary but as a series of meditations on pivotal moments that illuminate a journey through exile, protest, to the reconstruction of faith. Gushee presents Job's witness amid inexplicable suffering as pointing to the faithfulness of relentless, even confrontational questioning of God. Drawing on a wide range of voices and traditions, Gushee's close reading of Job refuses both reductive theodicies and brittle certainties without yielding to despair, offering instead a compelling vision of faith that can sustain solidarity, truth-telling, and hope in a fractured and wounded world."

—The Rev. Canon Prof Luke Bretherton Regius Professor of Moral and Pastoral Theology University of Oxford

"Widely read and profoundly thoughtful, David Gushee guides the reader through the Book of Job, passage by passage, in a compelling, complex, and highly provocative manner. He champions both the theological critique of Job and the profoundly moral lesson that, in a troubled and challenging world, we cannot leave it to God but must take responsibility. Anyone who has ever read the Book of Job, should read it through again with Gushee's book."

—Edward L. Greenstein, professor, Bar-Ilan University author, *Job: A New Translation*

"*Job in Exile* is a brave and ethically compelling companion for all who have been wounded by suffering and estranged by religious certainty. David Gushee, as a scholar-practitioner-activist of our times, gives spiritual refugees a wise, compassionate guide for wrestling toward truth, justice, and a more honest faith."

—Stacey Floyd-Thomas, E. Rhodes and Leona B. Carpenter Chair and Professor of Ethics and Society, Vanderbilt University Divinity School

"David Gushee brings his customary blend of astute intelligence, spiritual sincerity, and ethical passion to this study of the Book of Job, showing that whether or not the book is a midrash of Wisdom literature and the prophets, it is a gusher of spiritual daring that never runs out."

—Gary Dorrien, author, *Over from Union Road: My Christian-Left-Intellectual Life*

"Post-evangelicals will recognize the Job Gushee reveals: scorned by his faith community for an integrity that dares question dogma, Job discovers wisdom that can only be found in the ash heaps of comfortable religion."

—Rebecca Bell, lead pastor Threads Church, Kalamazoo, Michigan

"With exegetical rigor and hard-won moral clarity, David Gushee unlocks the Book of Job as a rich resource for anyone wrestling with oppressive, unjust, or abusive uses of faith and Scripture, whether in the academy or in lived experience. Biblical scholars, public theologians, and spiritual refugees alike will find in these pages both a credible guide and a deeply liberating companion."

—Dion A. Forster, University Research Chair and Professor of Public Theology and Ethics, Vrije Universiteit Amsterdam; Extraordinary Professor of Systematic Theology and Ethics, Stellenbosch University

"Shakespeare's plays are often set in contemporary contexts, thus illuminating things in both the text and ourselves. In reading the ancient biblical tale of Job as a guide for contemporary spiritual refugees, David Gushee creates the same effect. We see the complexity and profundity of this great story anew, and we gain fresh insight, compassion, and hope for those of us whose spiritual and religious journeys have been marked by change and loss. In *Job in Exile,* Gushee is the Bible teacher, the ethicist, and the pastor the church needs today."

—Steve Watson, pastor, Reservoir Church author, *All Flesh Shalom: Larger, Freer, More Loving Readings of the Good News of Jesus*

Job in Exile

Job in Exile

A Guide for Spiritual Refugees

David P. Gushee

ORBIS BOOKS
Maryknoll, New York 10545

The publishing arm of the Maryknoll Fathers and Brothers, Orbis seeks to explore the global dimensions of the Christian faith and mission, to invite dialogue with diverse cultures and religious traditions, and to serve the cause of reconciliation and peace. The books published reflect the views of their authors and do not represent the official position of the Maryknoll Society. To learn more about Maryknoll and Orbis Books, please visit our website at www.orbisbooks.com.

Published by Orbis Books, Box 302, Maryknoll, NY 10545-0302.

Manufactured in the United States of America

Library of Congress Cataloging-in-Publication Data

Names: Gushee, David P., 1962- author
Title: Job in exile : a guide for spiritual refugees / David P. Gushee.
Description: Maryknoll, NY : Orbis Books, [2026] | Includes bibliographical references.
Identifiers: LCCN 2026002486 (print) | LCCN 2026002487 (ebook) | ISBN 9781626986923 trade paperback | ISBN 9798888661437 epub
Subjects: LCSH: Bible. Job | Job (Biblical figure) | LCGFT: Commentaries
Classification: LCC BS1415.53 .G87 2026 (print) | LCC BS1415.53 (ebook)
LC record available at https://lccn.loc.gov/2026002486
LC ebook record available at https://lccn.loc.gov/2026002487

To the Seeking the Kingdom Class

First Baptist Church, Decatur, GA

In loving gratitude

Contents

Preliminary Notes

Translation of Job is notoriously difficult. Comparing Bible translations often makes me wonder if translators were actually looking at the same text. I began by using my preferred English translation, the New Revised Standard Version (usually cited as NRSVue = updated edition, 2021), and have kept it near at hand. I also found the New American Standard Bible (NASB) helpful because of its tendency toward the most literal rendering of the Hebrew, as it often also doesn't smooth out the textual difficulties.

During the exegesis process, however, I began to frequently use and soon preferred the version of the Hebrew Bible offered by the 1985 Jewish Publication Society translation (NJPS). What makes it preferable, in my view, is that it seems *braver,* more willing to translate passages in a way commensurate with the radicalism of the book of Job, not amending or softening the text to protect pious sensitivities. Frankly, it also seems right that I should use a translation of the book of Job that comes from the Jewish community.

Many commentators also offer their own translations. I cite these commentaries as standard books in the Works Cited at the end of this book.

The book of Job and thus the NJPS use male pronouns for God. The NJPS, further, capitalizes male pronouns when it concludes that they refer to God: He, Him, etc. Biblical Hebrew does not distinguish capital and lowercase letters, so capitalization is itself a translation decision.

While quite concerned that many who are spiritual exiles find gendered male pronouns for God problematic and potentially harmful, after careful consideration I retain this practice here, using male pronouns for God in a few places when quoting the biblical text—though not when offering my own thoughts. I do so only when it is necessary to make clear who Job or his friends are talking about when it's otherwise difficult to discern who is being referenced.

* * *

Hebrew Transliteration

This book employs a hybrid Hebrew transliteration style, using the Society of Biblical Literature's Academic style for consonants and its General Purpose style for vowels. In this way, the consonants are easily identifiable for scholars while simplifying the vowels for the general reader. Note the following partial pronunciation guide:

ʾ	(not pronounced)
ʿ	(not pronounced)
ḥ	ch (Scottish *loch*)
ṣ	ts
ś	s
š	sh
ṭ	t

Abbreviations

Biblical Books

Hebrew Bible/Old Testament (HB/OT)

Gen	Genesis	Song	Song of Songs
Exod	Exodus	Isa	Isaiah
Lev	Leviticus	Jer	Jeremiah
Num	Numbers	Lam	Lamentations
Deut	Deuteronomy	Ezek	Ezekiel
Josh	Joshua	Dan	Daniel
Judg	Judges	Hos	Hosea
Ruth	Ruth	Joel	Joel
1–2 Sam	1–2 Samuel	Amos	Amos
1–2 Kgs	1–2 Kings	Obad	Obadiah
1–2 Chr	1–2 Chronicles	Jonah	Jonah
Ezra	Ezra	Mic	Micah
Neh	Nehemiah	Nah	Nahum
Esth	Esther	Hab	Habakkuk
Job	Job	Zeph	Zephaniah
Ps(s)	Psalm(s)	Hag	Haggai
Prov	Proverbs	Zech	Zechariah
Eccl	Ecclesiastes	Mal	Malachi

New Testament (NT)

Matt	Matthew	Gal	Galatians
Mark	Mark	Eph	Ephesians
Luke	Luke	Phil	Philippians
John	John	Col	Colossians
Acts	Acts of the Apostles	1–2 Thess	1–2 Thessalonians
Rom	Romans	1–2 Tim	1–2 Timothy
1–2 Cor	1–2 Corinthians	Titus	Titus

Phlm	Philemon	1–3 John	1–3 John
Heb	Hebrews	Jude	Jude
Jas	James	Rev	Revelation
1–2 Pet	1–2 Peter		

English Bible Translations

CEB	Common English Bible
CSB	Christian Standard Bible
Douay-Rheims	Holy Bible translated from the Latin Vulgate
ESV	English Standard Version
GNB	Good News Bible
HCSB	Holman Christian Standard Bible
ISV	International Standard Version
JPS	Jewish Publication Society Version, 1917
KJV	King James Version
LB	Living Bible
LXX	Septuagint, ancient Greek translation of the HB
NAB	New American Bible
NABR	New American Bible, Revised Edition
NASB	New American Standard Bible, 1995
NCV	New Century Version
NEB	New English Bible
NET	New English Translation
NETS	New English Translation of the Septuagint, 2d ed. 2009
NIV	New International Version
NJB	New Jerusalem Bible
NJPS	*Tanakh: The Holy Scriptures: The New JPS Translation According to the Traditional Hebrew Text,* 1999
NLT	New Living Translation
NRSV	New Revised Standard Version
NRSVue	New Revised Standard Version, Updated Edition
REB	Revised English Bible
RSV	Revised Standard Version
TNIV	Today's New International Version

Introduction

The Irresistible Book of Job

Job is one of the most difficult, provocative, and challenging books in the Bible. Many adventurous believers have made a serious effort at interpreting it, while others have stayed as far away from the book as possible. With Job, it seems to be either one or the other. The daunting questions raised by the book mean that it is not for the casual reader. But for those willing to wade in, it is a feast!

The book of Job tells the story of an exceedingly wealthy, morally upright, religiously devout ancient Near Eastern man whose glorious life is shattered—with God's permission—as a test of his character and devotion to God. Violently and rapidly losing his possessions, servants, children, and health, Job suffers catastrophically.

At first, Job responds with perfect submission. His friends Eliphaz, Bildad, and Zophar come from afar to comfort him, sitting with him on an ash heap in silence for seven long days and nights. When Job speaks again, his submission turns to protest: in graduating steps of increasing intensity he directly challenges God's justice. The friends likewise gradually intensify their challenge to Job even as they defend God, implicating Job as the ultimate source of his own miseries.

Job and his friends end up at a bitter impasse, as Job defends his innocence and demands to hear directly from God. Following an intervention from a young interlocutor, God finally does appear, with a response whose relevance to Job's plight has been debated ever since the book was written. After his encounter with God, Job *appears to be* humbled and satisfied by God's response. God then declares Job vindicated. His friends, in turn, are repudiated. The story ends with Job getting new children and being blessed by God with exactly double the number of his earlier possessions.

The book of Job evokes intense questions about God, ethics, community, suffering, and more. Here are just a few of them:

The story opens with an angelic being convincing God to allow an orchestration of extreme suffering and loss for Job. Is this "blessed orchestration of suffering" how we should understand the source of Job's suffering, and our own?

Job initially responds with perfect acceptance and submission, not uttering a word of protest. Is this what God expects of believers who suffer?

Job rapidly shifts stance, from perfect submission to angry protest. What should we make of that shift? Is protest an expression of piety, or a violation of it?

Job's protests offer the most intense sustained critiques of God seen in the Bible. Is Job an over-the-top heretic, or are we to take him as raising legitimate questions? And is his form of questioning appropriate under the circumstances?

Job's friends constantly defend a doctrine that the good prosper and the wicked suffer, and that this explains Job's plight. What are we to make of this ancient claim, which sometimes seems to fit with reality yet so often turns out to be deeply incompatible with reality?

Job constantly defends his innocence, and the text affirms that he is indeed upright: a person of integrity, innocent, blameless. But is any human being truly *blameless*? And being blameless, during the unfolding of the book's events, is there still room for moral growth? Does Job reveal himself to be a person who has something more to learn?

When God finally appears to Job, He takes Job on a detailed tour of the creation and asks Job whether he was there when it was made or if he understands how it is sustained. Is this really even an answer to Job's tormented questions about suffering?

The story ties neatly in a bow as Job is vindicated. But *which* Job is vindicated, the submissive Job of Job 2, the protesting Job of Job 3–31? Or the version of Job presented at the very end of his encounter with God in Job 42:1–6?

Were Job's friends wrong to defend God from Job's attacks, relying as they did on religiously traditional moral-order-of-the-universe claims?

If they were wrong, what do we make of those claims when they appear not only in the book of Job but also elsewhere in the Bible?

In the end, what is the book of Job attempting to teach us? And why was this singular book included among the others in the canon of the Bible?

* * *

Few biblical texts provide as many head-snapping contradictions and interpretive challenges as the book of Job. Among the biblical texts, no other book is as morally and theologically complex, drawing so many to this maddeningly complex book, which legendary Jewish rabbi-scholar Martin Buber called "one of the special events in world literature."[1]

Robert Gordis, a brilliant twentieth-century Jewish biblical scholar who devoted decades of study to Job, articulates the mysterious drawing power of the book of Job this way:

> Some years ago an American scholar declared that just as the humblest actor harbors a secret ambition to play Hamlet, so every biblical student nurtures the hope of some day writing about Job. The truth is that Job is a perennial challenge to every reader and biblical scholar. This "Mount Everest" of the human spirit continues to defy even the most intrepid and confident of climbers and probably will never yield all its secrets. For every aspect of the book poses problems that each reader and student must solve for himself.[2]

Yes, this is one of the reasons I seek to join those who have sought to scale Mount Job. But there is also another critical reason.

A Postevangelical Ethicist's Reading of Job

Job is a book that belongs first to the Jewish people and the Hebrew Bible. Anyone venturing a serious examination of the book must read it within its original literary and communal context and attend to its long history of interpretation within the Jewish community.

Job is also part of the Christian canon and has attracted two millennia of Christian interpretation, with its own context that also challenges

Christians attempting to read the book today to attend to these earlier readings and the varied history of interpretation.

Like any truly transcendent work of human civilization, Job also belongs to the world. It is not only rabbis, priests, theologians, philosophers, and biblical scholars who have been drawn to the book. The more I read in Job research, the more I discovered exactly how many well-known intellectuals and artists felt as compelled as I did to take on this book. Psychologist Carl Jung, theologian Søren Kierkegaard, and playwright Archibald MacLeish all wrote about Job. It turns out that Job is not so much a man or a book as it is a long continuous tradition of reflection.[3]

Some might consider my scaling of Mount Job a task far outside of my field of Christian ethics. It is true that I have found few other Christian ethicist working in the Job literature. But this is odd, because the book of Job is suffused with ethical themes, as one would expect in a book long classified among the Wisdom writings of the Hebrew Bible. The ethics of humans and the ethics of God are profoundly challenged in the book of Job, as we will continually see.

While some biblical scholars have been raising questions about the coherence of "Wisdom" as a category of books in the Bible,[4] there are good reasons why the Jewish and then Christian traditions have offered such a category and grouped certain books together in the canon. Certainly, the concerns addressed in the biblical texts (formerly) known as Wisdom books are suffused with ethical themes. These books, most clearly the book of Proverbs and the intertestamental book called Wisdom, are filled not only with moral exhortations but also with a vision of a divinely given moral structure to the universe and therefore to human life and with the promise of reward for those who align their lives with the grain of the universe—and punishment for those who do not.

But the book of Job also presents what can be considered a challenge to the Wisdom tradition, or is at least a stark variation within that tradition, one that contests a reliable, divinely given moral order rather than proclaiming it. More precisely, as Job scholar Carol Newsom points out, through the book's use of dialogue both sides of that argument are heard and re-heard. "Dialogue is at the heart of the book of Job," argues Newsom.[5] If we see Job as part of the Wisdom tradition, we can see that it was a dynamic and contested tradition rather than a static one. The book of Job both adds to the complexity of the tradition and uses what Newsom calls a "polyphonic" approach: host all those different voices within the book.

Amidst his great and unmerited suffering, the character Job both defends his own moral integrity and attacks the idea that God reliably delivers justice to human beings. The book of Job therefore destabilizes one of the most important bases for historic moral exhortation and behavior. It is not the only biblical book that does so, but nowhere is the attack more sustained. As a Christian ethicist, I have felt drawn to take up this conversation for several decades.

Ethics is not just about individual behavior but also about community. My reading is that the community around Job—which includes but is not limited to his three friends—turns on him when his challenges to their beliefs prove more troubling than they can bear. Job is a pious and respected member of a religious community (that is, a human community shaped by a shared religious worldview and ethos) until his terrible life experience forces him into a state of spiritual exile as he presents disorienting challenges to that community's orthodoxy.

This dimension of Job is what caught my attention in 2019 when I taught the book in my Sunday School class because by that time, and especially in that class, I found myself among a community of those who had left or been pushed out of their former religious communities in some branch of conservative American Protestantism. The reason we had left or been pushed out was because our experiences—and our religious interpretations of the same—challenged our former church communities seriously enough that we were forced into exile. That was certainly true of the Seeking the Kingdom class at First Baptist Church. At least 30 percent of the members at that time were LGBTQ+, with a significant number of attenders also people of color in a historically white denomination and this particular historically white Baptist church.

Together we saw a pattern emerge in Job, a pattern often seen in contemporary religious life. Defenders of religious orthodoxy often seek to crush any dissent to tradition offered by believers whose life experiences ultimately lead them to challenge their tradition's claims.

But just as with Job's friends, the answer to this concern almost always comes down to this: *We who hold tradition* are the holders of fixed and certain truths within that tradition. Under no circumstances will we allow *another's* experiences to prevail over our traditions. No evidence can pierce the armor of Orthodoxy and Absolute Truth as we have understood it.

The book of Job is precisely about this challenge, as the defenders of orthodox tradition encounter real life in the embodied suffering of a particular human being.

What makes Job even more interesting is that the character Job himself gives every evidence of having been deeply embedded in, even a leader of, the very communal religious tradition that he now challenges.[6]

Because I now write this meditation on Job as one of the religious exiles, as someone pushed outside of the community of evangelical Christianity, this book is an offering of one spiritual exile's interpretation of Job. While I write as a postevangelical, I sense the vantage point I explore also applies to people in other religious communities who find themselves heirs to a tradition that they love but now must leave.

Just as postevangelicals often find that challenging one part of tradition requires them to challenge much more of it, Job does too. He must reconsider what he believes about God, about reality, about morality, about community, about injustice, and about tradition.

Job as a Crisis-Driven Challenge to Religious Orthodoxy

A close reading of the book of Job suggests that the work itself is a kind of postorthodox writing, or at least a serious challenge to the received Jewish orthodoxy at the time of its composition. The book contains challenges to specific sacred texts that by the time of Job's composition had likely already attained the status of Scripture in the Jewish community. It certainly contains challenges to broadly shared theological assumptions. Indeed, some scholars suggest that it challenges the entire Jewish legal/covenantal tradition.

This idea that Job is a book questioning antecedent biblical theology and sacred texts is debated. In part, the veracity of that claim depends on when the book is believed to have been written. But I concur with the biblical scholars who follow relevant clues within the book itself related to language, intertextual references, and major themes in placing the composition of Job during or after the Exile (587–538 BCE), when the Jewish people were crushed by the Babylonians, the Temple destroyed, the monarchy annihilated, tens of thousands murdered or perished, and surviving leaders taken into exile.[7]

The idea that the author of Job reflects *both* personal and communal suffering—as if he had suffered through the catastrophe and lost many and much in the process, along with his community—is a compelling one. Liberation theologian Gustavo Gutiérrez writes, "The Book of Job . . . could have been written only by someone who had suffered in flesh and spirit. Job's protesting lament bears the seal of personal experience."[8] And Buber writes, "It is true it is a personal fate that is presented here, but the stimulus to speaking out, the incentive to complaint and accusation, bursting the bands of the presentation, are the fruit of suprapersonal sufferings. Job's question comes into being as the question of a whole generation about the sense of its historic fate."[9]

More recently, biblical scholar Alexander Breitkopf has argued, "The book is not in its essence a story of an individual from a long time ago and a faraway place but rather a story of identity and identity formation for a devastated people who had found themselves in a devastated landscape."[10]

The situation facing that community was powerfully imagined two generations ago by Hebrew Bible scholar John Bright, who argued that after the Exile, "Israel as a whole clung to the orthodox equation in its most stringent form: sin leads to physical punishment, righteousness to material well-being, in this life. But this neat orthodoxy, though not without its truth, was simply not adequate to cover the case. . . . The problem could not be suppressed."[11]

Job thus deals with a crisis raised by the dissonance between the majority voice of the legal-covenantal-prophetic tradition and the bitter experiences of the heirs to that tradition.

To do so, the book's author(s) had to then deal with the entirety of the foregoing tradition. Hebrew Bible scholar Ellen Davis argues that the book of Job is "marked by multiple echoes of other parts of Scripture," not just in the Wisdom literature (as historically understood) but also in the prophets.[12] She writes, "The book of Job is thus a midrash of gigantic proportion, an imaginative expansion of an earlier scriptural tradition."[13]

The claim holds weight, and it makes for another dimension of the book of Job's fabulous complexity. A book whose setting is envisioned as the ancient human past, and that involves only characters who exist before the birth of the Jewish people, was probably written by Jewish author(s) rather late in the canonical game, late enough to engage acutely important questions of Jewish theology and identity—in light of tremendous historical suffering on the part of the Jewish people—and even to challenge what had emerged as sacred Jewish Scripture, in multiple genres.

As it does this, Job connects powerfully with the questions being raised today by many on the other side of a religious orthodoxy that holds as a tenet that it is almost always wrong to question Scripture and/or tradition, which are often described not just as authoritative but perhaps even infallible. That such claims are not plausible, and not even necessary for robust faith, could hardly be more clearly demonstrated than by reading a book *within the biblical canon itself* that challenges Scripture and tradition. The book of Job itself demonstrates that the best way to show respect to ancient canonical texts is to wrestle with them!

Approach: Meditations on Pivotal Moments in Job

At the beginning of this project, I considered writing an entire commentary. As I write I am looking at the more than two dozen commentaries that I have assembled that treat the entire book of Job, verse by verse. They are very impressive achievements, involving scholars who have devoted their entire lives to studying the Hebrew Bible and/or the book of Job. While impressed by such formidable, specialized knowledge, it became clear to me that commentary writing should be left to the experts.

While I have read widely in the scholarly literature on Job and have indeed undertaken a verse-by-verse exegesis in the quiet of my study, this book develops a series of meditations for the reader not on the whole text, verse by verse, but on *pivotal moments* in Job. These pivotal moments, in *my* judgment as a postevangelical Christian and an ethicist, reflect the same concerns that first motivated me to enter close study of this book.

As I introduce each of these moments, I offer relatively brief reflections mixing scholarship with heartfelt personal reflection. This book of meditations is written to be accessible to all, requiring no technical expertise on the part of the reader—though occasional deeper dives into translation challenges will be necessary.

There will never be a single interpretation of the book of Job. I do not believe it was written with such a purpose in mind. Biblical scholar J. Richard Middleton has written, "The text of Job remains fundamentally polyvalent and will undoubtedly continue to exercise interpreters for millennia to come."[14] All we can offer are *readings* of Job. I am offering mine. I will join those who attempt to read Job for itself, not to force a harmonization of the book of Job with other texts in the canon—or with the kind of fragile orthodoxy that the book itself attacks rather than reinforces.

About the profound challenge of interpreting the book of Job, Robert Gordis writes:

> The interpreter of Job must possess the elusive ability to penetrate to the spirit and intent of a work of genius. The book is too profound and complex an achievement to yield up all its secrets easily; but if we approach it with knowledge, humility, and insight, we may be able to enter the precincts of this noble temple, sacred to beauty and truth.[15]

This Mount Job presents quite a challenge. Together, let us meet the challenge, make the attempt, and discover the precincts of the noble temple.

I

The Prologue and First Soliloquy of Job (Job 1–3)

1

The Blameless Job and His Family (Job 1:1–5)

There was a man in the land of Uz named Job. That man was blameless and upright; he feared God and shunned evil. Seven sons and three daughters were born to him. . . . That man was wealthier than anyone in the East. It was the custom of his sons to hold feasts, each on his set day in his own home. . . . When a round of feast days was over, Job would send word to them to sanctify themselves, and, rising early in the morning, he would make burnt offerings, one for each of them.

—selected from Job 1:1–5*

The Greatest Man of the East

We meet the man Job and his story with the first words, *There was a man in the land of Uz*. A more literal translation of that phrase reads, "A man there was in the land of Uz, Job was his name." Biblical scholars consistently note the unusual idiom here. This way of starting connotes storytelling rather than historical narrative. The way we would read "Once upon a time" rather than "The United States was attacked on September 11, 2001." This way of setting the scene signals to readers that "what we have here is a tale and not actual history."[1]

But if so, it is a tale the narrator then takes pains to locate in a particular place. No one really knows where Uz was, though scholars know where it wasn't: *Israel*. Scholars scatter placement of Job, variously, in

* All translations are from the New Jewish Publication Society Bible (NJPS) unless otherwise noted.

Edom, northern Mesopotamia, Arabia, or Syria. Perhaps the best answer is to accept "the East" (Job 1:3). He was not Israelite, not Jewish, but a man of the east—or, more mythic-seeming in print, "the East."

Not only his place but Job's name has been hashed over by scholars. The Hebrew is normally transliterated today as *iyyob*. Scholars have attempted to attribute meanings to the name based on etymology. Three common suggestions link the name to these phrases: "Where is the (divine) father?," "the persecuted one,"[2] and the one treated as an enemy.[3] All are certainly themes of the book, but the text itself offers no comment on the meaning of Job's name.

Scholar Marvin Pope cites examples showing that Job was "a fairly common name among western Semites in the second millennium B.C."[4] There is but one reference to the name in the Hebrew Bible outside the book of Job, in an obscure corner of the prophet Ezekiel (14:12–14), where Job is associated with Noah and Daniel (or Dan'el), paragons of righteousness in the ancient world. Both righteousness and ancientness offer relevant links to the book of Job.

The first thing we learn about Job is, indeed, his remarkable virtue. The description comes in two striking pairs, a fact that was noted by biblical scholar Edouard Dhorme in the first major Job commentary of the twentieth century. Job is "blameless" (Heb: *tam*), which means his virtue is complete, finished, and whole.[5] In Gutiérrez's meditation on Job, he translates the term as "a man of integrity."[6] He is also "upright" (*yašar*), which means honest, straight, just, righteous, consistently excellent in his conduct, notably in his treatment of others. Job is exemplary in terms of demonstrating the moral virtues honored in his community—and in many communities.

To say that Job "feared God and shunned evil" is another familiar pair in the Wisdom literature (Prov 3:7; 14:16; 16:6). The righteous person shows reverence for God by actively shunning evil—turning away from evil, not dabbling with evil.

Job is also immediately described as a person blessed abundantly. Dhorme noted that the grammatical construction of the key sentence can be read (or perhaps should be read) to link the description of Job's virtue with the blessings described in the next two verses. Built into the translation, it would read like this: "Job feared God and shunned evil, *and so* he was blessed with seven sons and three daughters," and a whole lot more.[7]

Job's abundant blessings indeed begin with his children—seven sons and three daughters. Sons were valued more than daughters, further evidence of Job's good fortune, that is, in a patriarchal society.

With a mythical, fable-like symmetry, Job's material prosperity also comes in sevens, threes, and tens—in this case, adding up to thousands of animals, which together indicate that Job has agricultural, trade, pastoral, and mercantile interests.[8] It all adds up to Job being, by comparison with all his neighbors, the "greatest man" (Heb: *gadal*), the "biggest man,"[9] that is, the wealthiest man, "in the East."

English translations, including the NJPS, occasionally obscure Job's vast servantry (some of them almost certainly *enslaved persons*) by using the term "household" rather than "slaves" or "servantry."[10] Let us note here, then, that Job's vast wealth is, in part, built, secured, and measured by slaveholding. This means that Job's reputation for piety and virtue occurs within a social context in which enslaving other humans was not seen as morally problematic. This is an issue we will return to because it is relevant for thinking about Job's moral character and behavior.

The fantastic wealth of Job and his family is indicated by the behavior of his sons, who are grown, as they appear to have households of their own. There is no mention of wives or grandchildren for Job's sons, though this does not mean that the author envisions none. Sometimes children are not noted in biblical texts even where they are likely to have been present. If Job has grandchildren, the tragedy soon to come is even worse than the text says.

Some scholars suggest that these sons host daily feasts, one hosted by each son on his designated day of the week, each one inviting their sisters. More scholars read this elliptical section to refer to occasional feast days or weeks connected with birthdays.[11] The general idea is of a happy, affluent, intimate group of young adult siblings who enjoy throwing good parties for one another.

Job is not at these events in his son's houses, but being the pious man that he is, and in his role as high priest of his own primeval family (in ancient times, before there were temples, laws, priests, etc.), Job makes a point at regular intervals to gather his family together for an event in which he makes a burnt offering to atone for any sins that his children may have committed during their feasting times together. He is especially concerned that his children might have ended up "cursing God in their hearts," perhaps under the influence of "the heat of wine."[12]

Job has no evidence that his children have committed any sin, but out of a sense of moral responsibility for his family, Job sacrifices preemptively on behalf of each child. The fact that Job summons the children to these sessions also functions as a reminder of the standards of piety and integrity expected of them.

A Blessed and Privileged Man at the Center of His Community

So, what do we make of the beginning of the book of Job?

The author begins by spinning a fable of a long time ago in a land far, far away. The central figure is not Jewish; indeed, the story is situated in such a way that all things Jewish are in the future. This is the tale of the greatest man in the primeval, proverbial East, the land of wisdom. He is beyond reproach in every way, pious in relation to God, just in relation to people, always proactively avoiding anything evil, guarding the sanctity even of his children.

Job is religiously and morally *the best*. Perhaps as a consequence, Job is also the most abundantly blessed man in his entire region, with massive holdings in every form of wealth in his society. Soon we will see that his neighbors believed that Job's material blessings were in fact divine rewards for his blameless life. Certainly, Jewish readers would have understood that "while the text never tells that he gained his wealth because of his faith, it can be presumed in a system of reward and punishment."[13]

Job's blamelessness and integrity will come to be challenged, indeed eventually will be dismissed altogether, by the friends who once knew and honored him. It is essential to refuse to accept any diminishing of this original claim of Job's piety and integrity, as well as his outstanding regional reputation. This is where the story starts, and the terrific force of the tale lies in large part because Job's moral greatness is the unquestioned presupposition of the story.

Imagine the social and, one might say, political consequences for the character Job of having the deserved reputation both of moral greatness and of massive material wealth.

It is hard not to imagine that Job is routinely honored as the political, moral, and spiritual center of his community. He is a man at peace with himself and his family, respected by all, "a man in the prime of life . . . at the peak of his mental and physical powers,"[14] standing at the very pinnacle of his world.

Job is also a man who at the beginning of the story almost certainly holds to the widely held local theology related to how things happen in this world, a theology that his friends will soon speak aloud. This theology is that pious and good people are rewarded by God for their virtue—and the greater the visible abundance, the greater the virtue being rewarded.

Consider Job's privileges for a moment. He is not a woman, not a child, not enslaved, not poor, not a stranger. He is also not what might be called an epistemic outsider. That is, he believes what others believe in his community, with more reason to do so than most. He is "a man in full,"[15] the patriarch in his prime, wealthy, powerful, honored, authoritative, confident, respected, and religiously and morally *secure.*

It doesn't get any better than this.

Four Great Losses Soon to Come

The suffering that will soon come to Job is not just going to be about *his lost family and lost wealth.*

Job's suffering will also be about *his lost social power and status.*

But there's more to lose.

Job will also suffer due to *his lost ability to accept the theology that once contributed so greatly to his sense of self, his view of God and of the world.*

And finally, Job will suffer due to *his lost place in his community* because of his inability any longer to accept their theology in light of his new reality.

These last two losses are less visible but no less real. Some of us can identify deeply with Job here. It is one thing to grieve great losses within the convictional framework of one's community and with their full moral support. It is quite another to find that framework shattered and that beloved community turning against you when you are no longer able to accept the worldview you once shared with them. This is, very often, the postorthodox, postevangelical, postreligious exile experience of those shunned by religious communities of origin. It can be devastating.

But we are getting ahead of ourselves. Let's take it one step at a time.

2

God Permits the Adversary to Afflict Job (Job 1:6–12)

One day the divine beings presented themselves before the Lord, and the Adversary came along with them. The Lord said to the Adversary, "Where have you been?" The Adversary answered the Lord, "I have been roaming all over the earth." The Lord said to the Adversary, "Have you noticed My servant Job? There is no one like him on earth, a blameless and upright man who fears God and shuns evil!" The Adversary answered the Lord, "Does Job not have good reason to fear God? Why, it is You who have fenced him round, him and his household and all that he has. You have blessed his efforts so that his possessions spread out in the land. But lay Your hand upon all that he has and he will surely blaspheme You to Your face." The Lord replied to the Adversary, "See, all that he has is in your power; only do not lay a hand on him." The Adversary departed from the presence of the Lord.

—Job 1:6–12

We Meet the Adversary

Calamity soon will befall the greatest and most virtuous man of the East. How he responds to that calamity will be the focus of the book of Job.

The source of the calamity is identified in this crucial section of the text. The narrator tells us about a meeting of the "sons of Elohim," variously translated into English as heavenly beings, divine beings (NJPS), divine council, or angels. The idea that the nonhuman realm "up there" includes not just one God but multiple gods or entities of distinct types, levels, and powers is one of the oldest ideas in the world's religions, including in the ancient Near East.[1] That these beings would meet in heavenly council from time to time is also an idea present in ancient Mesopotamian and Canaanite religion and is clearly a metaphor drawn from political developments in the ancient world (cf. Gen 6:1–4; 1 Kgs 22:19–23; Ps 89:7; Job 38:7; Dan 7:9–14). In this text, these heavenly beings are subordinate to God.

In this scene of the gathering of the heavenly counsel, notice how in Job 1:6–8, the text refers to God by the holy biblical name, something exceedingly rare in the rest of the book of Job. By tradition, the translation of God's holy name is rendered "Lord" in English Bibles.

In this narrative where the Lord and others gather, critical biblical scholars note that this scene marks a specific moment in the Jewish adaptation of the earlier regional religious idea of a polytheistic divine council. It is one of the steps on the way from polytheism to monotheism, or perhaps a marker of the transition having already occurred, as evidenced by the fact that these beings "present themselves before God" like royal courtiers before their king.[2] There is no question of a council of equal divine beings.

In later Jewish and Christian traditions, the preferred reading identified these figures as *angels*. This was the term used in the Septuagint (LXX), the first Greek translation of the Hebrew Bible, completed in the second century BCE, and how some English translations, such as the NIV, now render it. But the modern English-speaking Christian reads the word "angels" within an entire tradition of Christian piety that had not developed at the time the book of Job was written. Thus, a simple English translation of "angels" can be quite misleading.

Some scholars suggest that this is not just a routine meeting of the heavenly council but, in an idea found in pre-Israelite ancient Near Eastern religion, a pivotal meeting on a particular day—New Year's Day. This is the day on which "the divine council gathers . . . to assess the year that has passed and to decide the destinies of nations and peoples for the year that approaches."[3] If these scholars are right, it makes more sense of the scene. In Jewish interpretation of the book of Job, the idea that this day is New Year's Day—Rosh Hashanah—appears as early as the ancient Jewish targums, two millennia ago.[4]

One of these heavenly beings is called *ha-śaṭan*, variously rendered in English translations as "the Satan," "the adversary," "the challenger," and "the accuser." The term is a title, not a name, and *ha* is a definite article, so "Satan" is a misleading translation. Some scholars treat him as a regular member of the divine council. Others read him as an intruder. Job scholar C. L. Seow has described him as "a hypostasis . . . a projection of divine doubt about human integrity."[5]

With the *śaṭan,* we again catch a crucial religious concept at a specific moment in its development. Scholar Marvin Pope describes the concept: "The term is a title and not yet a proper name. The figure here is not the fully developed character of the later Jewish and Christian Satan or Devil. . . . The Satan is one of the members of the divine court and comes with other members to present himself . . . and report on the fulfillment of his duties."[6]

What are those duties? The *śaṭan* is indeed the adversary—the accuser, skeptic, doubter, maybe even prosecutor. He goes "to and fro" (1:7), "roaming," checking out human affairs. Scholar N. H. Tur-Sinai suggests that the best parallel is to a royal secret service official, going to and fro to spy out the loyalty of the king's subjects, "including those who may appear to be utterly loyal."[7]

There are a handful of other passages from the Hebrew Bible that might help us understand what is going on here, at least in the history of Jewish theological development.

In 1 Kgs 22:19–23, the prophet Micaiah describes a scene in the heavenly court in which Yahweh seeks a "spirit" who will entice the evil king Ahab to his doom. Such a spirit volunteers for duty.

In the late text Zechariah 3, *ha-śaṭan* presents as a clearly adversarial figure intent on accusing the innocent high priest Joshua, and for such intention God rebukes him.

In the also late text 1 Chronicles, a late rewriting of ancient Israelite history, the text describes the *śaṭan* as inciting David to take a census, against God's will (1 Chr 21:1). But in the much earlier 2 Samuel, from which 1 Chr is drawn (and edited), it is God who angrily incites David to take this census (2 Sam 24:1).

So we can see how, over the centuries of Jewish theological development, the *śaṭan* develops a role in which he partly takes over from God the role of bringing trouble into human affairs. This foreshadows later, fuller development of the concept in early Christianity, for example, where we see (e.g., in the Gospel accounts) a quite vivid theology of Satan as chief adversary to God's Son.

This later move has the potential development of sparing God's moral reputation, as God is not described as bringing evil or trouble. But it does so at the cost of introducing a kind of cosmic dualism that is foreign to the Hebrew Bible.

As we return to the scene developing in Job, we find God addressing the accuser, suggesting he "consider my servant Job." God describes Job with the same exalted attributes the narrator offered earlier in v. 1: blameless and upright, fears God and shuns evil. God also describes Job as incomparably good, the best human being anywhere, not just in the East: "There is no one like him on earth."

Why would God want the accuser to notice Job? The text does not say. It is a fateful suggestion indeed. It is as if God wants to taunt the adversary with the very existence of one profoundly good human being.

But then the *śaṭan* does what adversaries do: He casts doubt, raises questions, insinuates a potential accusation. "Does Job not have good reason to fear God?" (1:9). And what is that "good reason"? Because God has "fenced him round" (1:10), protecting him from all threats, blessing him and his household so greatly. Take all that away, and Job's piety and virtue will dissolve. The pious man will blaspheme God "to your face" (1:11). The accuser is so sure of this that he makes it a vow/curse, rendered by biblical scholar Francis Andersen as "I'll be damned if he doesn't curse you to your face!"[8]

The power of the adversary's challenge should not be dismissed, but neither should it be taken at face value. It is true that according to the story Job is the wealthiest and greatest man in his world. Further, Job 1:2, as we saw above, may be read to suggest that Job's many privileges come to him from God as reward for his piety and virtue.

"Knowing" that this is how the world works—that the good are blessed by God—the reader could surmise that Job may have "feared God" precisely because he had been divinely rewarded for it.[9] This then invites the logical question: If Job were not rewarded for his piety and goodness, would he remain pious and good?

Gustavo Gutiérrez describes this as the question of whether Job's piety is "disinterested" (intrinsically motivated) or reward based.[10] Those who do things to receive a reward will stop doing them when the reward stops. Some readers think this is the main theme of the whole book of Job. But Job 1:1 never once suggested that Job was blameless and devout because he was looking for or had received divine reward.

Yet this is precisely what the adversary wants to test. And God responds to this challenge—sometimes described as a wager—by releasing Job's affairs into the *śaṭan*'s power, permitting him to attack "all that he has," though not Job's physical person. Thus commissioned, the adversary leaves the presence of God and sets to work.

A Theologically Appalling Story

What we make of this set-up to the book of Job carries considerable significance for the way we interpret the whole book.

Clearly, the heart of the book is how the pious, virtuous Job will respond to calamitous suffering that destroys everything that he values. Why this suffering "really" falls upon him is less important than *that* it falls upon him—and how he responds to it. One way we can know this is that once this disturbing backstory is introduced and dispatched as a scene, what follows is almost entirely about Job's response to his suffering. It is never about how that suffering was introduced.

A way to read this story of a wager between God and the accuser is simply as a fanciful backstory for the readers of, rather than the characters in, the book of Job. The latter are never informed of this meeting of the divine council, and no character in Job ever offers this story as an explanation for what has happened. There is never even a suggestion after Job 2 that it is the adversary rather than God who is responsible for Job's suffering, and *ha-śaṭan* never appears again in the narrative. Hebrew Bible scholar Ellen Davis says, with some asperity: "No serious reader imagines that the opening scene of a boastful God making a bet with 'the Satan' is a reliable representation of the workings of the universe."[11]

Hebrew Bible scholar Norman Gottwald put it this way:

> It looks as though the author of Job chose this contrived "limit situation" to give readers a necessary viewpoint "above" the awareness of Job and his friends. . . . Probably the author was not troubled by this potentially demonic view of deity. . . . He seems to have wanted to make only one point: sometimes there is suffering totally beyond our ability to understand it and we should at least spare ourselves and others the stupidity and cruelty of imposing meanings that will not fit.[12]

Not all scholars agree. Some think that the story intends to teach that God "is in the right in having the problem probed."[13] Biblical scholar H. H. Rowley offers a take that reads like special pleading: "It is the evidence of God's complete trust in Job that he is willing to stake himself on the unwavering integrity and piety of his servant."[14] Job himself might have preferred not to be the object of such complete trust, if this was the result! This bends over too far backwards to defend the indefensible in the name of piety.

That bending-over-backwards tendency appears so consistently in treatments of the challenges posed by the book of Job that it requires a descriptive term. I use terms like *pious, traditionalist,* and *apologetic.* Pious-traditionalist-apologetic readings of Job try to smooth out or explain away the threats to orthodoxy, tradition, and piety posed by either the character Job or the book itself. I challenge such readings, as the text and narrative themselves problematize these types of readings.

Marvin Pope doesn't offer credence to any version of traditionalist apologetics: He describes what God authorizes here as simply a "cruel experiment."[15] For Pope, readers should simply detach the prologue from the main body of the book and consider the latter rather than the former. That goes a bit far, but it shows how deeply objectionable at a moral level many readers find this prologue to be.

Still, there are other readings.

Biblical studies scholar Kathryn Lopez proposes that the "frame story," including this prologue, is "not an uncritical retelling of a folktale but rather a highly sophisticated parody of one, written by the author of the poetry"[16] to follow the prologue. This approach integrates both the authorship and purpose of the prose tale, including the accuser narrative, with the bulk of the book.

Hebrew Bible scholar Tod Linafelt, in a study comparing what he calls the "prose narrative" (Job 1:1–2:13; 42:7–17) and the "verse dialogue" (3:1–42:6), says that all the action of the book is in the prose narrative, while all the emotion, depth, passion, direct discourse, and intrapersonal penetration of the book are in the verse dialogue. Linafelt argues that "there is poetry in the book of Job . . . because one can do things in ancient Hebrew verse that one cannot, by convention, do in ancient Hebrew prose."[17] So for Linafelt both the prose narrative and the verse dialogue have their different and crucial roles in the book of Job.

These latter approaches contribute to what is sometimes called a "final-form" reading of a biblical book. Rather than dismissing parts of the text due to an imagined editing process, we read the book as it stands and try to make sense of it. That, too, forms my approach, even as I retain an awareness of the editorial issues associated with the book of Job. Working with the whole of Job—rather than dismissing portions of the text—is work I perceive as important. To dismiss elements of the text doesn't require us to wrestle with it at a profound level. It also positions the modern reader as not needing to respond to the historic text of the book of Job as it stands—an approach that would set us apart, or above, preceding generations of readers.

Job as a Fundamental Challenge to Any Just-World Theology

Related to final-form and a commitment to the whole text of Job is not so much the question of whether there is such a thing as disinterested righteousness but instead what we are to make of the ancient theology of divine reward and divine punishment. This is the most important theological question raised by the book of Job. Sometimes this quandary is called the "doctrine of temporal retribution."[18] I want to broaden the concept and call it *just-world theology*.[19] It's the theme I witness coursing through the entire book. And it opens crucial questions about the character and activity of God in the world.

As the words themselves suggest, the idea here is that the world is just, by God's design. God demonstrates this justice by the rewards that come to the good and the harms that befall the evil, whether immediately or eventually.

This theme is one of the central through-lines of the Hebrew Bible. God establishes the covenant with Israel, a covenant laced with promises of reward and punishment. And the historical books interpret events accordingly. The prophets warn of earthly divine retribution for impiety and disobedience. In the Wisdom literature, the corresponding idea is expressed through the assertion of built-in consequences of human actions more than direct divine intervention to reward or to punish, but the idea that a just moral order prevails by God's will is a consistent theme.[20]

The book of Job is a dissenting text to the canon embedded within the canon itself. That itself is significant. The book of Job is a foray into a post-just-world theology, in itself a challenge to the just-world theology found throughout other parts of the Bible. It questions any worldview that envisions a simple, clear, consistent moral structure to the world that is enforced justly by God on human beings in this life.

The fact that such a critique is found within the Hebrew Bible—and thus the Christian canon as well—is an enormous gift to everyone who takes the Bible seriously and also takes human suffering and earthly injustice seriously.

After the Holocaust, the very existence of the book of Job became even more important to Jews and Christians who found their faith at the point of being shattered by that enormous evil.[21] In Job, they found that they did not have to leave Scripture to ask their questions. The questions were embedded within the Bible itself.

Writing of the Holocaust survivor Elie Wiesel, his student and friend Ariel Burger said,

> Job was Professor Wiesel's favorite book of the Bible because it spoke so deeply to his own experience—Job, whose inexplicable suffering foreshadowed that of Wiesel's generation and whose demand for justice gave Wiesel ammunition for his own quarrel with God; Job, whose refusal to concede God's victory and his own guilt forces God to become visible. Wiesel began teaching the book of Job to other orphans like himself when he arrived

> in France [as a teenage Holocaust survivor] . . . the experience of wrestling with this difficult text with other young people so soon after the war was crucial to his growth as a teacher.[22]

Throughout our study we'll see that Job is both a fundamental challenge to just-world theology and a searching exploration of what theology might look like without that frame—an exploration of essential importance to a great many of this world's sufferers and survivors.

3

Job's Catastrophes and Submissive Response (Job 1:13–22)

One day, as his sons and daughters were eating and drinking wine in the house of their eldest brother, a messenger came to Job and said, "The oxen were plowing and the she-asses were grazing alongside them when Sabeans attacked them and carried them off, and put the boys to the sword; I alone have escaped to tell you." This one was still speaking when another came and said, "God's fire fell from heaven, took hold of the sheep and the boys, and burned them up; I alone have escaped to tell you." This one was still speaking when another came and said, "A Chaldean formation of three columns made a raid on the camels and carried them off and put the boys to the sword; I alone have escaped to tell you." This one was still speaking when another came and said, "Your sons and daughters were eating and drinking wine in the house of their eldest brother when suddenly a mighty wind came from the wilderness. It struck the four corners of the house so that it collapsed upon the young people and they died; I alone have escaped to tell you."

Then Job arose, tore his robe, cut off his hair, and threw himself on the ground and worshiped.

He said, "Naked came I out of my mother's womb, and naked shall I return there; the Lord has given, and the Lord has taken away; blessed be the name of the Lord." For all that, Job did not sin nor did he cast reproach on God.

—Job 1:13–22

Job's Blessings Devoured in a Single Day

Having received God's permission to bring disaster upon "all that [Job] has" (1:11–12), the *śaṭan* arranges the blows to fall in one horrible day. That day is the feast day of the eldest brother. Rowley suggests that this means the beginning of the young adults' cycle of feasts, with Job having just offered his preventative sacrifices to sanctify his children and therefore no possibility of there being legitimate divine retribution for unaddressed sins.[1]

Earlier we heard that some scholars suggest that these feast days might have been birthday parties. Thus the attack on Job may well begin on his eldest son's birthday.[2]

The *śaṭan* arranges for the assaults to fall upon Job with the same symmetry of his earlier blessings. There are four attacks, two from humans and two from what we today would call "nature," but in biblical terms could be called "heaven" (1:16)—or, indeed, "God" (1:16).[3]

The reader does not witness the escalating disasters but receives news of each along with Job, keeping the mood breathless and our focus on the escalating assault on Job.[4] That news comes in dreadful waves, so quickly that even while one "was still speaking" (1:16, 17, 18), the next hammer blow falls.

The Sabeans (v. 15) steal the oxen and donkeys and put the attending servants to death "with the mouth of the sword,"[5] while a big raiding party of Chaldeans (v. 17) likewise steals the camels and kills their attendants.

The "natural" attacks begin with "God's fire [that] fell from heaven (v. 16). Some scholars label this a massive lightning strike; biblical scholar Norman Habel sees parallels within the Hebrew Bible (Gen 19:24; Num 11:1; 1 Kgs 18:38), clearly signaling to Jewish readers that this is fire *from God* and would be viewed as such by anyone who heard about it.[6]

The decisive blow is a tremendous wind (*ruaḥ gedola*)—akin to a cyclone—that comes from the wilderness and instantaneously destroys the house in which Job's children are feasting, killing "the young people"—that is, killing Job's children, their attending servants, and any grandchildren.[7]

I Alone Have Escaped to Tell You

The attacks that fall on "all that Job has" come from the heavens, the earth—every direction. The assault is cosmic and comprehensive. Job's wealth and economic status are destroyed in a single day. It will become clear that his honored place in his community has been ruined. Many of Job's servants have been killed. And, of course, most heartrending to him, Job's children are all dead. If there were children's spouses, they are dead. If there were grandchildren, they are dead. What remains to Job is his own immediate household—though no longer the means to support it—and, we will soon see, a grief-stricken, embittered wife.

I alone have escaped to tell you.

The book of Job combines attacks from the heavens and attacks from the human realm in one comprehensive assault. But the scope of devastation is not entirely unknown in human history, with natural disasters intensifying in our era of accelerating climate disruption and destruction of lands and whole communities.

Job's Grieved but Entirely Submissive Response

Job apparently received all his bereft servants while in the seated position (1:20). Having been pummeled by the fourth, final, and most devastating blow, he finally arises. Dhorme suggests that the Hebrew words here signal rapid movement—first up from his chair and then into two traditional rituals of mourning and two movements of worship.[8]

First, he tears his outer "mantle," or robe, which upper-class men wore over their tunics.[9] The robe was ritually torn as an expression of grief, both in traditional Jewish culture (Gen 37:34; Josh 7:6; Ezek 9:3, 5; Esth 4:1) and in other ancient cultures.

Then, Job cuts off his hair. The shaving of hair, pulling out of hair, and even the lacerating of scalps were widely practiced rituals of mourning in the ancient Near East, in classical Greek texts, and in the Hebrew Bible (Isa 15:2; 22:12; Jer 7:29; 16:6; Amos 8:10; Mic 1:6).[10] Gordis suggests that Job's actions fall within the parameters of Jewish Law and would be recognized as such by Jewish readers, even though (as we recall) the characters are not identified as Jews.[11]

Then Job "threw himself on the ground," as well anyone might after having such devastating blows fall on them. But scholars mostly agree that this was not a fall like a collapse into grief.[12] This was a fall into worship; thus the striking NJPS translation: "Job threw himself on the ground and worshiped" (v. 20).

Just like supplicants literally laid on the ground or bowed low repeatedly before the all-powerful kings of the ancient world, so did many worshipers of God in Scripture (Gen 23:7, 12; Exod 18:7; 1 Kgs 2:19; 2 Sam 1:2; 9:6; 14:4; 2 Chr 20:18; Acts 10:25–26). Many do so even today, across religious traditions. Casting oneself on the ground in this way is a sign of utter submission to God.

Finally, we encounter Job's famous saying, which reads like ancient poetry (and I will render it as such). In this prayer, Job uses the unique Hebrew name for God for the only time in the book other than in 12:9.

Naked came I out of my mother's womb [and]
Naked shall I return there;
The Lord has given,
And the Lord has taken away;
Blessed be the name of the Lord.

There is no evidence of an exact saying like this in the ancient world, though similar lines appear in a few other places in Scripture. Consider Eccl 5:15: "As they came from their mother's womb, so they shall go again, naked as they came; they shall take nothing for their toil, which they may carry away with their hands."

Then, Sir 40:1:

Hard work was created for everyone,
  and a heavy yoke is laid on the children of Adam,
from the day they come forth from their mother's womb
  until the day they return to the mother of all the living.

Also consider 1 Tim 6:7. In some ancient manuscripts, it reads: "For we brought nothing into the world, and it is certain that we can take nothing out of it."

Scholars agree that "naked I shall return there" represents a subtle identification of the mother's womb with the earth to which all our bodies return—ashes to ashes, dust to dust (cf. Eccl 12:7). This theme will recur in Job.

We come to the end of the chapter with the affirmation that Job did not sin in response to his suffering, nor did he "charge God with folly,"[13] "ascribe corruptness,"[14] or "speak insult."[15] Job passed his test. But it turns out, this was only the first test.

The Impossible, Inspiring Job

Emily Dickinson once wrote a poem with this title line: "After great pain a formal feeling comes."[16] Job has just received a barrage of news that signals the destruction of everything he holds dear, everything that has defined him. His initial reaction is to turn to formal gestures of grief recognized in his culture.

The text is spare and the prose rapid, but these actions would not have been instantaneous. Job becomes noticeably quiet and then acts with deliberateness. He rises, perhaps assembling his remaining household, takes off his outer mantle in their presence, and tears it to pieces. With some assistance, he gathers the needed implements and shaves every bit of hair off his scalp and his face, leaving him shockingly naked to public view. This would have taken some time.

Only after these gestures, still in full view of the survivors in his world, Job falls prostrate to the ground, offering his bodily submission to God his king. Job had been a regal figure in his world. Men had bowed before him. Now Job prostrates himself before his Maker.

Finally, Job borrows or creates a poem. This poem speaks rock-hard and absolute truth about the human condition, truth recognized in many cultures; We come into the world with nothing. Everything we receive during our earthly sojourn is, in a sense, a loan. Loans can be called.

Job's first words speak ultimate truth about the human condition. His complete refusal to charge God with wrongdoing or to do anything other than express gratitude for life's good gifts has left a staggering impact on the religious imagination. This is the patient Job, the submissive Job. And some readers choose to remember and honor only this version of Job, as if the rest of the book, full of Job's complaints, did not exist.

But the rest of the book very much does exist.

Maybe this was Job in shock, in his first stage of grief. Maybe it was the next assault that pushed Job over the edge. It may be that Job was so overwhelmed that all he could do was to default to the formal mourning traditions of his culture. It may be that the author/editor of the book of Job has not adequately stitched together the submissive-Job prologue with the complaining-Job remainder of the book.

But as we close the opening movement of the book, behold our brother Job.

Lifted to the heights by the good gifts of God, now brought to the depths with these good gifts *taken from him in one day*, Job responds with perfect submission to God. No wonder many pious believers still think of this Job and look to him for inspiration.[17]

But—no wonder such perfect submission remains entirely out of reach for most of us. This is not how human beings really act. It is certainly not how human beings really feel when they lose everyone they love.

Real, normal, flesh-and-blood human beings give their hearts away to those we love. We are vulnerable because we love. Think of Benson Boone's raw lyrics as he considers the loss of his loves: "I want you, I need you, oh God / Don't take / These beautiful things that I've got."

Job has lost all his children in one day, perhaps also their spouses and his grandchildren. I think of my children, and my grandchildren, and how deep my connection to each one is, how deep my love for them is. If they were all taken from me—if even one were taken from me—as two of them almost were—how could I simply submit to such loss the way Job does? I could not.

I cannot quite believe that such a response is even admirable. It is, at least, not quite human. And for Job, too, it does not—it cannot—last.

4

God Authorizes Further Afflictions for Job (Job 2:1–8)

> *"[Job] still keeps his integrity; so you have incited Me against him to destroy him for no good reason." The Adversary answered the* Lord, *"Skin for skin—all that a man has he will give up for his life. But lay a hand on his bones and his flesh, and he will surely blaspheme You to Your face." So the* Lord *said to the Adversary, "See, he is in your power; only spare his life." The Adversary departed from the presence of the* Lord *and inflicted a severe inflammation on Job from the sole of his foot to the crown of his head. He took a potsherd to scratch himself as he sat in ashes.*
>
> —Job 2:3b–8

Destroyed for No Good Reason

Job 2:1–3a offers an artful echo of 1:6–8, with the lines repeated almost exactly. But just a few things have changed. Job's children, servants, and wealth are now gone. The adversary doesn't bother to report any of this. And of course, God knows it.

God's repeat of 1:8 when describing Job can now be read to have a triumphant quality. Despite *the śaṭan* having "incited" God to "destroy him," Job "keeps," or "clings"[1] (2:3, Heb: *azaq*), to the integrity that the accuser has challenged.

God admits that this ruinous attack on Job was "for no good reason." Norman Habel translates *hinnam* here as "all for nothing," a translation that includes a note of sadness: "You incited me to make him suffer so much, all for nothing."[2] The adversary had used the same word in 1:9 to suggest that Job's earlier integrity had been "not for nothing"—it was because God had so blessed and protected him. Now God turns the phrase back on the adversary: You made him suffer so much for nothing.[3]

Note that God squarely takes responsibility for the attack. The *śaṭan* was the inciter, but "from God's point of view it was he who had destroyed Job."[4] Hebrew Bible scholar John Hartley suggests that this is why the *śaṭan* does not appear in the epilogue (or indeed, anywhere after Job 2)—Job's issue is with God, and rightly so, as God is the one responsible, in God's full acknowledgment here.[5] At this point, if the text has God taking full responsibility for the attacks on Job, we must attribute them to God as well, however uncomfortable that might be for the traditionalist believer.

Still, it is important to note that this is the only instance in the Hebrew Bible where the verbal construction "incite against" (Heb: *wattesiteni bo*) is used with God as the object. The *śaṭan* has provoked God to be incited against Job, unjustly. The Talmud says this: "Were it not written in the Bible, it would be impossible to say: God is like a man whom someone tries to incite and who in the end is incited."[6]

Far from chastened by God's challenge, the *śaṭan* doubles down. Impudently flinging out the phrase "skin for skin," he argues that Job's integrity will collapse if God attacks Job bodily, in "his bones and his flesh."

The phrase "skin for skin" may just have been a local proverb. But the adversary's implication seems to be that when the attacks pierce Job's own skin and even go to his "bone and flesh," then he will *really* be tested. Does this reflect a cynical understanding of human nature, that a person can lose all his children, but this will matter less to him than his own skin condition? Are human beings really that self-absorbed? I, at least, can venture a reluctant acknowledgment of times in which my own bodily maladies, including a humiliating skin condition, have utterly dominated my consciousness. The *śaṭan* is onto something.

The adversary promises that after this renewed attack, this time on his body, Job will at last do what the *śaṭan* predicted the last time—curse God to his face. God authorizes the deepening of the assault on Job, requiring only that the *śaṭan* not kill Job. Honesty requires acknowledging that this is little different than a despot ordering the torture of a prisoner, as long as he is kept alive.

A Sickened Job Sits in the Ashes

The attack on Job is immediate: "a severe inflammation," an awful skin disease (Heb: *šeḥinra'*), variously translated with terms such as *burning rash, boils,* and *eruptions*. Most translators assume intense itchiness, which accounts for the scratching and scraping that Job does, familiar to anyone who has attempted not to scratch bug bites, rashes, psoriasis, or poison ivy. The adversary afflicted Job with a miserable skin condition likely to evoke revulsion in onlookers.

If Deut 28:35 is taken as an intentional parallel, Jewish readers would associate Job's suffering with a direct divine curse:[7] "The Lord will strike you on the knees and on the legs with grievous boils of which you cannot be healed, from the sole of your foot to the crown of your head." God is punishing Job! This is what everyone would assume, especially after everything else that has happened to him.

Job scratches himself as he sits "in ashes" (v. 8). This could be at home, with the ashes as a ritual symbol of his mourning. However, the Septuagint substitutes that line with "and sat upon a dung heap outside the city." This led to a traditional belief among Jews and Christians that Job by now has moved to the dunghill that existed outside of the perimeter of an ancient Near Eastern town. Dung heaps were covered with ashes because dung was periodically burned.[8]

Such dunghills, which could grow exceptionally large, eventually acquired other purposes and meanings. These were the places the contagious sick were removed to from the mainstream community, where mourners went to grieve, and outcasts dwelled.[9] According to the fourth-century church father John Chrysostom, a traditional Arab location for Job's dunghill served as a pilgrimage site even during Chrysostom's lifetime.[10] On this traditional reading, Job has moved from the penthouse to the outhouse, in two chapters.

Job was indeed extremely sick, and not just with boils. Bible scholar Laura Quick argues that "the book of Job provides the most complex and detailed descriptions of illness in biblical literature." Besides the boils, Job will eventually report "loss of appetite (6:7), sleeplessness (7:4), a ruptured kidney (16:13), and fever (30:30)."[11]

Perhaps Job has been forced to move to the dunghill by his community, fearing a contagious condition or signaling that he is now an outcast cursed by God. Or perhaps to Job it seems precisely the place where he now belongs.

A Terrible Depiction of God

This second assault on Job makes for a riveting story, but it also presents a terrifying theology. If read on its face, we are to believe that God again calls the *śaṭan*'s attention to the innocent man whom the accuser, authorized by God, had already attacked so grievously. This is supposedly to test Job's character. But the real question emerging by this point in the story is about God's character, not Job's.[12] What kind of God allows himself to be "incited against" human beings, especially paragons of virtue and faith like Job?

If we follow the scholars who suggest that the prologue can be read merely as a fablelike setup for the suffering of Job, then we do not need to take too seriously the theological implications of that fable. Our story needs an innocent person who suffers; all the better if this is a great man who suffers greatly. And yet, the story *does* exist in the final form of the book of Job. Are everyday readers really supposed to ignore it?

Because the parameters of perceived faithfulness in pietistic tradition require that such stories not be challenged, those within the tradition are left trying to defend the indefensible, to protect God's "honor" and the text's perceived authority. Many postorthodox, postevangelical, and other spiritual exiles are people who simply endured one too many such defenses of the indefensible.

Still, the laments and dialogues that follow this prologue in the book of Job include searching efforts to interrogate not only the character of Job but also the character of God—and indeed the character of the relationship between God, humankind, and the world. So it is best to not simply dismiss this staggeringly disturbing picture of a God who allows himself to be incited to inflict grotesque harm on an innocent man.

Humiliating Suffering Inscribed on Skin

Maybe the *śaṭan* was right. Maybe you can lose all your children but still not feel as personally assaulted as when your own body is ravaged by a humiliating disease from head to toe. Picture Job, having already shaved his head and facial hair as a gesture of grief, now "naked" before the world, with a disfiguring skin condition dominating his personal appearance.

Chronic health issues are traumatizing; our bodily experiences are our soul's experiences, and if God is to care about human beings this must involve caring about our bodily sufferings—even more so when our bodily sufferings are interpreted by our faith community as divine vengeance and by our neighbors as simply disgusting. Based on a (mis)reading of Paul (cf. Rom 8:13; 1 Cor 9:27; Gal 5:16–17), many evangelical Christians were taught a body/soul dualism and a kind of gnostic detachment from our bodies. But as early as the text from Job, we see faith as an embodied faith. Job's bodily suffering helps drive this point home.

Behold: The man who had stood astride his world as a wealthy, bearded, mantle-wearing paragon of virtue and piety now sits bald, his mantle torn by his own grieved hands, his skin covered with ugly boils. He is a broken man scraping his broken body with broken pottery,[13] quite likely sitting with the homeless, leprous, and outcast on an ashy dunghill outside of the town he once dominated.

God has destroyed Job's life, with staggering comprehensiveness.

5

Job's Wife Makes Her Misery Known (Job 2:9–10)

His wife said to him, "You still keep your integrity! Blaspheme God and die!" But he said to her, "You talk as any shameless woman might talk! Should we accept only good from God and not accept evil?" For all that, Job said nothing sinful.

—Job 2:9–10

Job's Wife Also Incites Him to Curse God

We now meet Job's wife for the first time. She has survived, but in her profound pain, she also becomes an inciter of Job against God. In the face of the tremendous suffering that has come to her own "bone of bone and flesh of flesh" (Gen 2:23),[1] Job's wife urges him to abandon the "integrity" she knows Job is lauded for in his community as a role model, and she invites him to go ahead and curse God before dying, or to curse God and invite God's bringing death upon him. Religious tradition has often treated her as a villain. This is both cruel and far too simple. Job's wife is a fellow sufferer, hit just as hard as her husband, with the same losses but without the same prior status. He becomes the center of the story; she is consigned to invisible suffering.

The Hebrew word *barak,* which means "bless," is sometimes piously used in the Hebrew Bible as a euphemism for "curse"—and has been artfully deployed with this potential double meaning several times in Job to this point (1:5, 11; 2:5). (If that doesn't compute, think of how in the United States South, you can sometimes hear people use these words similarly, "Why, I *blessed the guy out* who cut me off in traffic.") So far Job has met every curse upon him, and every invitation to respond to God with a curse, only to meet both with blessing. The whole book, in one sense, is about whether Job blesses or curses God in response to what God has done to Job.

Job rebukes his wife, describing her as acting "shameless" (Hebrew root: *nbl*). The rebuke is rendered as brutally as it sounds here in most translations: NRSVue: "foolish"; Goldingay: "villainous"; Scheindlin: "disgraceful"; Alter: "base."[2] It is a harsh judgment indeed.

Against the provocation both of his own further suffering and his brokenhearted wife, Job again articulates perfect submission to God, when both "good" and "evil" come from God's hands. He remains sinless in his response to the suffering that has come his way. And now we have learned that even though she has survived the assaults on the family, Job's wife is too angry, too hurt, to be of support to Job. His isolation is deeper than we knew. And so is hers.

Reconsidering Job's Suffering Wife

Job's wife deserves much more sympathetic attention than the text itself offers her. This is the only time we meet her in the authorized Hebrew text of Job. She is not an attractive figure as she stands. It was easy for her to become a figure of scorn in Christianity, where stalwarts such as Chrysostom, Augustine, Thomas Aquinas, and John Calvin heaped judgment upon her. She ranked with Eve on the top-ten list of feminine inciters of good men to sin. Augustine called her the *diaboli adjutrix*—the Devil's adjutant, reading the person of Job's wife within a set of misogynist stereotypes.

The Jewish tradition did better. We can see the difference already in the Septuagint (LXX), which inserts a longer speech than the one present in the Hebrew text (2:9). This is almost certainly because the LXX editors added it rather than that the final Hebrew version of Job dropped it.[3] Because this fragment adds much to our encounter with Job's wife, I include it here:

> Then after a long time had passed, his wife said to him, "How long will you persist and say, [9a] 'Look, I will hang on a little longer, while I wait for the hope of my deliverance?' [9b] For look, your legacy has vanished from the earth—sons and daughters,

> my womb's birth pangs and labors, for whom I wearied myself with hardships in vain. [9c] And you? You sit in the refuse of worms as you spend the night in the open air. [9d] As for me, I am one that wanders about and a hired servant—from place to place and house to house, waiting for when the sun will set, so I can rest from the distresses and griefs that now beset me. [9e] Now say some word to the Lord and die!"[4]

This addition—which was treated as sacred Scripture everywhere the Septuagint was read—profoundly humanizes Job's wife and distances her from the caricature of a diabolical woman.

In the LXX, Job's wife is the first to name the grievous loss of their children. She makes clear something that the Hebrew text of Job never really does—once children are gone, there can be no real hope of full divine deliverance—because dead children cannot be brought back.

Further, Job's wife reminds first her husband, and then all oblivious men, that she was the one who had borne each child through pregnancy and childbirth. Her embodied memory includes the memory of pregnancy, labor, and birth, of harrowing sorrow and suffering, of the intrinsic risks of pregnancy and childbirth. With every one of her ten children *now all dead*—all that suffering and risk was *in vain!*

While Job sits on a wormy dunghill, apparently choosing to spend his nights there "in the open air," his wife is the one who has been rendered homeless, reduced to a servant in others' houses, where once she was mistress of the greatest household in the East. The text suggests that while he has been so disabled by his grief that he spends all day and all night on the ash heap, somebody must earn a living to feed the couple. So that is what she does. While he gets to be the visible mournful sufferer, she is forced to leave home and go get a job.

She is suffering so much she just wants the pain to end. She invites Job to go ahead and invite his own theological "euthanasia" by cursing God, perhaps hoping that one more bolt from the sky will end her life as well.[5]

Bible scholar David Clines redeems much bad biblical commentary as he speaks movingly of Job's suffering wife:

> Solely because of the social structures of her time, her own well-being has been wholly dependent on Job's. She has relied on him

> for her economic existence, her social status, and for her moral standing in the community. But now, at a stroke, she has lost everything. . . . All of this in addition to the sudden loss of her ten children.[6]

Job's wife looks upon a ruined, diseased, ravaged man, and her own ruined life. In her brokenhearted grief, which she can articulate in words before he can, she groans out the despair that is the most natural response to the assault on this family—an assault that has come from the hand of God. While we think of Job as the suffering one, Job's wife has been collateral damage, cruelly wounded in the divine attack on her husband.

To slander Job's wife as now somehow his greatest misfortune, the Devil's helper, is religious misogyny, and something the Christian tradition has often done. She too is broken. Job is not alone in his grief; she shares it. But she has come to a certain conclusion about the religious implications of their experience, and she is ready to say so.

Indeed, it is Job's wife who raises the question that the entire book of Job will go on to explore: Is it really an act of "integrity," as biblical scholar Gerald Janzen asks, for Job to remain pious, unquestioning, and unprotesting, thus "denying the implications of [his] own experience, [his] own sense of what makes sense, [his] responsibility as a moral being" in the face of the calamities that have come upon him?[7] Job's wife is immediately unwilling to do this. How is it that this makes her bad, and Job good?

For now, Job rejects her question and remains submissive to God, without sin, verbal or otherwise. Perhaps it is because he's just that virtuous and devout.

Entering this story with a bit of imagination, however, we can look at it a different way. Think of a man who has not yet had the opportunity to fully process what has happened to him and his family. This includes his wife's apparent break with conventional faith, her readiness to give up on hope, her despair before and with God.

What if it is Job's wife, based on her embodied experience as a grieving mother, who has simply gotten ahead of him in processing her trauma?[8] Perhaps Job needs a bit more time. Surely his friends will help. Until they start talking.

6

Job's Friends Join Him in Silent Mourning (Job 2:11–13)

When Job's three friends heard about all these calamities that had befallen him, each came from his home—Eliphaz the Temanite, Bildad the Shuhite, and Zophar the Naamathite. They met together to go and console and comfort him. When they saw him from a distance, they could not recognize him, and they broke into loud weeping; each one tore his robe and threw dust into the air onto his head. They sat with him on the ground seven days and seven nights. None spoke a word to him for they saw how very great was his suffering.

—Job 2:11–13

Job's Friends Grieve for Him and with Him

The narrator does not tell us how long it took for news of the downfall of the greatest man of the East to reach his three friends. Surely such news would have traveled fast.

The names of the men and of their places are not intrinsically important in the story. The name Eliphaz and the place Teman have Edomite connections, but the other names and places are more obscure.

The effect of these details, though, suggests this is an international gathering and that the friends have come from a considerable distance. The Edomite origin suggests that the men hail from a land known for its sages. Christian readers might think of the three wise men from the East. It feels like that kind of gathering.

Most scholars suggest that the friends did not meet by accident but instead agreed to first gather and then to journey together to see Job.

According to H. H. Rowley, the Hebrew root term *nud,* translated "console" here in Job 2:11, literally means "to move to and fro," and then evolved to mean "shake the head" or "rock the body to and fro."[1] The history of the term may suggest culturally agreed-upon, embodied rituals of consolation. The friends intend to grieve with Job, to comfort him, in the manner prescribed by their culture.

It is a good thing that these friends are going to see him. He needs support amid his great suffering, and he needs community amid his social isolation. Sometimes the most important thing we can do for other people is just show up.

The scene exudes high drama. As the friends approach the ashy dunghill on the outskirts of town, they spot Job from afar. His appearance is beyond recognition (2:12). Their distinguished old friend has no mantle, no hair, no beard, no servants, no animals, no children, and a devastating skin condition. The narrator feels no need to narrate these details. The scene is more powerful for *not* being described.

Whatever rituals of grief the friends had planned on their arrival, these appear to be superseded by spontaneous expressions of sorrow for their friend. Upon first seeing Job, they "broke into loud weeping." They each tore their robes, just as Job had. Then they "threw dust into the air onto their heads."

This latter act may reflect a small textual error that combines one ritual where mourners threw dust on their heads to signal extreme grief, and another where people threw dust in the sky to signal extreme anger and disdain.[2] Norman Habel, however, suggests the possibility that "their action recalls the magical or symbolic act of Moses (Exod 9:10) throwing ashes heavenward to produce the same sort of 'boils' as those that now afflict Job."[3]

In other words, this could be a gesture of solidarity, saying by their actions, *May such boils come upon us as upon our friend*. This is a moving idea.

Conditional Friendship?

Readers who know what happens in the rest of Job may wish to dismiss the sincerity and concern of Job's friends.

But just as the narrator wants us to begin the story with firm trust in the integrity and piety of Job, the text suggests the first actions are of community care: We are supposed to begin this part of the story with firm trust in the integrity, piety, and *loving solidarity* of Job's three friends with their suffering brother.

To dismiss the sympathy and sincerity of Job's friends is retrospective interpretation. It also misunderstands the complicated dynamics of friendship, at least friendship within a religious community. We must begin with the evidence we have before us: Job's friends are true friends, real friends, concerned friends.

They are also friends *within the context of a community that holds a firmly shared view of God and the world.* When Job finally does speak, he eventually challenges their view of God and the world. His challenges then pose a profound test of these friendships.

That's because friendships embedded within communities in which shared theological belief is viewed as essential often *turn out to be conditional.* If someone in that community questions or abandons core shared beliefs, friendships often are withdrawn. This is a unique feature of friendships among deeply devout people of a certain type. It can cement ties very deeply when shared belief exists, but it can also shatter ties when shared belief evaporates.

But that gets ahead of our story.

In this first scene, the friends seem unimpeachable. They express their high regard for Job by traveling hundreds of miles to "console and comfort him." Going as a group signals the sense of an international delegation. Their intentional action expresses high respect for Job as a figure of regional stature.

Their shocked reaction to what has become of their friend rings with authenticity. He must indeed barely resemble the man they once knew. Their gestures of mourning are less ritualistic than immediate and visceral. Notice that they sit with Job on his ash heap. It's not exactly the Holiday Inn. They go to where their friend is, and they sit in the ashes with him.

Seven Days and Nights of Silence

Notice that contrary to 1:21 and 2:10, when the friends find him, Job is no longer articulating words of submission to God. He has gone silent. They join him in that silence.

Citing Talmudic sources, David Clines argues that Jewish tradition prescribed silence for mourners upon arrival, until the bereaved chose to speak.[4] Job remains silent for seven long days, and thus the friends do so as well. They will not speak until he does.

Sometimes the best ministry is the ministry of quiet presence, though spiritual companions know it does not usually last 168 hours. But neither do people usually sit on ash heaps having lost every child and most possessions while facing a deeply disfiguring health crisis without the support of their spouse.

Holocaust survivor Elie Wiesel spoke of silence in his own journey, reminiscent of Job. After losing his mother, father, little sister, and countless other family members, neighbors, and friends, Wiesel was taken as a teenage refugee to France.

When later telling his story, Wiesel always recalled that upon his liberation from Buchenwald and transport to France in 1945, he vowed to remain silent about his experiences for ten full years. The silence was finally broken by the publication of the famous book that American readers know as *Night*.[5]

In talking about *Night*, Wiesel said that the initial Yiddish version of the book was over nine hundred pages. But in the end, he decided that the book needed to relay the story with fewer words. What resulted was a very thin volume whose silence mixed with speech is central to its extraordinary power.

It is plausible to think of Job's week of silence as preceded by *months* of silence, during the period his friends learned of the bad news, planned a visit, gathered for it, and traveled to him. Think of it as something like Wiesel's vowed period of silence. Sometimes words feel like desecration. Sometimes silence is not just the best but the only proper response.

Job's friends are to be honored for sitting with Job on the ashy dunghill for seven agonizing days and nights of silence. They enter his suffering and join him in the silence of his response. It is their best moment.

Soon, though, Job will find words. And after that, so will his friends.

7

Job Curses the Day He Was Born (Job 3:1–12)

Afterward, Job began to speak and cursed the day of his birth. Job said:
Perish the day on which I was born,
And the night it was announced,
"A male has been conceived!"
Why did I not die at birth,
Expire as I came forth from the womb?
Why were there knees to receive me,
Or breasts for me to suck?

—Job 3:1–3, 11–12

The Deepest Despair: A Wish Never to Have Been Born

The silence ends, as "Job began to speak and cursed the day of his birth." The phrasing is formal, signifying an important discourse. A similar formulation—"he opened his mouth and began to teach them"—is used to open the Sermon on the Mount (Matt 5:2 NASB; cf. Acts 8:35).[1] But whereas that discourse of Jesus began with statements of blessing, this one begins with what the narrator aptly calls a curse, though Job himself does not use that word.

Job does, however, certainly lament that he was born. Not only that, Job goes on to lament the night that he was conceived. For that matter, he would prefer that the day of his birth not exist on the calendar at all.

The only similar passage to Job's in the Bible is found in Jer 20:14–18. Both signal the deepest despair:

Accursed be the day
That I was born!
Let not the day be blessed
When my mother bore me!
Accursed be the man
Who brought my father the news
And said, "A boy
Is born to you,"
And gave him such joy!
Let that man become like the cities
Which the Lord overthrew without relenting!
Let him hear shrieks in the morning
And battle shouts at noontide—
Because he did not kill me before birth
So that my mother might be my grave,
And her womb big [with me] for all time.
Why did I ever issue from the womb.
To see misery and woe,
To spend all my days in shame!

The poetry that sweeps into the beginning of the book of Job is majestic, artful, and devastating, though at points exceedingly difficult to interpret.

Job alternates polarities, some explicit, some implicit: day and night, birth and death, light and darkness, joy and sorrow, fertility and barrenness, blessing and curse. Scholars see multiple allusions to the creation story in Genesis 1, but here with bitter reversal. "Let there be light" (Gen 1:3) becomes "Let that day be darkness" (NRSVue). The celebration of the goodness of life and light that exudes from the creation account becomes here a lament over both and a plea for death and darkness.

The abundance of words for darkness is striking. Job makes clear that he wishes God's creative activity of bringing light from darkness, day from night (Gen 1:1–5), had never happened. At least in relation to the day of Job's birth, and possibly in relation to his entire life, Job wants creation reversed.[2]

This text expresses Job's despair as Job wants his "day," his birthday—the day one's life is honored by loved ones—entirely "erased from the calendar."[3] He cries, "May it not be counted among the days of the year" (3:6). *I wish I had never had a birthday.*

But that also means, nine months before, there should have been no cry of celebration in the night for (presumably) the joy of sex (3:7) and the conceiving of a child who would later become accursed. Job's thinking now turns to logic laced with anguish. If the day of his birth is to be cursed, so also must be the night of his conception. If the daytime celebration of his birth is to be hushed, silenced also must be the "joy (of love)" that fateful night.[4]

In all cultures, certainly in the Hebrew Bible, sex, fertility, children, light, and life are seen as joyful gifts to be received with celebration. Job, in his misery, is reversing all such celebrations. As far as his own miserable life is concerned, give him barrenness, infertility, darkness, and death.

Contemporary writer James Parker writes about this section:

> Howls of despair are a biblical staple, but Job's self-curse—the special physics of it, the suicidal pulse that he sends backwards, like a black rainbow, toward the hour of his own conception—is singular. Dispossessed of everything, he is choosing nothing. That first prickle of my existence, the point of light with my name on it? Turn around, All-Fathering One, and eclipse it. *Delete.*[5]

Verses 11–12 follow closely from 3:10. The flow of thought is captured by Dhorme: "Since the doors of the maternal womb were not closed, he might at least have been an abortion or have died at the moment of birth!"[6]

Or, if not blessed by being stillborn, aborted, or born dead, Job could have wished for a birth in which no "knees" greeted him, no breasts fed him. Most scholars believe both refer to the mother—to either knees parting at birth or the knees of a mother's lap where a child is held and nestles to feed.[7] It could also refer to the father "taking the child in acknowledgment that it is his."[8] It is striking how reticent Job is to articulate words like "mother" or "father," but instead speaks of body parts, only "knees" and "breasts." It is as if he cannot bear to remember that there was once a particular mother and father who loved him.

Sometimes Only Job 3 Suffices to Articulate Human Misery

"I wish I was never born." How many people suffering the excruciating sorrows possible in this life have ever reached a nadir so low that these words have emerged from their mouths?

I went there once. It was when my wife, Jeanie, lost her second consecutive pregnancy at midterm. We lost two babies in fourteen months. When reaching for Scripture adequate to describe the depths of my own sorrow, I turned to Job 3: *I wish I had never been born.* We were young then, and I did not yet know that this first sequence of sorrows too painful to bear would be followed by others. But for us the sorrows were spread out over time, preceded and followed by many good days and rich blessings.

The character we met in Job 1 once enjoyed a life full of happiness and joy, light and life. All his days were good, the blessings rich. That man never imagined that one day he would be sitting on a dunghill, childless and destitute, scratching his oozing sores and concluding that it would have been better if he had never been born.

Job is not going to kill himself. Never does he consider doing so. But he wishes that God had never seen fit to create the night on which he was conceived and the day on which he was born.

Job's Critical Engagement with Scriptural Motifs—and God

Job never addresses God here. He never addresses his friends, either. But before God, and with one reference to God (v. 4), he offers a lament that almost amounts to a negation of the Hebrew Bible's story of creation.

This is the first but not the last time in this book when the author has the character Job seize a familiar biblical text or motif so that it can be challenged or negated. We will see that this remarkable book offers regular engagement with, critique of, and even sarcastic riffs on other parts of the Hebrew Bible.

This will be the case even though in the narrative world of the book of Job the events occur in primeval time; none of the characters are Jews, because there are no Jews yet, which means that in Job's world there is no Hebrew Bible. But that very Bible is in fact being engaged throughout the book of Job, by a Jewish writer, fully shaped by and interacting with the Jewish biblical tradition. It's ingenious, really.

For those of us raised with pious instruction about the univocality of the Bible, about its singular, entirely consistent message, the way Job riffs critically on Scripture is shocking and deeply instructive. *Job is a critic of the canon from within the canon.* Does this give the rest of us similar freedom to engage sacred Scripture with critical reflection and openness to dialogue?

But Job's critical reflection goes even deeper. Consider: Who do Job and his friends believe created the world? Who brought light out of darkness? Created the conception and birth of children? Who is being challenged when Job asserts that it would have been better if he had never been born? Who is being critiqued if Job asserts that it would have been preferable if creation itself did not exist?

In his very first discourse, Job is implicitly challenging not just the creation narrative but also the God who created the world.

8

Job Begins to Notice Other Sufferers (Job 3:13–26)

For now would I be lying in repose, asleep and at rest,
With the world's kings and counselors who rebuild ruins for
themselves,
Or with nobles who possess gold and who fill their houses with
silver.
Or why was I not like a buried stillbirth,
Like babies who never saw the light?
There the wicked cease from troubling;
There rest those whose strength is spent.
Prisoners are wholly at ease;
They do not hear the taskmaster's voice.
Small and great alike are there,
And the slave is free of his master.

—Job 3:13–19

Small and Great—Alike at Last in Death

As he turns to think of death, Job begins to imagine his companions in that long repose. The first group that comes to mind are the elite—the kings, counselors, and wealthy nobles (cf. Ezra 7:28; 8:25).

And within that contemplation of the elites, how to read the phrase translated "rebuild ruins for themselves" (*bonim ḥorabot lamo*) is very much contested. People might rebuild ruins, but not if they are dead. Something beyond the literal is going on here. Among the most interesting translation options are these:

- Pope: "Who built themselves ruins"[1]
- Terrien: "Built desolate places for themselves"[2]

- Scheindlin: "Build rubble heaps for themselves"[3]
- Kravitz and Olitzky: "Build those places now in ruins"[4]

Notice the discrepancies in verb tenses ("build" vs. "built"), signaling translators' struggle with the Hebrew participle, which lacks an inherent time reference. Both the translation and the interpretation of these verses depend on what verb tense translators choose—past or present, so the time element must be determined by context. Here the past tense makes the most sense:

> *With the world's kings and counselors who built ruins for themselves,*
> *Or with nobles who possessed gold and filled their houses with silver.*

Job is talking about the fate of the elite dead, which is the fate of all the dead, but perhaps more striking because Job contemplates his situation as among the elite. His fate—and theirs—is this: All their ambitious projects, all their money-making ventures, eventually amount to nothing. Their grand palaces fall into ruins. Their money goes to others. Everything comes undone. "Built themselves ruins" notes Robert Alter is a "brilliantly compact formulation of the futility of all human endeavor."[5] Job isn't alone in his ruminations. Another ancient text, the *Gilgamesh Epic,* also speaks to the folly of human building projects and the way in which both people and their projects end in decayed ruination.[6]

After another reference to wishing he had never been born—this time specifically a stillbirth (v. 16)—Job again ponders what for him would be the blessed rest of death. Thinking of Sheol, normally understood in Israelite tradition as "the lowest part of the underworld to which the dead descend in unremitting darkness and gloom,"[7] Job's mind populates that place with a broad cast of characters.

He envisions these in pairs linked by relation of power and subordination: the wicked or "troubled" (Heb: *rešaʿim*) and the weary (v. 17), the prisoners and their "taskmaster" (v. 18), the small and the great (v. 19a), the slave and his master (v. 19b). Job's point, in effect, is that those who have dominated, and those who have been dominated, finally enjoy the fundamental human equality in death that they never experienced in life. Death is the great equalizer (cf. Eccl 2:16; 9:2). All suffering ends there. Yet another reason death is to be preferred.

Job Sees from Below for the First Time

The author by now has us deeply involved in Job's extraordinary misery. Job is explicitly invoking and then reversing every understanding of blessing and curse that existed in the ancient world (and still exists today in contemporary culture): Life is good. Death is bad. A child born alive is a blessing, very good news. A child born dead is a tragedy, very bad news.

But Job is so miserable that he articulates a shocking reversal of the norm. For him, everything (normally) good is bad; everything (normally) bad would have been good. Job is not cursing God. But in effect he is cursing life. Because God is the author of life, Job's words are shocking. As biblical scholar Samuel Balentine writes, "The notion that one should prefer the oblivion of Sheol to life is virtually unprecedented in the Hebrew Bible."[8]

The articulation of this level of despair in the book of Job, and therefore in the biblical canon, is an important contribution. It helps readers who have hit bottom feel seen in Scripture. *The Bible and the God who inspired it understand me, even here and even now.* This is an especially important word for spiritual exiles, those emerging from a version of Christianity that emphasized the piety-to-blessing ratio of Christian experience that those lacking joy feel as communal rejection of their experience of and relationship with God.

Now Job thinks of death as rest, a rest he desperately seeks. And as he thinks of death, he begins to imagine other dead. First, he imagines and seems to mock the privileged dead, who lived such full, rich, powerful lives and now lie in the dust, their dreams come to naught. But then his focus broadens to the dead who had been at the bottom of society, paired with the dead who had been their oppressors and who no longer hold power over them. With some insight, Job sees that only in death have these paired groups reached equality.

If we correctly surmise that Job himself had been among the highly privileged, a kind of prince among men in his world, it's appropriate to wonder *whether Job's suffering has begun to affect his moral vision in a way that shows promise of growth* (not that Job cares) amid the very ruins of his own life. Both the narrator and Job—not to mention God (1:8, 2:3)—are confident of Job's blamelessness and integrity. *But some dimensions of moral maturity can be learned only through suffering*, including suffering the loss of privilege and place. And this is what Job is now experiencing.

The flow of thought in the text here suggests Job has first considered his own (former) life and all its wealth and power, the sum of everything he had been so laboriously building. Seeing its utter ruin, Job has now found his pursuits futile, with death preferable. In this first move he identifies with the kings and nobles of the world, who had been his peers; after all, he was the greatest man in the East (1:3).

But then Job looks to the society's margins, now visible to him from his location on the ash heap. He begins to *see* all the overlooked people in his (former) world, the troubled, the weary, the prisoners, the enslaved, the "small." As theologian Gustavo Gutiérrez writes, Job gradually broadens his perspective from his own suffering to the suffering of all the world's "nonpersons." He starts attending to "the suffering and injustice that mark the lives of the poor."[9]

This could include Job's own slaves, some of whom perished in Job's calamity. While it is not absolutely clear from Job 1:3 that among his vast workforce were people that Job had enslaved, it comes clear later, in Job 31, because Job uses the words for male and female enslaved persons (*ʿebed* and *ʾamâ*, respectively). The fact that Job had owned humans, perhaps a substantial group of enslaved human beings—even if common in his time and place—is a relevant fact to consider when thinking about the moral integrity, and the moral journey, of the man Job.[10]

Beginning now, Job articulates some identification with those whose life experience had once been remote to him. Samuel Balentine captures the idea: "Job no longer identifies with the titled and the prosperous. His affiliation now lies with . . . those at the bottom of the social scale."[11] They will be equal with him in death. Indeed, on the dung heap outside of town he is now equal with them in life. Having one's privilege shattered opens the lens to see the world and other people very differently.

Rabbi Moshe Eisemann points in this direction when he writes:

> Perhaps suffering has a different function. Perhaps it is meant to stimulate a search. Perhaps, when Zophar says that we are called to suffer for sins of which we cannot know, he means only that we cannot know of them as long as we live superficial lives. Perhaps, goaded by pain, we can become aware of new vistas, deeper, more intimate visions of ourselves, our responsibilities and abilities. Perhaps, through them, we may even aspire to meet our God anew.[12]

In Christian tradition, Dietrich Bonhoeffer articulated this as he wrote to a group of fellow conspirators against Nazism at Christmas 1942:

> It remains an experience of incomparable value that we have for once learned to see the great events of world history from below, from the perspective of the outcasts, the suspects, the maltreated, the powerless, the oppressed and reviled, in short, from the perspective of the suffering . . . we learn, indeed, that personal suffering is a more useful key, a more fruitful principle than personal happiness for exploring the meaning of the world in contemplation and action.[13]

These words from Bonhoeffer form a type of skeleton key to mature Christianity in a suffering world. Those in spiritual exile from a Christian culture and identity, who have experienced the hard but salutary loss of religiously legitimated comfort and privilege, come to the words of Bonhoeffer with a kind of knowing, a recognition of being known. It's also why Job speaks so compellingly to those in spiritual exile.

Job 3 offers the devastating account of a man so miserable that death would be far preferable to the so-called life he now endures. As we read further in Job 3, we see that Job is so miserable that he longs for death as for buried treasure (3:21–22). Every terrible thing that Job had ever feared amidst his once good life has now actually happened to him (3:25–26).

Job 3:23 (NRSV) reads as if Job is a man caught in a maze, at night, in the dark, with neither God nor people anywhere near to help him escape. "Why is light given to one who cannot see the way, whom God has fenced in?" He is both lost and trapped. In his agitation he seeks a way out, but there is, as Jean-Paul Sartre would say, *no exit*.

Job Is Beginning to Ask Why

As Job's astonishing opening speech ends, it's important to ask: To whom is Job talking? It does not appear that Job is talking to his friends. Recall that they are with him; they have sat silently with him for a week, and they are now the first to hear him verbalize any reaction to his travail. But there is no evidence that Job is addressing his comments to them or seeking a response from them.

But neither is Job directly addressing God. The only time Job clearly names God is later, in v. 23. Before that, Job speaks in a strangely dissociated, impersonal way. He opens by addressing the day of his birth, then the night of his conception, and says they would have done far better to have never existed. He does not refer directly to mother or father but speaks indirectly of a generous womb, knees, and breasts that gave him the life that he so wishes had never begun. He does not name the children that he has lost. The only others he refers to are categories of people whose prideful hopes, or daily miseries, all finally end in the grave. This first speech of Job is a soliloquy, which begins with a self-curse, moves into a series of hopeless "why" questions, and ends with the shattered recognition that his worst fears have all come true.

After days or even months of silence, the interior work of suffering is articulated as Job begins to ask the critically important question, *Why?* Eventually, Job will train his sights more closely on God. For now, the battered Job hurts too much to address God at all. There is no second person voice here, no "You." There is Job, in his utter isolation and grief, roaring out an anguished hatred of his life, his miserable *WHY?* to no one in particular—to the silent void where God and blessing, piety and children, wealth and privilege, community and honor, used to be.

II

The First Cycle of Speeches between Job and His Friends (Job 4–14)

9

Eliphaz Reminds Job of His Past Role and Past Beliefs (Job 4:1–11)

See, you have encouraged many;
You have strengthened failing hands.
Your words have kept him who stumbled from falling,
You have braced knees that gave way.
But now that it overtakes you, it is too much;
It reaches you, and you are unnerved.
Is not your piety your confidence,
Your integrity your hope?

—Job 4:3–6

Eliphaz Exhorts Job to Regain His Confidence and Hope

Multiple commentaries point out that Job 4 is notoriously difficult to translate. By now we are used to this, but it is helpful to recall this as we turn to Job's three friends.

As we move into the long dialogue chapters of Job (4–31), we'll direct our attention somewhat selectively to sections that are especially apt or important to a spiritual exile reading of Job rather than attempt to comment on every verse of the book.

As we read these words from Job's friend, this "oracle of Eliphaz," it's unclear where it precisely stops. Different commentaries place the ending in different places. And biblical scholar Robert Alter identifies Job 4:12–21 as, rather, a speech of Job.[1] But most scholars place the first speech of Eliphaz as running throughout chapters 4–5, and we'll do the same.

One of the first things Eliphaz does is reflect on *his own* dilemma, that is, his need to speak but his fear of offending or upsetting his friend Job.[2] This humble opening note reflects kindness and compassion. But he goes on to "venture" a word anyway, and the dialogue begins.

Recall how in his first soliloquy Job did not directly address either his friends or God. But he did break his silence, which may have seemed to Eliphaz—likely the senior of the friends, named first in Job's list of friends—to authorize him to also speak a word. He turned and spoke to Job, in what looks like the first of many mistakes made by Job's friends. Because if they were not being addressed, they had no need to respond. As so many counseling and pastoral-care-oriented books about Job have noted, compassionate silence is often the best response to suffering.[3] While the friends practiced that, unfortunately, by the time Job starts speaking, they race in to talk as well.

Eliphaz starts by reminding Job of his past beliefs and past role in his community. In 4:3, the Hebrew word *yasar,* translated "encouraged" ("instructed" in the NRSVue, "reproved" in the Alter translation), also carries the sense of "disciplined."[4] This suggests that Job once had a spiritual leadership role in his community that included reproof or discipline of those straying in their beliefs or behavior.

Before the calamity struck, we met Job as among the wealthiest and most prominent people in his region. As a respected figure in his local community. As reputed for his integrity and piety. But now we also meet a man *who had a religious and moral leadership role.* People turned to him when they faced religious and moral questions and difficulties, and they took his instruction seriously. For those with a church background, imagine someone in a senior lay elder or deacon role who also happens to be the biggest donor in the church.

Note that the poetic parallelism in Job 4:3–4 also goes on to describe Job's role in supporting, strengthening, and bracing up those who were stumbling, weakening, collapsing, and falling. These are tender descriptions. Job had been not just a teacher and exhorter but an encourager and a strengthener. He helped people who were staggering under life's burdens find the strength needed to carry their heavy loads.

In the book of Job, the first word of reproof from a friend comes next, in v. 5. Eliphaz now gently rebukes Job for not responding well to trouble when it finally comes his way. Job's once strong and confident faith, Eliphaz says, which provided the basis of his counsel to others, has given way to Job being "unnerved" (Heb: *tibbahel*), translated as "impatient" by NRSVue.

Job has come undone, and to Eliphaz, this is regrettable. He wants to buck up his friend. And Eliphaz thus attempts to play the role for Job in a time of trouble that Job had played for others under his spiritual care.

And so, in 4:6, Eliphaz tries to take Job back to the touchstone of his (former) confidence by affirming Job's piety and integrity, the very same combination of attributes ascribed to Job at the beginning of the book. This is encouraging—at this point, no one is questioning Job's piety and integrity. Instead Eliphaz is citing that piety and integrity to support his friend. Unfortunately, that will soon change.

Verse 7 continues Eliphaz's reminders of Job's past beliefs, as he employs two rhetorical questions:

What innocent man ever perished?
Where have the upright been destroyed?

Eliphaz uses these questions to make the argument from (supposedly) shared experience that no one has ever seen an innocent or upright person destroyed. Verses 8–9 go on to make the same argument in reverse, by articulating the classic proverbial sowing/reaping argument. The claim Eliphaz makes is that the one who sows evil reaps evil (cf. Gal 6:7).

Eliphaz then adds a more theological layer, though, as he says that those who do evil are destroyed by a "blast" from the "breath" of God. This is not just the sowing and reaping language common in the Wisdom tradition, but instead a picture of a God who identifies and destroys evildoers by active intervention, more commonly seen in the historical and prophetic sections of the Hebrew Bible, though also not absent from the Wisdom literature.

Job Can't Believe the Proverbial Certainties He Once Taught

Eliphaz's description of Job's (former) role in the community is tantalizing. Eliphaz does not tell us much. But it does seem that Job had been a respected teacher, encourager, and guide. It is an appealing picture: Job the wise elder, offering not just instruction but also support.

In his former life-situation of blessing and abundance, of communal respect and leadership, Job had been there for those who were hurting. In his strength, he had comforted the weak.

One can assume that in this laudable role, Job had once offered the kinds of verities that Eliphaz now is about to repeat. We can know this because of the manner in which Eliphaz reproves Job here. You once encouraged and supported those facing a hard time that challenged their faith, but now that it "overtakes you" (4:5), it is too much for you; you are impatient, dismayed, unnerved. Job, brother, you are falling apart, and you of all people should know better.

The implication is that *Job does not appear able, from his radically new position of brokenness, to believe the proverbial certainties, the just-world theology, that he once offered to others.* Eliphaz hopes Job will get his act together and return to the old certainty that the innocent are vindicated and the wicked destroyed, in God's good and morally orderly world.

Eliphaz seems completely oblivious to the fact that life sometimes crushes our certainties and that suffering can be so grave as to put us in an entirely different epistemological location than before that suffering came to us. Just as Job once spoke to those who came for counsel, Eliphaz now speaks as a nonsufferer to one gravely suffering. And it is Eliphaz who sets the tone for the other friends in the dialogue that follows. In this way, he is unwilling to make space for Job to offer honest lament and honest questions about the calamity that has struck him.[5] Eliphaz only wants to rush him back to his old certainties.

With Eliphaz's words, we witness the beginning of a major motif in the book of Job: As Newsom puts it, "the way claims to knowledge are authorized . . . the book stages a conflict between different ways of grounding and authorizing knowledge."[6]

When the strong and blessed offer comfort to the weak and miserable they often do so *while separated by an invisible but quite real experiential chasm.* They cannot know what the recipient of their words is experiencing because they have not experienced it.

Many spiritual exiles from the church and faith communities have experienced this very thing, being instructed, even in the guise of pastoral encouragement, to return to old verities that are no longer believable because life experience has annihilated them. What is more galling to the suffering than to be instructed like this by one's (ex-)friends, as they employ vocabulary and patterns of thought you no longer share, but the friends continue to instruct you and won't/don't/can't realize the harm they reenforce, despite your very clear protestations.

Eliphaz offers Job just-world theology, asking him to knuckle under to it. He does so not as a fellow sufferer but as one who looks on from above.

Those of us who have experiences of "comfort" offered from the suffering-free zone of *above* are aware that such comforting words do far more for the comforters than the suffering ones. They help comforters believe that such suffering has not come to them, because they are among the innocent and therefore immune.

We sufferers know something different, because our knowledge has been the product of awful experiences that have not (yet) touched the lives of our comforters.

It is interesting that in this first round of dialogue Eliphaz offers the factually dubious claim that one can routinely see the sowing/reaping principle working out right before our eyes. When have you seen the innocent perish? When have you not seen the wicked destroyed?

What world is Eliphaz living in? Not the world at all, with its realities. Instead he is living in a *religious worldview* that requires a sow/reap belief, all evidence to the contrary notwithstanding.

As Eliphaz seeks to comfort Job in v. 6 with what seems like praise: "Is not your piety your confidence, your integrity your hope?" he affirms—in public—Job's reputation for piety and virtue. By doing so, he also inserts the implicit claim that in the end, in this just moral universe over which God presides, if you are as pious and virtuous as you have appeared to all of us, God will vindicate you.

What Eliphaz does not realize is that Job's suffering is already far too great for such a claim to be plausible to him. Job is not going to be comforted by any claim that his own piety and integrity will protect him—because his travail has already shattered that claim.

10

A Ghostly Challenge to the Possibility of Human Goodness (Job 4:12–21)

Can mortals be acquitted by (NRSVue: *righteous before*) *God?*
Can man be cleared by (NRSVue: *pure before*) *his Maker?*
If He cannot trust His own servants
And casts reproach on His angels,
How much less those who dwell in houses of clay,
Whose origin is dust,
Who are crushed like the moth,
Shattered between daybreak and evening,
Perishing forever, unnoticed.

—Job 4:17–20

A Vision in the Night

In the second section of Job 4, Eliphaz reports the terrifying visit of some kind of ghostly apparition (vv. 12–16) that speaks a specific, relevant message to him (vv. 17–21). Commentator H. H. Rowley points out that the author intentionally makes the talk of Eliphaz's encounter with the apparition feel "spooky,"[1] and on close reading it is indeed frightening.

It is odd to encounter the ghostly language of Eliphaz's vision in the Bible, where divine visitations, supernatural dreams, and visions in the night do not sound like this. However, this way of speaking was common in the ancient Near East, where the story is situated. Recall that Eliphaz is situated as a Temanite, an Edomite foreigner (Job 2:11; 4:1) and that he and the other friends have traveled from afar. And again, while nowhere in the book of Job is any character identified as Israelite or Jewish. Thus it might not be a surprise that he makes an argument that sounds foreign to a Jewish perspective.

We see that Eliphaz experiences the ghostly apparition "amid thoughts from visions of the night" (4:13, NRSVue). A sympathetic reading suggests that Job's friend Eliphaz is not sleeping well; he is having unsettled and uneasy thoughts about the crisis afflicting his friend Job. The appearance of a semivisible "spirit" gliding by his face shakes him to his bones and sets all his hairs on end.

Why does Eliphaz share this vision with Job? Why does he report an uncanny or supernatural visitation with a specific message? Might that be his way of enhancing the authority of his message? Eliphaz may be reaching for a supernatural visitation to buttress claims he is making in his first speech. Hebrew Bible scholar John Burnight argues that the falsity of Eliphaz's claims, together with the supernatural authority he cites for them, show him to be not just "profoundly misguided" but also perhaps a "false prophet"—and certainly a "presumptuous" one.[2]

The function of the apparition in vv. 17–21 heightens the question of whether mere mortals can be righteous (4:17a, *ṣadaq*) or pure (4:17b, *ṭaher*) before God. The NJPS translation twice renders the Hebrew here with judicial language, not of being "righteous" or "pure" but of being "acquitted" or "cleared" by God. But the question remains: Can any human being be viewed as righteous or innocent before God?

If vv. 17–21 are taken as the speech of the apparition, the mysterious visitor is, first, arguing from the flaws of the angelic beings, making a "how much less" move to compare angels with altogether mortal, dusty, frail, quickly forgotten, unwise human beings. Second, the visitor reminds Eliphaz of the fragility and brevity of human life and of how humans perish forever and without anyone taking notice of our lives.

But because there are no quotation marks in Hebrew, we do not know where the voice of the apparition ends and the commentary of Eliphaz begins. If, for example, the apparition simply raises the question as to whether a person can be innocent or righteous (or acquitted) in v. 17 and the rest is Eliphaz's commentary, that makes it possible to read the passage differently.

Hebrew Bible scholar Douglas Miller suggests that the language here is of a genuine encounter with a spirit or God, but Eliphaz takes it as an attack on Job, launching into his conventional rhetoric on the flaws and frailty of human nature.[3] If we have a genuine divine voice here (v. 17) asking Eliphaz "who can be righteous before God?" then Eliphaz has the chance to realize that it is Job, sitting right before him, who is one such person. Instead, Eliphaz assumes this apparition's question is a rhetorical question, launching him into reinforcing their community's conventional theology.

Interestingly, much later in the book, Elihu also claims divine inspiration that justifies his disparagement of Job (32:8, 18–20; 33:4). This would mean that Job 4:17 and Job 32–33 serve as ironic bookends, missed opportunities to see Job for who he is and to learn something theologically by taking the righteous Job seriously.

Paradoxes of Human Moral Goodness

Even if we take v. 17 and vv. 18–21 as separate voices, the voice Eliphaz experiences in the night in v. 17 whispers a question that the reader must take seriously in the context of this book: Can any human being be understood as righteous, or innocent, before God?

The visitor (or Eliphaz) offers two arguments to support a negative answer to the question. The first is that God finds even the angelic beings guilty of error; so, certainly, lowly humans have the same problem. The second is that human beings are creatures of dust who live in clay houses (v. 19). Yasir Saleem, a scholar publishing on Job, argues this is likely a reference to the second creation story in Genesis (Gen 2:4b–24), a key example of an intertextual allusion in Job.[4] Eliphaz goes on to compare humans to moths that get crushed underfoot, and to people who drive tent pegs into the ground expecting a prolonged stay, only to be sorely disappointed. Most of us die forgotten, having learned no wisdom during our brief sojourns (vv. 19–21).

Many Christians, unfortunately, read the famous question in 4:17—asking whether any human can be right/pure/innocent before God—in the context of Paul in Rom 3:10–12 (quoting Ps 14:1–3 and alluding to Eccl 7:20), as he makes his case for each and every person being a sinner in need of the savior, Jesus Christ. Paul is quite certain that no one is righteous, that all need a savior. This became a central theological foundation stone in Christian theology.

But the entire premise of the book is that Job is in fact "blameless and upright" (1:1). This judgment is made by *God* twice, who attributes this description to Job (1:8; 2:7). In the prologue (Job 1–2), as Job responds with perfect submission to God, and we, as readers, see him do this, we hold this as our own evidence of his piety and integrity as well. And Job is finally vindicated in the epilogue as well (42:7–9).

So, for this book, the idea that Job is blameless, a person of integrity, both pious and moral, carries not just the narrator's authority but God's authority. The ghostly apparition does not have such authority—unless we interpret the visitor as an angel or as God, neither of which option seems to fit with the description of the experience by Eliphaz.

Frequently Christian readers and commentators want to read the apparition's question in Job 4:17 as simple divine revelation in full alignment with Romans rather than reading it within the context of the complex dialogical structure of the book of Job.

Still, the question the apparition raises does not go away. Can anyone with a suitably searching understanding of the human condition *really* accept that a human being can be innocent, blameless, entirely unindictable before God? Job's moral goodness was apparent to his community and confirmed by both the narrator and God. Okay, fine. But is there *no* sense in which he can be described as morally flawed, guilty, or less than entirely innocent? Can that really be said of any "creature of dust," especially if we take into view the story of the entry of sin into the world in Genesis 3?[5]

This raises the profound question of whether *innocence* and *guilt* are the only way or the best way to understand the human moral condition. In future chapters we'll look at the texts showing Job *growing in his moral vision* through his experience of suffering. We already saw glimpses of this in 3:17–19, as Job's attention shifted to other sufferers on the previously unfamiliar (to him) bottom rungs of society.

One can be a person of moral integrity without obvious acts of wrongdoing on one's record, without having a fully formed moral vision. One can keep every commandment but still not stand in solidarity with the poor. There are dimensions of moral depth that can only be reached through the veil of tears, through suffering, through marginalization.

This is also what is happening in the New Testament story of the man (tradition calls him the rich young ruler) who asks Jesus how to gain eternal life (Mark 10:17–31/Matt 19:16–22/Luke 18:18–23). The man says he has kept all the commandments from his youth, and Jesus does not challenge him on that. Yet Jesus goes on to challenge him to sell all he has, give to the poor, and then follow him into the itinerant ministry (Mark 10:17–31). This is the "one thing" that the man lacks, and the one thing he is unwilling to do (Mark 10:21).

We are in the realm of moral paradox here, or at least moral complexity, and that is part of the message of the book of Job. What if pre-calamity Job had some of the same moral blind spots as the rich young ruler? What if Job (like the rich young ruler) could be described as *innocent,* in terms of sinful action, while not yet fully *righteous,* in terms of reaching a passion for justice that can only be envisioned by those who have emptied themselves (or have been emptied) of their privileges?

There's a tendency in traditional Christian communities to think in terms of moral purity/perfection/sinlessness/innocence, something the Wesleyan/Holiness traditions treated as a legitimate goal and the Lutheran/Reformed traditions treated as an impossibility, and thus as the grounds for their entire theology of salvation in Christ.

The perfectionist strand in Christian theologies is simply different from a Hebraic understanding of righteousness/justice. The Hebraic understanding of righteousness is that of living in the fear of God. This includes addressing one's failures, with repentance, and ritual sacrifice, and living by Torah. So, there is no thought in the Jewish tradition of being morally perfect, but there is a path for the flawed human to still be *right before God.*[6] In this sense, the terms "innocence" and "righteousness" may not mean the same thing, and we will need to hold that clarity and caution, not treating them as synonymous when discussing Job.

In the last part of the ghostly speech, there is also the mention of the humble makeup and profound fragility of the human being. Every human is dust, living in a house of clay, easily and quickly dead. But is this statement about the makeup, fragility, and brevity of a human life even relevant to the question of Job's innocence? How is the fact that we are mortal, embodied creatures who share dust and clay with all other creatures even relevant here?

Perhaps this is what is going on: Much human wrongdoing emerges from our embodied neediness, fragility, and mortality. Our needs drive many of our actions, including actions in which we take what we need at the expense of others. Our fear of death creates anxiety for ourselves and for those we love. This anxiety is morally problematic even as it motivates morally problematic behaviors. Human actions so often demonstrate our endless quest to secure our lives, accompanied by an increasingly weak concern for people outside our narrow circle.

Now add to this picture the more abstract but nonetheless profound human desires for recognition, status, and honor. It is hard to deny that the fear of dying, and of dying "unnoticed" (4:20), is at least part of what motivates such desires and the actions that follow. People will do morally problematic things to obtain even shabby forms of recognition and honor, including taking brutally competitive actions to elevate ourselves over others in zero-sum games. Jesus's moral teaching aims precisely at inoculating his disciples against these anxiety-driven, competitive, status-seeking behaviors—through a relentless focus on seeking God's approval alone.[7] And how many humans succeed at this project?

The book of Job is rewarding our efforts to probe its mysteries. Let us continue our journey with the text and with Job, the man at the center of the mysteries.

11

Don't Be Angry—Trust God's Justice (Job 5:1–16)

Vexation kills the fool;
Passion slays the simpleton.

I myself saw a fool who had struck roots;
Impulsively, I cursed his home:
May his children be far from success;
May they be oppressed in the gate with none to deliver them.

I would lay my case before God,
Who performs great deeds which cannot be fathomed,
Wondrous things without number . . .
Who raises the lowly up high,
So that the dejected are secure in victory;
Who thwarts the designs of the crafty,
So that their hands cannot gain success.

—Job 5:2–4, 8–9, 11–12

Eliphaz Articulates Just-World Theology

In Job 4 we saw that Eliphaz made two moves that opened the dialogue between the friends and Job. He encouraged Job to remember his past role as teacher and provider of comfort to others in trouble. He also reported seeing a ghostly apparition who raised the question of whether any human is righteous before God.

Now as we turn to Job 5, we find that Eliphaz again makes two arguments. The first argument is that God is in fact just and has created a just world. (This argument is made so many times in the book of Job that we will only review those that are significant arguments or turning points.) The second argument, considered in the next chapter, is that God is disciplining Job through suffering, and that after such divine discipline comes healing.

In 5:2, the word translated "fool" is *ʾewil*, a particularly harsh insult. Eliphaz is saying that religious/moral idiots, fools who rebel against God and do wrong, who are neither pious nor blameless, will pay the price. It is possible that in this little couplet in v. 2, Eliphaz is *both* warning Job not to be such a "fool" and launching into the just-world theology recitation that follows.

Eliphaz's message in 5:3–7 can be summarized this way: The fool may build a home that seems permanent and successful, but in the end, it will be ruined. His children will be unsuccessful; his community will turn its back on them. His harvest will be devoured, his wealth destroyed. He will reap the consequences of his wrongdoing, which spreads its damage like fire or contagion.

A great many difficult translation decisions are embedded in the little summary I just offered. Without getting bogged down in technical linguistic arguments, this seems a good place to linger with one example of how difficult it is to translate—and thus interpret—the book of Job.

Many devout readers raised in conservative religious traditions were never told how important translation decisions are, and thus how provisional our theological conclusions should be when based on biblical texts especially subject to difficult translation choices. How many times did we all get lost in what postevangelical pastor Ken Wilson calls *linguistic-grammatical quicksand*—and didn't even know we were lost.

So, follow along as I detail my work related to translation decisions in this text. And I invite you to engage the process, too. Check it against the translation you are reading, check it against the paragraph above, or bring other resources to the project. For those who are spiritual exiles from communities that rarely challenged biblical texts, even the wide swath of difference between the translations opens up space for curiosity and questions.

I will quote the NJPS translation and then describe the translation challenges.

Verse 3. *"I myself saw a fool who had struck roots; impulsively, I cursed his home."* The translation issue here is whether *Eliphaz has cursed* the home of a fool who has found some success or whether he has *witnessed* justified misfortune falling upon him/it. Many modern translations and scholars have shifted toward the "I cursed his home" reading. But is Eliphaz really claiming that he has cursed the homes of fools? Is this what righteous people do?

Verse 4. *"May his children be far from success; may they be oppressed in the gate. . . ."* This is probably the city gate, the place for legal proceedings and sometimes even executions. There is painful irony in the "children killed at the gates" line, given that public execution was part of a justice system, but Job's children died without a chance to defend themselves.[1] The idea here is that the fool's children will lose everything and be rejected by their community.

Verse 5. *"May the hungry devour his harvest, carrying it off in baskets."* Translations vary wildly. The basic move is a curse on the *prosperity* of the fool and his family, but whether the curse is theft, famine, drought, or seizure is not clear. Robert Alter thinks the text is corrupt, damaged through the copying process beyond clear reconstruction.[2] Even beyond issues of translation are layers of textual errors and changes. In this instance, I follow the NJPS, and read the verse as the hungry devouring the fool's harvest through theft.

Verse 6–7a. *"Nor does mischief spring from the ground (ʾadamah). For man (ʾadam) is born to [do] mischief."* Job scholar C. L Seow wants us to see that the agrarian language here is *coded* in Hebrew to remind us of *ʾadam/ʾadamah* in Genesis 3.[3] It is easy to see this connection in the Hebrew, as the terms are right next to each other.

But if there is an allusion here to Genesis 3, that makes the actual teaching even more debatable. If misery/evil/trouble/suffering/mischief (all of these are sometimes used in 5:6a to translate the Hebrew *ʾawen*) does *not* come from the ground, that must mean it is attributable to humans, who are "born to [do] mischief" (NJPS). With that reading, 5:6 would be saying that neither God nor the earth is to be blamed for human misery and evil. It is human responsibility, period. The cursed ground is not the problem.

But also note the different connotations attempted by the English words in the last paragraph. If words like misery, trouble, suffering, or oppression are used, the meaning could be that awful experiences are just part of the human condition. This would not be about moral agency but the "cursed" nature of the world.[4] But that would undercut the moralizing that Eliphaz and the friends generally do in the book of Job. Therefore, I have not read the text in that way; but it is a plausible reading.

Verse 7b. *"Just as sparks fly upward."* This phrase (Heb: *ubene rešep yagbihu ʿup*) contains the name of a Northwest Semitic god Resheph, the god of the underworld and pestilence. So the text can be translated as "sons of Resheph," but no one would have any idea what that means.[5]

Most often the line is rendered today as "like sparks flying upward." The NRSVue goes with "just as sparks fly upward," while also offering a marginal note for 5:7: "Or *birds;* Heb *sons of Resheph.*" This same phrase is used in Deut 32:24, there translated into English as "consumed by plague" or "devoured by burning heat." The phrase is again deployed in Hab 3:5, where it is translated as "plague" or "burning coals."

The metaphorical sense in Job 5:7 could be that human suffering comes from bad human choices that spread like sparks during a spreading wildfire or like disease during a contagion. The overall sense of Job 5:6–7 would be as I have rendered it above, that bad things happen to people because of their folly and not due to random chance or the brokenness of the world.

Bible nerds like me can get lost in these details. And while this level of detail may not seem to matter to most people, it is the very process of puzzling over the details, while acknowledging uncertainty and taking personal responsibility for translation choices and their impact, that makes the work important, that affects our Scripture reading and understanding. When as readers we aren't willing to look under the hood, as it were, related to translation and choices translators and translation boards make, we surrender an aspect of our engagement with Scripture that both challenges Scripture and our own relationship to it.

Eliphaz Urges Job to Lay His Case before a Just God

Eliphaz next suggests that if he were in Job's situation, he would "resort to God" and "lay [his] case before God."

It is true that, so far, Job has not articulated his cause or his concerns to God. The only words we have from Job thus far, after the prologue, are the bitter laments in Job 3. It is early yet, but Eliphaz could have a point—Job should seek God and not just curse the day of his birth.

And Eliphaz is convinced that his God is a good God. The description of God in vv. 9–16 is quite attractive, quite Jewish, and quite a challenge to how Christians so often describe God because of the way it centers the justice of God.

God's deeds, says Eliphaz, are "great," "wondrous," and beyond numbering. A very brief description of God's care for creation begins the recitation in v. 10. But the remainder of the poem speaks of the active work of God in the world to reverse the fortunes of the crafty schemers and the lowly poor.

The description beginning in 5:11 sounds much like Mary's Magnificat (Luke 1:39–56), more than a bit like Jesus's words in the Beatitudes (Matt 5:3–12), and like many of the Hebrew Bible texts on which these New Testament texts are based (like Ps 37). God is one who frustrates the evil plans of the "strong" (5:15) and the "designs of the crafty" (5:12). God elevates "those that are lowly" (5:11a), "saves the needy . . . from the clutches of the strong" (5:15), and offers "hope for the wretched" (5:16). This is because God shuts "the mouth of wrongdoing" (5:16).

It is to this God that Job is invited by Eliphaz to seek out and commit his cause. Recall that Job's sufferings (Job 1:13–19) have combined "natural" disaster with brazen attacks by two groups of human enemies. Though he had been rich and prosperous, recent events have indeed brought him low, have indeed caused him great mourning, and could indeed be described as the result of the "designs of the crafty."

This is an appealing picture of God that Eliphaz offers, even though it comes a bit late to offer this kind of comfort to someone in Job's position. Both "natural" disaster—and isn't God in charge of creation?—and human schemes have taken all of Job's children *already*. Job's life experience has *already negated* these happy claims about God. Claims about God's active involvement in this world to advance justice and prevent evildoing are encouraging, but they can be cold comfort when the one addressed has just experienced vast injustice and evil.

Eliphaz says, "I would seek God, and to God I would commit my cause." Here Job would have reason to respond: *I have no cause left. Everything I cared about has been taken from me.* If Job is now going to seek God—and, we will see, he is going to do so—it will be for a quite different kind of conversation.

There are times when the old religious verities—even very appealing ones like the active justice-making of God in the world—run up against human experiences that negate them. What does "religion," faith, theology, or prayer look like then? That is what the book of Job continues to wrestle out.

12

Do Not Reject the Discipline of the Almighty (Job 5:17–27)

> *See how happy is the man whom God reproves;*
> *Do not reject the discipline of the Almighty.*
> *He injures, but He binds up;*
> *He wounds, but His hands heal.*
>
> —Job 5:17–18

He Injures, but He Binds Up?

Organized as a kind of beatitude, the start of the third section of Job 5 (5:17–18)—still in Eliphaz's voice—suggests that blessed are those "whom God reproves," because after the wounding will come the healing. What follows in Job 5:19–26 describes the many mercies that will come to Job in the future. Finally, v. 27 asserts collective authority for these claims—we have examined this matter, and we all see it this way.

The interpretation of suffering as divine discipline, akin to parental spanking, is certainly a familiar understanding in the Hebrew Bible (cf. Deut 32:39; Prov 3:11–12; Hos 6:1) and has worked its way into many of our religious traditions. When bad things happen, the idea implies, we should look at these events not as curse but as blessing. That is because our parental God cares enough about us to discipline us. Yes, this reproof "injures" and "wounds" us, but the one who hurts us is the one whose hands will later "bind up" our injuries and "heal" us. After we have learned our lessons, blessing and deliverance will flow our way. In this theological understanding, the full process represents the love of God.

A familiar argument for evangelicals and those from more conservative traditions, the idea is often bolstered by the widely quoted Heb

12:4–11, which makes a similar move, at length. The text of Hebrews alludes to Prov 3:11–12. Another text, Jas 1:2–4, was also popular in evangelical subcultures, advancing the theme that suffering is spiritually salutary. And God as divine disciplinarian, inflicting punishment or allowing suffering for our good, is not an insignificant strand of thought in both the Hebrew Bible and the New Testament. However, it does raise acute issues about the character of God.

Why the Divine Discipline Argument Is Grotesque

When it comes to Job, there are four obvious problems with this claim.

The first problem is that it assumes Job has done something worthy of such discipline. Yet Job is blameless and innocent. An innocent child does not need to be spanked. The very analogy, then, goes back to the assumption that Job has done something wrong. So unless we believe that a sound whipping is a good idea even for a child who has done nothing wrong, the claim falters.

The second problem is that the suffering Job endures can hardly be accepted as akin to spanking. Job has lost everything, including his material possessions, his health, and his children. *You did wrong, I need to punish you, so I will permit the killing of all your children.* That would be the behavior of a cruelly abusive God, not a lovingly corrective parent. Carol Newsom puts it plainly: "When the logic of the metaphor is fully developed, what emerges is the image of God as abusive parent."[1]

And that is the third problem with this move—the overall picture of God here is indeed abusive. A God who wounds, strikes, injures us badly enough to draw blood is an abuser. The idea that the same one who gashes us later puts the Band-Aids on is not comforting, carrying the same patterns as domestic violence. How is a child supposed to relate to a parent who has abused her for no reason? Is she supposed to be comforted by the medical care offered by her abuser afterwards?

This picture of God raises painful issues about both God and unfortunately still-prevalent approaches to disciplining children. Pity the child who must suffer brutality in the name of discipline, and in the name of God. Jewish scholar Nehama Verbin puts it starkly: "Job experiences God as an abuser."[2]

The fourth problem here is that the comprehensive promise of protection offered in vv. 19–26 is lovely but far too late. Deliverance from famine, war, slander, violence, starvation, wild animals—it is all too late for such promises, at least for Job. The apparent promises of safety in the created order, of peace, harmony at home, sexual virility (the apparent NJPS reading of v. 24b), and many descendants (v. 25) are, at this point, almost grotesque. The idea that Job will reach his old age in robust health and vigor (v. 26) is a slap in the face to a man facing both the grief and the intense physical suffering he now endures.

Everything promised to Job for God's future kindness to him has already been negated in his current experience. And if it should all come to him in the future, would that negate the cruelty of his current unjust suffering? When we come to the very last verses of Job, we will consider this issue again.

The final appeal here is to collective authority, the community's shared tradition—"see, we have inquired into this and it is so; hear it and accept it" (v. 27). But it is precisely what Job has experienced that makes such collective authority epistemically meaningless.

We have all studied this. Fine.

But for Job and for many spiritual exiles who have reached such a point, the answer is: You may have studied this; you may call it true; but *we cannot hear it and accept it.* Because we know what we have experienced, as it is inscribed on our bodies and our souls. There is no going back to the old verities, and it does not matter how loudly you proclaim your expertise or the community's consensus.

The impulse to attribute even grotesque suffering to divine corrective discipline never goes away. I recall reading, in shock, some early versions of Holocaust theology in which even the annihilation of six million Jews was treated as divine reproof for the purported sins of the Jewish people.

One such argument was made by highly traditionalist Orthodox Jewish writers, including Rabbi Elchonon Wasserman of Baranovitch, as the Holocaust was looming, and Rabbi Joseph Isaac Schneersohn, the Lubavitcher Rebbe, after the Holocaust. The sins that were supposedly being reproved included assimilation, secular nationalism, and the accusation that those punished had abandoned Torah.[3] The lesson to be learned was to return to more traditional and rigorous Torah observance.

Suffice it to say that this explanation—a classic religious response to trauma—did not prove persuasive to most Jews after the Holocaust. Indeed, it was roundly rejected. Most Jews simply could not accept that divine discipline was the explanation for the killing grounds of Babi Yar or the gas chambers of Auschwitz. Even if the paradigm of divine discipline of Israel for sin was still meaningful to them, the experience of the Shoah simply did not fit.

Nor will Job accept this explanation, as he enters the dialogue with his friends.

13

God Shot Me with Poisoned Arrows—and I Protest (Job 6:1–13)

Then Job said in reply:

If my anguish were weighed
My full calamity laid on the scales,
It would be heavier than the sand of the sea;
That is why I spoke recklessly.
For the arrows of the Almighty are in me;
My spirit absorbs their poison;
God's terrors are arrayed against me.

Would that my request were granted.
That God gave me what I asked for;
Would that God consented to crush me,
Loosed his hand and cut me off!
This would be my consolation,
As I writhed in unsparing pains:
That I did not suppress my words against the Holy One.
—Job 6:1–4, 8–10

Poisoned, Anguished, Nauseated

We come to the moment when Job offers his first response to a speech from one of his friends. He does not respond in the "you" voice at first. Like his opening soliloquy in Job 3, his words are directed to the universe or to himself. Edward Greenstein suggests that Job responds as if Eliphaz isn't there at all—thus he is being rude—yet he plays with much of the imagery of Eliphaz's speech.[1] As his speech continues, later in the chapter, we see Job's shift to a direct address to the friends.

In v. 2a, the first key Hebrew word is *kaʿaś*, with English translations varying between words like "vexation" (NRSVue), "anguish" (NJPS), misery, passion, anger, grief, and turmoil. Job is overwhelmed and undone.

Job acknowledges that his first round of "words" has been "rash" (NRSVue, NASB) or "reckless" (NJPS). However, Greenstein uses the term "a garble," a word associated more with stammering incoherence than anger.[2] (The Hebrew word here is *laʿaʿ*, a word used only one time in the Hebrew Bible. Such *hapax legomena,* as they are called, make translation even more difficult.) Job may be acknowledging the possibility of (being accused of) verbal wrongdoing after his stunning first speech. This will become a major theme of the book.

Job's striking phrase "the arrows of the Almighty," in 6:4, finds parallel uses in Deut 32:23; Pss 7:13 and 38:2; Lam 3:12–13; and Ezek 5:16. The idea that God as archer would fire arrows at people in judgment is not unprecedented, but when used elsewhere in the Hebrew Bible, these arrows represent just punishment (except perhaps in Lam 3). But Job is *innocent.*

Notice that these arrows are poison tipped (the Persians used these, an act considered a war crime today), and, to Job, they remain "in me," lodged permanently inside him. Job views himself as a person impaled (by God) with poison arrows, slowly dying of their toxins. If you want to deepen your understanding of his emotional state, picture Job this way.

The sense of 6:5 appears to be that Job would not complain if he did not have reason to do so. Just as animals do not complain when given the food they need and want, Job would not complain. In the verse (6:6) that follows, translations are all over the place, but the overall idea of vv. 6–7 is that the "food" Job is being fed makes him sick—or maybe that his situation is like trying to eat when you are sick (NJPS).

Don't miss the animal images, metaphors, and comparisons. Biblical scholar Brian Doak argues that "the plant and animal metaphors constitute the primary terms of debate within the Dialogues. . . . These attempts at narrating nature have implications for the formation of the discrete human being and the human community within Job and the Bible more broadly."[3]

Job is probably using the idea of nausea metaphorically. The fact that the term *nepeš* is used here in v. 7 suggests this reading. This very significant Hebrew word is usually translated "soul" or "spirit" or "self." The NJPS simply says "I" here, whereas NRSVue says "My appetite." But it doesn't seem like Job is speaking literally. He is probably describing soul sickness, not physical sickness.

Looking back over my own life, I can remember just a few times when I felt so sick at soul that I also felt sick in body: A kind of *life-nausea* consumed me. The worst of these were three life-threatening crises involving our dear children. They all survived, and these crises are in the past. But Job's children are all dead. No wonder he is nauseated. No wonder he feels like a man walking around with poison arrows in him.

This Unjust Attack on Me Is from God

Job goes much further than he did in Job 3 in blaming his unjust suffering on God. The words are shocking, really—God has attacked him with poison arrows. "The terrors of God" are arrayed against him (6:4b). There are no niceties here about "when bad things happen to good people." This is Job blaming God directly for attacking him like a warrior, like a terrorist.

Commentators reflect considerable diversity of perspective on what to make of Job's response. The issue is present in most faith-based treatments of the entire book of Job—and whether (from the perspective of piety) Job has gone too far. There are good reasons why devout parents do not put the book of Job readily into the hands of their children and youth.

Translators smooth out 6:8 for readability. The Hebrew is redundant and emotive, like something from a Disney musical. If you pull the Hebrew directly, you get something like, "O that I might, I might, I ask for the thing I long for, my desire to be granted." We can interpret this as the poet being poetic, but also we can see the desperation of Job in what we read as an overwhelmed stammering earnestness, maybe even a garble.

The request that Job stammers out is clear enough: He wants God to crush him, release him, kill him. He is not asking for recovery, but for death.

Submission or Protest? A Crucial Translation Decision in Job 6:10

Verse 10 is very difficult to translate, and translation choices say much about how radical Job's critique of God is understood to be—or allowed to be.

The verse *may* be read to start with the idea that Job would feel consoled by God being kind enough to go ahead and take his life. He might even "exult" (NRSVue) while "writhing" in unrelenting, unsparing pain on the way to death, because at least he would know his ordeal was soon to end.

But the verse can also be read to suggest that Job's consolation has to do with *his response* to what God has done to him, not to the fact of his imminent death.

Even here, though, we see two fundamentally different translation choices. The NRSVue gives what might be called the pious option: Job's consolation is that he has not "denied the words of the Holy One" (6:10b). And most current English translations take that route—the idea being that Job feels consoled because, despite all his terrible suffering, he has never denied, disowned, or violated God's words/commands.

But for NJPS, the (tentative, footnoted) translation decision for 6:10 is this:

> *Then this would be my consolation,*
> *As I writhed in unsparing pains:*
> *That* ***I did not suppress my words against the Holy One.***
> (emphasis added)

The difference is acute: from "I have not denied the words of the Holy One" to "I did not suppress my words against the Holy One." The latter would be a statement of protest-unto-death, *not* of resigned piety.

Rabbinic scholars Leonard Kravitz and Kerry Olitzky say of v. 10,

> The classic commentaries struggle with Job's expression of faith in the midst of his pain and are looking for a realistic way for its expression in the text. Even pious scholars find his faith unsettling and disturbing. Lashing out at God would be a natural and expected response from someone who has suffered as has Job. Had Job lashed out at God, the book would not have been published. Critical to the book of Job is the notion that Job, in some manner, has accepted what has happened to him.[4]

But that interpretation assumes that the correct reading of the passage—and of the book overall—is something more like the pious submission of the NRSVue rather than the stubborn protest-unto-death of the NJPS. The latter offers the much more challenging notion that Job finds consolation in never suppressing his words of protest against God, to the very end of his ordeal.

On this reading, which I share, Job is saying: While my friends were urging me to confess wrongdoing that I had not committed, to offer submission to the justice of my supposed punishment, *I refused to do so.* I died having never ceased my protest against God's unjust attack on me.

Pious Jews and Christians often have appeared to and remain intent on finding a way to translate Job (6:10 and beyond) so as not to offend pious sensibilities. They want Job here to say that he has not denied—and unto death will never deny—the words of a holy God, despite everything that has happened to him. That is a plausible reading based on the ambiguities in the Hebrew, but it does not seem to reflect Job's spirit.

Instead, Job is saying that until his dying breath he will never cease using his words to protest any notion that he (and his loved ones) have deserved their fate. The NJPS translation has Job not just protesting the words of his friends—so far, Eliphaz only, but the hits will keep on coming—but directly protesting against God himself.

Many traditionally devout believers—Jewish, Christian, Muslim—are reluctant to indulge in such brazen words of protest. But Job himself blazes the trail. He is relevant today not for the mistaken idea that he submits without protest to his suffering but for quite the opposite reason. Job shows that in times of horror, suffering, and injustice, protest is precisely how the believer's dialogue with God remains open.

On this point, Job is not alone in the canon. Virtually every major character comes to an experience of crisis and doubt of some kind. This includes Abraham, Moses (Exod 5:22–23; Num 11:10–15), Jeremiah (Jer 12:1–4; 20:7–10), Habakkuk, Malachi, the disciples Thomas and Peter. Even Jesus cries a stark lament psalm (Ps 22) from the cross. Consider also Rev 6:10 (NRSVue): "They cried out with a loud voice, 'Sovereign Lord, holy and true, how long will it be before you judge and avenge our blood on the inhabitants of the earth?'"[5]

If this is the case, why is it that so many orthodox, traditionalist believers have been taught that unprotesting submission is the only expression of true piety? What damage has been done by such teaching!

Elie Wiesel said in a lecture that I had the privilege to witness: "You can be a Jew for God, you can be a Jew against God, but you can't be a Jew without God." That is the spirit we see in this text, and in the book of Job—and it speaks profoundly to those of us who are among the spiritual exiles.

14

You Have Failed Me as My Friends (Job 6:14–23)

Those who withhold kindness from a friend
forsake the fear of the Almighty.

—*Job 6:14 NRSVue*

For the despairing man there should be kindness from his friend;
Lest he forsake the fear of the Almighty.

—*Job 6:14 NASB*

A friend owes loyalty to one who fails
Though he forsakes the fear of the Almighty.

—*Job 6:14 NJPS*

Job's Friends Are Like a Dry Wadi to a Thirsty Traveler

By now, Job feels deeply let down by his friends. Even if only Eliphaz has spoken, he has spoken to represent a common authority. In a moment, we will consider a hugely important translation choice in 6:14, but let's look ahead a bit to see where the text is going.

In an extended metaphor in vv. 15–20, Job compares his situation to that of a caravan of desert travelers desperate for water taking a detour to find a wadi (desert riverbed) that they think they can "count on" (6:19). But "when they reach the place, they stand aghast" (6:20), because there is no water. Job, in effect, is saying that he is dying from thirst in his own spiritual desert, and his friends are "as nothing" to him (6:21a). This extended metaphor finally yields a direct second-person address from Job to his friends: All I wanted from you was a bit of water for my thirsty soul, but it was a mirage; you offered me nothing.

Job's diagnosis is that the reason his friends are proving so worthless to him is because "you see my calamity and are afraid" (6:21b). What exactly are they afraid of? Three possibilities emerge:

a God will decide to punish them if they "also" get out of line.
b Allowing themselves engagement with Job's frightening questions will impact their own conventional theology.
c Losing their illusory sense of security, by identifying with Job in his distress, means they would have to close the gap between themselves and Job; they would have to disrupt their pious dreams.

This last point reminds me of various times, decades ago, I was tempted to process the tragic early deaths of people of my generation by giving myself reasons why that kind of thing would never happen to me. My instinct was to think that *this kind of thing happens to others because they don't take proper care of themselves,* or whatever illusory story my fearful self could concoct to draw a line of security separating my safe self from their dead selves.

Christian theologian Sameer Yadav writes:

> The problem with Job's abasement is that if it is truly unmerited . . . and truly an experience of the sort that warrants the despair Job expresses, then it can strike anyone, anywhere. This would force Job's friends to recognize themselves as inhabiting the same uncontrollable and chaotic world that Job inhabits as one that makes them equally vulnerable to his fate, and this terrifies them. Their dialect of divine providence has been constructed precisely to impose order on the chaos.[1]

A primal fear reaction. That's what Job is nailing in his friends. As Yadav argues with reference to 6:21, the friends are offering a "toxic positivity about the human relationship to God's providential guidance of the world" that is little more than "a defensive strategy of terror management."[2]

By vv. 22–23, Job further rebukes his friends, saying, in essence, I did not ask you for money; I did not ask you for any physical help or rescue from my enemies. All I asked for was your compassionate friendship in my suffering, and you failed me.

On the Problem of Friendship Being Contingent on "Right" Belief

It is worth, now, zeroing in on crucial translation differences related to Job 6:14.

Translators mainly agree that Job is accusing his friends of failing him. More specifically, their failure is in practicing *ḥesed,* a central moral obligation in biblical ethics, translated variously into English as kindness, loyalty, and steadfast/covenant love.

Everything else about the verse, though, is disputed. The three translations cited at the start of this chapter help us see where the disputes lie. Job may be saying:

a. You friends have forsaken the fear of the Almighty (*El Shaddai*) in withholding *ḥesed* toward me during my distress (NRSVue).
b. I am despairing and need you to do better in practicing *ḥesed* toward me so that I do not forsake my fear of the Almighty (NASB).
c. You should practice *ḥesed* toward me despite my being in such great distress that I am (at risk of) forsaking the fear of the Almighty (NJPS).

The NRSVue and NASB readings are (again) more conventional; the NJPS is (again) more provocative. Within the multiple translations on my desk, judgments are split, though most take the more conventional view.

All three translations (and more besides) are possible from the elliptical Hebrew. On the more conventional readings of v. 14, Job accuses his friends of withholding *ḥesed* toward him and thus either abandoning "fear of God" or failing Job so that he does so. One might say that in the name of defending God's reputation they have abandoned God's moral command and thus what true reverence requires.

On the more provocative reading, Job suggests that his friends owe *ḥesed* to him *even now,* even in a moment when Job's great distress has caused him to forsake his traditional submissive reverence to God. But his friends have not offered the *ḥesed* that Job deserves.

In other words, NJPS Job is saying that true friendship should not be contingent on whether I am satisfied with the current state of your theology or spirituality. A faithful friend, even within a religious community, offers kindness, loyalty, and love (*ḥesed*) "even" to the friend who is struggling deeply with God, faith, and theology—*perhaps especially to such a person, because their need is so acute*. True friendship is not contingent on "right" belief! Here we circle back to this crucial issue.

This reading of Job 6:14 has enormous implications for spiritual exiles and those deconstructing readers of Job. Job's complaint about his friends failing him is something that pastors and ministers of those spiritual exiles from more traditional communities hear a lot. The exiled realize that these church people who they thought *loved* them in their church or faith community were only willing to love them for the sake of what the individual could give to the church or how far in agreement to traditionalist views they were willing to stay.

What happened when the struggling or questioning individual came forward? Too often, either their faith community "friends" disappeared or they created an us/them schism between the true piety of the faith community and the faltering of the one they then exiled.

The experience of being rejected for asking hard questions or coming to unwelcome conclusions is common in traditionalist religious circles, as friendship turns out to be contingent on somebody's idea of theological or moral orthodoxy. This is what Job experiences, and he calls his friends on it.

Who can find those friends who will not abandon us if we do not end up believing all the same things? So many friends, and all of Job's, leave each other "high and dry" when crisis comes. They are of no help, because they are too busy judging others for having the "wrong" theology.

For those of us who are the spiritual exiles, as we build new communities of faith and friendship, will we be able to avoid replicating the pattern that once so wounded us? Fiercely loyal, fiercely loving, not breaking off friendships within community when *we* cannot accept *their* theology or ethics anymore? How do we work proactively to create communities of faith that are not based on religiously contingent friendship, that are not re-versionings of purity tests, of the same old cancel culture?

15

Look Me in the Face and Say All This to Me (Job 6:24–30)

Now be so good as to face me;
I will not lie to your face.
Relent! Let there not be injustice;
Relent! I am still in the right.
Is injustice on my tongue?
Can my palate not discern evil?
—*Job 6:28–30*

On the Experience of Worthless Rebukes

In the second half of his speech, beginning from 6:24, Job asks what many spiritual exiles ask—especially those facing a deep precipice where deconstruction of faith awaits but also the fear of leaving faith communities. It's questions like these: *Can you just put it back? Can you tell me something that can help me go back to the faith I once had? Can you make it make sense so I can go back to my faith community or church, as though nothing just chasmed within me?*[1]

Paraphrasing a bit, Job says to his friends: *If you can teach me something that makes me understand how my actions or thinking have gone wrong, I will stop protesting* (v. 24). *What you have presented to me instead are words intended as forceful/powerful/honest reproof* (Heb: *mah nimreṣu* contains this whole semantic range). *But do you know what you have really offered me? Useless formulaic theological rebukes, while you treat my desperate words as if they were merely wind* (v. 26). Job's friends are acting as if he were some kind of straying adolescent just needing a firm orthodox rebuke to get back on the right track.[2] To Job, it feels like they are exploiting his vulnerability and selling him out to keep their worldview in order (v. 27).

Turn, I Pray, and Look Me in the Eyes

Job makes an interesting rhetorical move in v. 28 that most translations get, but some obscure. He is saying: Stop talking about me, or at me. Be kind enough to look at me. Look your old friend in the eyes. *Turn your face to me. I will not lie to your face.* Here the NRSVue repetition of the word "turn" in v. 29 has a poetic value and builds on v. 28 more than the use of the word "relent" does in the NJPS translation:

Turn, I pray; let no wrong be done.
Turn now; my vindication is at stake.

The climactic lines in vv. 28–30 bring the command for a direct gaze: Turn your face to me. Turn and look at me. Turn and look me in the eyes and then try to tell me what you know is not true, that I have done wrong, that I no longer can discern right from wrong, that I am worthy of the calamity that has struck me!

Even as Job's friends have turned their faces away from him and resorted to their conventional theological formulas because they are afraid of him, afraid of what has happened to him, afraid of the uncomfortable questions he is raising, Job begs them not to look away. He demands they turn their faces back toward him, to look him in the eyes as a human being, to engage with him in his miserable reality, to go on this terrible journey *with him*.

These verses call to mind the many LGBTQ+ young adults of Christian background that I have known, who describe the way their coming out to their families and faith community met with precisely this, a *turning away*, a refusal to engage them face-to-face, a resort to theological formulas amounting to rejection and condemnation.

Hester panim is a Jewish phrase meaning the hiding of God's face, traditionally as a manifestation of God's judgment on Israel.[3] An ancient concept from rabbinic theology, this phrase was retrieved in Holocaust theology to try to describe the felt experience of God's abandonment while the Jewish people were annihilated by their foes.

Many individuals and groups in faith traditions have experienced the devastating sense of God's absence. Many do so today, including Christians and Muslims experiencing the devastation of Gaza. The metaphor of God hiding God's face is a powerful one to describe this terrible experience not just of suffering, but of abandonment—by God, and by humans.

Throughout his travail, Job experiences *hester panim*. God hides his face from Job. When Job turns to his friends for succor, they hide their faces too. When we are suffering, we desperately need friends and fellow believers to turn their faces toward us, and to talk honestly with us, no matter if what we are saying is difficult for them to hear. For friends to respond in that way, it can feel like we catch a glimpse of God's face as well. But when they turn away, our sense of isolation and abandonment only deepens.

Tel Aviv University philosopher Nehama Verbin writes: "Job . . . does not merely suffer pain, disease, humiliation, and the loss of everything that he holds dear. His suffering and loss turn him into a stranger to his life; he becomes an alien in his world. The hinge around which his life was arranged, namely, the existence of a divine and just governance . . . collapses."[4] In this crisis, Job, who needs his friends to turn their faces to him while God looks away, only discovers that the friends now look away too.

16

Job to God: Please Do *Not* Look at Me (Job 7)

Truly man has a term of service on earth;
His days are like those of a hireling—
Like a slave who longs for [evening's] shadows,
Like a hireling who waits for his wage.
So have I been allotted months of futility;
Nights of misery have been apportioned to me.

Consider that my life is but wind;
I shall never see happiness again.
The eye that gazes on me will not see me;
Your eye will seek me, but I shall be gone.
As a cloud fades away,
So whoever goes down to Sheol does not come up;
He returns no more to his home;
His place does not know him.

What is man, that You make much of him,
That You fix Your attention upon him?
You inspect him every morning,
Examine him every minute.
Will You not look away from me for a while,
Let me be, till I swallow my spittle?
If I have sinned, what have I done to You, Watcher of men?
Why make of me Your target,
And a burden to myself?
Why do You not pardon my transgression
And forgive my iniquity?

For soon I shall lie down in the dust;
When You seek me, I shall be gone.
—Job 7:1–3, 7–10, 17–21

Sentenced to Misery in Life, to Oblivion in Death

Having swatted away his friend's useless words of rebuke that disregarded sensitive engagement with his experience, Job now turns to a stark description of what his life is like right now. His description at times shifts between his own life and a broader assessment of the human condition.

In 7:1–3, Job describes human life, and certainly his life, as a "term of service" (Heb: *ṣaba*ʾ). According to Jewish rabbi Ibn Ezra, this refers to warfare. Robert Alter says it refers to "army" or more broadly "any set term of service."[1] If the reference is to "hard labor," it could also be a connection to the curse in Genesis 3, or simply to the condition of enslavement. Human life, Job says, is (like) a sentence to hard labor for a term of miserable service that ends when God says it does.

And that's just his perception of the daytime. In vv. 3–4, and again in vv. 13–16, Job refers to the misery of his nights. Immensely weary, he cannot sleep. And later (7:14) he reveals that when he does sleep, he meets terrible nightmares. In the ancient Near East, sleeplessness is a common way to talk about suffering.[2]

It is my experience, and well-attested by others, that suffering manifests most painfully in the middle of the night. Lack of peace in my heart or relationships shows up in disrupted sleep. In a devastating cycle of daytime grief and nighttime sleep disruption, those experiencing these ongoing deprivations can attest to the additional pain of this cyclical form of torture.

In v. 5, the vivid description of Job's awful skin condition contains an Ethiopic phrase transliterated into the Hebrew and rendered by NJPS as "clods of earth." It is another *hapax legomenon*. Part of Job's ongoing misery is his wretched skin condition, which includes not just these clods of skin but also maggots crawling over him. Perhaps that is because by now he has spent "months" (7:3) on the dung heap?

In vv. 6–10 Job returns to a reflection on death. In v. 6, we see Hebrew word play with the remark usually translated "hope" (Heb: *tiqwah*), an exact homonym for the word "thread."[3] Both NJPS and NRSVue add "as/when the thread runs out" as a footnote. Using the image of thread running through a weaver's shuttle, Job suggests that the fragile thread that is his life will soon run out, or "snap off."[4]

Notice Job's distorted and shifting sense of time in these lines. In vv. 1–3, time is running slowly for him, like a prison sentence; but here in v. 6, at least in the NJPS translation, his days "fly faster than a weaver's shuttle."[5] Which is it? Perhaps both, depending on one's mood.

In this section, Job's ephemeral and miserable life—"my life is but wind"—will end soon and in misery. No one will ever set eyes on him again, as he will go "down to Sheol"—the place of the dead—and stay there. He will never return home. "His place does not know him." Note there is no reference to hope of eternal life here. But also, see how the text reminds us what it is like even today when you die. They come and get your body and before too long someone moves into your old house. You are gone and very soon forgotten.

Job Parodies Psalm 8!

The most remarkable feature of Job 7 is found in its last section, vv. 17–21. Many Jewish and Christian readers will recognize in them a familiar text, the beautiful lines in Ps 8:3–5 (NRSVue):

> When I look at your heavens, the work of your fingers,
> the moon and the stars that you have established;
> what are humans that you are mindful of them,
> mortals that you care for them?
> Yet you have made them a little lower than God
> and crowned them with glory and honor.

That text is a celebration of how a great Creator God, the one who makes the universe in all its grandeur, also chose not just to create human beings but also to declare them "a little lower than *elohim*" (variously translated as God, the angels, the divine beings, etc.). We are "crowned with glory and honor" and not by ourselves but by God! How glorious!

What a remarkable affirmation of God's love for and valuing of human beings!

In sentences that suggest the book's writings postdate and reference the psalms, Job says (7:17–19, citing NRSVue for comparison):

What are humans, that you make so much of them,
that you set your mind on them,
visit them every morning,
test them every moment?
Will you not look away from me for a while,
let me alone until I swallow my spittle?

The author of Job has the character Job offering a "savage parody" of Psalm 8![6] The embittered Job turns this beloved psalm of praise on its head: *What indeed is man, that you inspect him minutely for sins and then punish him severely if he does the slightest thing wrong? That is what you are doing to me,* says Job. Even if I *had* sinned—note that Job still does not concede he has sinned—what have I done to you? Why are you watching me so closely? Why are you targeting me? Why have you made my life such a "burden"? Why won't you forgive me?

Again, legendary rabbi-scholar Abraham Joshua Heschel reflects on Job: "The deepest human longing is to be a thought in God's mind, to be the object of His attention. He may punish and discipline me, only let Him not forget me, not abandon me."[7] But here Job, having reached such extremity of suffering, is asking precisely to be ignored by God for a while!

Even the reference in v. 20 to God watching Job reads as another sarcastic use of common scriptural imagery normally read as positive and encouraging. In numerous texts, God is called guardian, watcher, or protector, using the same Hebrew word (*noṣer*) here in 7:20 (cf. Deut 30:10; Pss 12:7; 31:23; 32:7; 64:1; Isa 26:3; 27:3).

Most evangelicals, and others raised in conservative religious traditions, were taught to see Scripture as speaking with one united voice. We were also taught to treat all Scripture with reverence. Here Job the character is deploying Psalm 8 and the God-as-Watcher motif sarcastically. This means one scriptural author, or one scriptural author's main character, is riffing sardonically on the words of other scriptural authors.

One voice within the Bible is negatively engaging the ideas of other voices.

Job scholar Will Kynes confirms this hunch. He says that "Job and his friends frequently attack each other through allusions to each other's words. This interpretive dispute spreads into their allusions to other [scriptural] texts, which are drawn into the dialogue and caught up in the conflict."[8]

In traditional Christian communities, this is something we are not used to seeing. We were never authorized to have this much freedom to engage the text.[9]

Notice that in Job 6:28 Job asks his friends to "be so good as to face me." But now, in Job 7:19, Job begs God to "look away from me for a while" and "let me be." Job wants God to turn his (brutal, terrorizing) divine face away from his miserable self.

Look at me, my friends. Please.
Do not look at me, God. Please.

These are the pained requests Job makes as chapter 7 concludes.

17

Bildad: Trust the Tradition, Not Your Experience (Job 8)

Will God pervert the right?
Will the Almighty pervert justice?
If your sons sinned against Him,
He dispatched them for their transgression.

Ask the generation past,
Study what their fathers have searched out
For we are of yesterday and know nothing.
—Job 8:3–4, 8–9

Structure and Flow

As we come to Job 8, the second of Job's three friends finally offers his first comment addressed to Job. Beginning with an impatient insult (v. 2), Bildad then moves directly to verbal brutality (v. 4) before making an appeal to ancestral religious tradition about the justice of God (v. 8) and illustrations from nature (vv. 15–19). The bottom line for Bildad is that because, by definition and tradition, God is in control and cannot act unjustly, Job's children must have sinned, which explains their destruction. Job may have done nothing wrong, but this did not spare his guilty children. Besides being a cruel thing to say to a grieving father, this does not even attempt to explain the remainder of Job's losses, including the loss of his possessions and his health.

Before we reflect more deeply on the implications of Bildad's words, let's notice a few more things about this chapter.

Chapter 8 is broken into three movements: Verses 1–7, which reassert the justice of God; vv. 8–19, asserting that this divine justice is a clear teaching of "the fathers," a teaching itself illustrated by nature; and vv. 20–22, the conclusion, a final assertion of God's just treatment of the wicked and the good, both getting what they deserve.

Bildad opens in v. 2 by dismissing Job's words as just "a mighty wind" (Heb: *ruaḥ*), the same word Job used in 6:26 when he complained that his friends are not taking his concerns seriously. At least on this point they agree!

Bildad goes on to posit the justice of God through a repeated rhetorical question: *Will God pervert the right? Will the Almighty pervert justice?* Then shifting to the use of the conditional "if" phrase that follows to suggest the possibility that Job's children sinned against God, he brutally says that the children would have deserved to be "dispatched" (Heb: *šalaḥ*) to death for these transgressions.

Job himself, however, appears to be viewed by Bildad as still worthy of the classic appeal he offers in vv. 5–7: If you seek God and remain blameless and upright, God will protect you and your home, and you will flourish. Eduoard Dhorme argues that Bildad thinks Job (or someone in his family) has made a lapse in piety or right living and has been punished for it. This means that Job's descent into the hell of his current situation will be temporary.[1] All will eventually be well. Once again, such an argument would sound ridiculous to a man who has *already lost everything.*

In the second section of the chapter, Bildad's poetry elevates as he urges Job to seek out the wisdom of the ancestors, those who would bring more authority to the situation than Job's own thoughts and feelings; after all, "we are of yesterday and know nothing" (vv. 8–10). Alter renders v. 9 as "we are but yesterday, unknowing, for our days are a shadow on earth."[2] *We are but yesterday.* Bildad delivers powerful poetry with truth to it. Unlike Eliphaz's reliance on a ghostly apparition in the night, Bildad refers to (seemingly) rock-solid ancient tradition.

In vv. 11–15, the impious man is compared to rushes without water—doomed to wither. That man may be confident in his life and its prospects, but in fact this is a confidence in "gossamer," an ephemeral spider's web, easily brushed aside.

Translators differ profoundly over whether vv. 16–19 are intended to describe the fate of the righteous or the wicked. Some, like NJPS, leave it ambiguous, as is the underlying Hebrew text. Some kind of analogy to nature is intended.

In this plant parable section, the language is usually gender-neutralized for the sake of modern readers, but the Hebrew makes the plants explicitly male, thus reading as more directly applicable to Job's fate or that of his sons.[3]

In the conclusion, vv. 20–22, Bildad offers another formulaic statement of the promised divine blessing of the righteous and punishment of the evildoers. It is encouraging that in his last words here Bildad assures Job that "He will yet fill your mouth with laughter, and your lips with shouts of joy" (8:21). The only wrong that Bildad sees is Job's complaining rather than trusting in God's justice. Even so, he has not attributed Job's suffering to his own sins.

The Epic Clash between Tradition and Experience

When I published my book *Changing Our Mind*, which took readers into an argument toward full LGBTQ+ inclusion in the church,[4] one of the many charges leveled against me was: *You are abandoning trustworthy ancient religious tradition based on untrustworthy contemporary experiential claims.* Many spiritual exiles who have moved to an inclusive position on this issue, or who have otherwise broken from traditional convictions, have faced such critiques.

As a Christian ethicist and pastor of orthodox instincts, I felt the force of this criticism. I still feel it today. I have always understood myself as standing within the lineage of a great tradition, and I feel a deep sense of responsibility to that tradition, a tradition I trace back both to ancient Israel and ancient Greece.[5] I preach exegetical sermons because I believe in the tradition that Christian proclamation should be based on the biblical texts, themselves enshrined by the "fathers" of the Jewish community and of the church as Scripture.

I am aware that today we live relative to the great tradition: We are indeed a shadow and know little.

The great British writer G. K. Chesterton once wrote: "Tradition means giving a vote to the most obscure of all classes, our ancestors. It is the democracy of the dead. . . . Tradition refuses to submit to the small and arrogant oligarchy of those who merely happen to be walking about."[6] To honor tradition means to honor our ancestors, those who built the temple that we now inhabit. It means anchoring ourselves in the best insights of the past. Honoring tradition provides a sense of stability in a constantly changing world.

If the reader does not feel the weight of these paragraphs, then the claims of Bildad will mean little.

Jews and Christians face the same challenge as every other human being in determining our epistemology—that is, our theory of knowledge. When it comes to how we know what we know in Jewish and Christian ethics, the ancient moral traditions of our respective faith(s) always play an authoritative role. Bildad here is saying what many have said over many centuries: Trust the tradition! Rely on its authoritative pronouncements!

And yet, *here they are,* the human beings whose life experiences bear eloquent witness against this immovable rock called tradition. If such dissenting voices are not silenced by the church, we discover that it is far more than one or two whose experiences require that they must dissent.

And if we truly listen, those of us who bear responsibility as stewards of religious traditions might feel the need, in the end, to propose an alteration of some aspect of the tradition we have inherited. We might conclude, with Catholic Bible scholar Roland Murphy, that "the real problem is to interpret experience and tradition together, to allow tradition to be improved in the light of experience."[7]

As Carol Newsom puts it, "For Bildad, the ancestors discovered truths that were valid for all time. Individual experience that contradicts those truths has to be wrong. Anyone who has ever lived through a time of change knows that it is not that simple."[8]

Gustavo Gutiérrez concurs, "Job becomes aware that the dividing line between himself and his interlocutors lies in the area of personal experience and of the thinking that experience yields. . . . His friends prefer to repeat ideas they learned in the past."[9]

Those who alter an aspect of tradition inevitably face stern criticism for selling out the ancestors based on the ephemeral confusions of the current moment. This is the exact criticism Job is already facing from his friends.

Job stands utterly alone in his challenge to tradition. But his friends see that this is what is developing in him and through him. And they are going to become increasingly committed to the idea that the worst thing happening in Job's life is not that he has lost his children and his possessions but that he has lost confidence in the tradition. And here they must attempt to stop him in his tracks.

18

Arbitrary Divine Power Is Destroying Me (Job 9–10)

He is not a man like me, that I can answer Him,
That we can go to law together.
No arbiter is between us
To lay his hand on us both.

Your hands shaped and fashioned me,
Then destroyed every part of me.
—Job 9:32–33, 10:8

Job Wants to Sue God— But He Knows He Would Lose

Job's response to Bildad appears to begin with a concession: "Indeed I know that it is so" (9:2a). But it is not clear what point Job is conceding, and he quickly moves on to a new thought: "Man cannot win a suit against God" (9:2b).

Among the translation decisions crucial in Job is the translation choice we meet at the beginning of Job 9, which sets the parameters for the entire interpretation that follows. Compare the crucial difference between these two renderings:

How can a mortal be just before God?
If one wished to contend with him,
One could not answer him once in a thousand.
(Job 9:2b–3 NRSVue)

Man cannot win a suit against God.
If he insisted on a trial with Him,
He would not answer one charge in a thousand.
(Job 9:2b–3 NJPS)

Robert Alter argues that the crucial Hebrew verb root *ṣdq*—from which we get *ṣedaqah and ṣedeq,* the central Hebrew terms for justice—"here and elsewhere means being vindicated in a court of law. Thus the opening line announces the metaphor of legal disputation that dominates this whole chapter and recurs later in Job's argument."[1]

We can see that NJPS translators clearly agree, translating all related words in Job 9—and throughout the book of Job—with a legal valence. Job imagines initiating a lawsuit against God, putting God on trial, a rather shocking idea! But NRSVue obscures this shocking yet clear move on Job's part by flattening out the language and even reversing, in v. 3, who is being asked to answer whom.

Can it be that even the mainline-Protestant NRSVue translation is unwilling to contemplate such a radical notion—a human initiating a suit against God?

Samuel Balentine, in his commentary on Job, agrees this text is clearly about putting God on trial. He argues that "in his second response, Job's 'bitterness of soul' (10:1) remains unabated, but he now begins to grope towards a centering idea that will provide the basis for sustaining the passion, hence the hope, which resides so tenuously inside his grief. What organizes his anguish into these chapters is the daring notion that he might put God on trial."[2] Carol Newsom puts it this way: "Even though Job happens upon the metaphor almost by accident . . . Job finds . . . a center in the metaphor of a trial with God . . . the very act of engaging in such an imaginative exploration of his situation vis-à-vis God gives Job a desire to live."[3]

"Job comes up with a notion that nobody has ever dared to express," writes William Safire, "the idea of defying God's judgment by bringing him before a court . . . Job has hold of a great idea: imposing a judicial discipline on the executive Authority."[4]

To the very idea, Rabbi Joshua Sperka bristles. He argues that the overall message of the book of Job is that it is humankind that is on trial, not God: "I am incensed at the flippancy of many writers on the Book of Job whose interpretation puts G-d on trial."[5] And while we will see that the idea that it is Job, or even humanity, that is on trial in the book of Job is a fascinating and fruitful one, it is worth questioning if it is offended piety rather than a fair reading of the text that prevents Rabbi Sperka and others from accepting that in Job 9 our character Job is contemplating a lawsuit against God.

But just as Job considers this, the wounded man is immediately daunted by the prospect, rendering his initial spark into tempered words:

- God's awesome power in creation means that Job would not be contending against a mere mortal but the Creator, Mover, and Destroyer of Creation and its elements (vv. 4–10). Job focuses first on God's destructive power in creation (vv. 5–7), only next on God's creative power (vv. 8–9).
- God is invisible and imperceptible and can "snatch away" without notice and in an instant (vv. 11–12).
- No one has the authority to challenge God; the one who does might just get struck down by God's fierce anger (vv. 12b–13).
- Facing God in "court" would be overwhelming and would make the plaintiff, Job, dumb with terror (vv. 14–15).
- If God did somehow show up at Job's summons (a subpoena!), God would not listen to Job's complaint (v. 16).
- If God did listen to Job, God would condemn him even though he is innocent; indeed, God would prove him guilty and mock him for his suffering (vv. 20, 23).

Job is aware that he would lose either a trial of strength or a trial in court against God (v. 19). It is obvious why Job would lose a trial of strength. He would lose a trial in court because in this lawsuit God would be both the accused and the judge (v. 15).

Indeed, it is also reasonable to surmise that Job also considers God his prosecutor. One could say that Job is countersuing God, who, for Job, is already quite unjustly acting toward him as both prosecutor and judge. There is an exceptionally good reason in all decent legal traditions why roles such as prosecutor, defendant, and judge are separated. As Alter suggests, "one detects a fundamental idea that will lead to Kafka's *The Trial*."[6] Job is caught in a nightmarish "legal system" in which he does not know the charges against him, has no representation, and is prejudged to be guilty.

It is in this context that Job makes his famous cry for a "mediator" (NRSVue) or "arbiter" (NJPS—Heb: *mokiaḥ*). Job needs help. He certainly cannot hope for success in arraigning God before God without some legal help!

While Christians have often caught a hopeful glimpse of Jesus the Future Mediator here, interceding between us and God, it would be best to hesitate before making this move. The God Job describes here is appalling.

Job Has Lost Confidence in God's Justice

In 9:22, Job makes this definitive and shocking declaration:

> *It is all one; therefore I say,*
> *"He destroys the blameless and the guilty."*

This is precisely the opposite of what the tradition teaches and exactly the reverse of what his friends are telling him (cf. Bildad in 8:20). Job is confident that he is "blameless" (9:21), but he is being "crushed" and "wounded" without cause (9:17). This forces Job to conclude that God is not just and has arbitrarily turned against him. This shocking discovery, based on hard experience, shatters the coherence of his former faith. Martin Buber concludes that "[Job] is no longer able to have a single faith in God and in justice. He believes now in justice in spite of believing in God, and he believes in God in spite of believing in justice."[7]

Then Job makes the broader declaration about God's character that the Divine "mocks as the innocent fall" (9:23). Further, "the earth is handed over to the wicked," and God "covers the eyes of its judges" (9:24). Because, after all, "If it is not He [who creates such an unjust world], then who?" Job ventures toward the idea that God is not simply unjust to him, but to the world.

These despairing judgments lead Job to further declarations of misery and dread. His life is ebbing away; he will not see happiness again; there is not even momentary diversion possible (9:25–28).

There is no way to make himself clean enough to please God, even were he to wash his hands not just with soap but with lye (9:30). This is such a bitter image, because if Job were to wash his hands with lye (Heb: *bor*) it would burn his hands off. Also notice the sardonic allusion to multiple other biblical passages calling on sinners to wash themselves clean (Isa 1:16; Jer 4:14). Job intensifies the bitterness by saying, in essence, that even if, through heroic effort, he was to get clean for God, God would respond by dipping him in "muck" (NRSVue "filth"; Heb: *šaḥat*), which while it may mean the grave, probably suggests excrement here (9:31).

Job Begins Addressing God Directly

The careful reader will notice that by 9:28, Job has shifted into direct address of God in the second person. More precisely, he adds direct address to God to his other pattern of describing God in the third person. The whole of chapter 10 is in this direct address voice. Job is challenging God, speaking to God. He describes how disgusted and bitter he is, articulating his complaints about God's unfair condemnation of him, his being found guilty without knowing the charges against himself (note God as prosecutor here), describing God as defrauding him (10:1–7).

He offers a lovely description of God as the life-giving and loving Maker of him and really of every human being (10:8–12a), which reads as a kind of happy midrash on Genesis 2. But Job does this only to set up the terrible idea that God only made him and provided for him to later destroy him, that God set Job up in a meaningful, happy, and prosperous life only to crush him in due time (10:12b-13), like the most sadistic parent ever.

Job begins to acknowledge the possibility that he has committed some hidden sin against God (10:14), but if so, he doesn't know what he has done wrong and, guilty or not, his suffering has shamed him and immiserated him as if he were guilty (10:15). And so, Job concludes (10:18) by reiterating his very first refrain: "Why did You let me come out of the womb?," once more asking for God to cease the ongoing assaults on him and let him sink into death quietly (10:16–17, 20–22).

The Terror of Arbitrary Power

Job has argued that even if he could take God to court, and even if God is at fault for Job's situation, Job can never be *ṣadaq* (just/righteous, 10:15) compared to God. In this courtroom there is no winning; God's status as God is a trump card that always wins.

Job raises a question about whether God is Just or whether God is simply Power. If God is simply Power, especially Absolute Power, then God can do whatever God wants to do, and no one can challenge God on any grounds. The question of God's justice is not relevant because God is not defined by justice, only by power. And because no one is as powerful as God, God always wins.

But Job is fully aware that this is not what his religious tradition has said about God. Job's friends, as spokesmen for the tradition, have been asserting repeatedly that God is just, not only powerful. That is why they continue to feel the need to interpret Job's situation as divine punishment for sin, whether Job's sin or his children's sin. This would mean that God is acting based on the principle of justice, not arbitrary power. Job is not at all convinced, and that is why his generalized lament over his suffering has now moved into a more specific protest directed to God Himself.

In the United States, we have had a political tradition in which the rule of law and the separation of powers was understood as limiting every official's exercise of power, including that of the chief executive. Careful readers of the Bible will not be surprised by the quest of a leader for unconstrained and absolute political power, because it surfaces often, from Pharaoh to Caesar (not to mention many Israelite kings, a fact well-known to the original readers of Job). But it is indeed an unhappy surprise when it happens in a declared democracy.

Many who have left conservative religious communities have done so in part as a response to the abuse of centralized, religiously sanctioned, patriarchal power. And those of us who have done so now wonder: Are our former co-religionists perhaps comfortable with unconstrained executive power because this also represents their vision of God's power?

Do they believe that the Ruler (perhaps also the Father, the Husband, the Religious Leader) can do whatever they want to do because God can do whatever God wants to do, and no underling dare challenge those in power?

Job will not kill himself, and God will not kill him. Thus Job begins his magnificent protest. Like Abraham challenging God's justice in Genesis 18, but from a position of much greater vulnerability, Job challenges God to be a God of justice, not just of arbitrary power. As Safire writes,

> I see Job's ancient challenge to the highest authority as a political metaphor for the modern dissident's principled resistance to authoritarian rule, as well as for his refusal to accept abuses of democratic power . . . the obligation of Man to hold even the highest authority accountable for injustice was first set forth in the most controversial, irreverent, and daringly subversive pages of the Bible—the Book of Job.[8]

19

Those at Ease Have Contempt for Misfortune (Job 11–12)

I am a laughingstock to my friends;
I, who called upon God and he answered me,
a just and blameless man, I am a laughingstock.
Those at ease have contempt for misfortune.
—Job 12:4–5a NRSVue

Zophar: Actually, God Has Gone Easy on You

Job's third friend, Zophar, makes his first appearance in Job 11. And most scholars agree that his tone is the most insulting of any of the three friends.

Zophar opens by claiming that Job's "multitude of words," his "prattle" (NRSVue: "babble"), his "mocking," may silence the crowd, but does not constitute vindication and richly deserves the "rebuke" that Zophar is now about to offer (vv. 1–3).

To Zophar, Job is contending that his "doctrine" or "teaching" (Heb: *leqaḥ*)—mistranslated "conduct" by NRSVue, choosing to follow the Septuagint—is "pure" and his life "innocent" (v. 4).

Both claims by Zophar are not fair. Job is not offering "teaching," as in doctrinal instruction, but protesting his immiserating experiences. As nurse-ethicist Janice Thompson puts it, "Job reveals how disabling change to the body is experienced as exile and as a new experience requiring new language."[1] Yet Zophar does not appear willing to engage Job as a suffering human being but instead only as theological combatant.[2]

Zophar joins Job, ironically, in wishing that "God might speak and talk to you Himself" (v. 5) and "tell you the secrets of wisdom" (Heb:

ḥokmah; v. 6). If God did that, he insists, Job would see that he knows little of "the mystery of God" (vv. 7–12)—which Zophar appears to be claiming to know rather well.[3] Among these mysteries is that God's wisdom is many-sided and beyond measure, that God deservedly has the power to indict any of his creatures, and that God knows the sinful secrets of each human heart.[4]

Moreover, if God did speak to Job, Job might just see that "God has overlooked for you some of your iniquity" (v. 6b), or in the more pungent NRSVue rendering, "God exacts of you less than your guilt deserves." All Job needs to do is—surprise!—turn humbly toward God (v. 13) and remove any "iniquity" and "injustice" that might exist in his life (v. 14). If he does so, God will respond favorably. Job will be (once again) unblemished (a reference to Job's skin condition?), secure, fearless, confident, and hopeful (vv. 15–19). Job will even "forget [his] misery" (v. 16 NRSVue). It will be like water under the bridge. But if he does not do this, Job will merit whatever disaster comes his way, as is the case with all the "deceitful," "hollow," and "wicked" (vv. 11, 12, 20).

Pause for just a moment and think about the callousness of Zophar's most memorable line: "God exacts less of you than your guilt deserves" (Job 11:6). Job has lost all his children, his health, appearance, prosperity, and reputation, and the support of his suffering wife. How is Job ever to forget such losses? What more could God do to Job if he were to "exact" of him what his supposed guilt *did* deserve? It is a statement of breathtaking cruelty, almost certainly uttered because Zophar feels that Job is now threatening communal convictions about the justice of God.

During the height of the AIDS epidemic, some Christians ascribed that deadly disease to God's punishment on gay men and IV drug users. Zophar's words are reminiscent of that terrible time. The idea that Job's suffering is far less than what Job's sins really deserve is unutterably cruel. But such messages are often communicated in traditionalist religious traditions. Is it any wonder many have fled such versions of God, of religion?

Zophar's logic is airtight—and merciless:

1. God is just.

2. God punishes the wicked and vindicates the innocent here on earth during their lifetimes.
3. Job is being punished.
4. Job must be wicked.
5. Job's self-defense and especially his questioning of God only make him more wicked.
6. Thus, God is for now going easy on Job, who deserves far worse.

As spiritual exiles, many of us have seen the lengths believers will sometimes go to, defending their mental picture of God or a conservative theological system built on certainty and rigidity. The introduction of questions, doubts, or even other perspectives threatens the whole machine, and traditionalists who will not listen to the suffering around them are system-prone to respond with fear, disgust, and defensiveness.

The Complacency of Those Who Are at Ease

Job's three-chapter response to Zophar (Job 12–14) begins bitterly: "Indeed you are the people / and wisdom will die with you" (12:2). It is interesting that NJPS adds [voice of] to its rendering, thus: "Indeed you are the [voice of] the people." Interpretations differ here, but it leaves the implication that Job is experiencing his increasingly combative friends as speaking against him not just on their own but on behalf of the whole community. But he refuses to accept that they know anything he does not know (v. 3). They are offering the common wisdom of the tradition, which Job knows and once believed. His experience has invalidated, or at least severely challenged, that common wisdom, and he needs to wrestle with that fact. But this is precisely what his friends and his community are not willing to do—or to allow him to do.

Job twice describes himself as a "laughingstock to [his] friend(s)" (v. 4; cf. similar statements in Jer 20:7 and Lam 3:14). This further confirms the idea that Job's suffering has expanded to include his loss of face in his community. He hears the collective comments of his erstwhile friends as representing a growing contempt for him. Those who began with a silent week sitting alongside him in the ashes of shared grief have now moved to a place of laughing at him.

Looking back at these first speeches of Eliphaz, Bildad, and Zophar, Job's judgment of his friends might seem a bit strong. While this is no fair description of the emotional tone of the speech of Eliphaz (chaps. 4–5) or Bildad (chap. 8), Job is not exaggerating, if we consider how a line like this from Zophar's speech is aimed at him:

A hollow man will get understanding
When a wild ass is born a man. (Job 11:12)

Job's sense that his friends and his community have moved into mocking him leads to the most striking statement in chapter 12. Let's take the whole verse as rendered in the NASB:

He who is at ease holds contempt for calamity
As prepared for those whose feet slip. (Job 12:5 NASB)

The Hebrew is difficult here, and translations differ.[5] In particular, translators differ in how they put Job 12:5a and 12:5b together, but the NASB seems most logical. Its general sense is widely shared in modern English translations. The idea is that complacent onlookers contemptuously view those facing calamity as having authored their own misfortune by allowing their "feet" to "slip" into sin—a familiar metaphor in Scripture (cf. Deut 32:35; 2 Sam 22:37; Pss 18:36; 37:31).

Seeing how his friends now view him, it appears as if Job is processing his growing alienation from them and the community they represent in the following way: *You spout the common wisdom to me because you are not experiencing the calamity that I am experiencing. I remind you that I am a just and blameless man (v. 4b) and do not deserve this cruel treatment from God. My defense of my innocence is threatening your complacent sense of safety. To distance yourself from my fate you have abandoned sympathy for my suffering. You are assuming that my feet have slipped into sin (v. 5b) and that I have earned my misfortune. If you were in my position, you could not say what you are saying. Those at ease have contempt for those who face misfortune.*

Job is naming with uncomfortable clarity a common human tendency. Say my colleague dies of a heart attack. He was younger than me, so it easily could have been me. But the reason that would not happen to me is . . . I exercise every day! That's it! I am safe!

This is a problem the great Danish theologian Søren Kierkegaard saw clearly:

> Perhaps you believe that such a thing cannot happen to you. Who taught you this wisdom, or on what do you base your assurance? Are you wise and understanding, and is this your confidence? Job was the teacher of many. . . . Are you powerful, is this your assurance of immunity? Job was reverenced by the people. Are riches your security? Job possessed the blessing of lands. Are your friends your guarantors? Job was loved by everyone. Do you put your confidence in God? Job was the Lord's confidant . . . there is no hiding place in the wide world where troubles may not find you, and there has never lived a man who was able to say more than you can say, that you do not know when sorrow will visit your house.[6]

This tendency toward spurious self-assurance quickly becomes laced with contempt when we feel the need to connect the calamity facing the other to moral wrongdoing of which we are innocent. Thus the spurious logic of the early Christian response to AIDS. Or those responding to pleas for mercy in light of the pain Christian LGBTQ+ people meet at the hands of traditionalists? It goes like this: *So you say gay people from traditional Christian churches are disproportionately depressed and suicidal. Too bad for them! If they would only obey God and abandon their sin, they would be fine.*

It is only a small further turn of the screw for this attitude to become one of sheer, direct mockery, a laughing at the misfortune of others. Because, after all, *those at ease have contempt for those facing misfortune*, especially a misfortune that the complacent believe could never happen to them.

Is Job by now identifying a former complacency on his own part? Remember the NJPS rendering: "In the thought of the complacent there is contempt for calamity." Perhaps Job is recalling times when, even as he was helping others, he sometimes found himself thinking about how he would never end up in their position because of his piety and integrity.

But now Job knows better. Job knows that God can take down anybody God chooses. Hebrew Bible scholar Thomas Wagner argues that

Job's chronic, miserable pain has "create[ed] a temporal divide in his personal identity over time." Through his catastrophic and now chronic physical and mental pain, he has also experienced "an increase in self-knowledge and a deeper understanding of the human condition."[7] Thompson says that, like many poets and theologians of disability, "Job seeks to reject the meaning others ascribe to their bodies."[8] For Job, there is no going back to the way he used to look at the world. But his friends have not experienced his experiences, and thus they remain complacent and oblivious.

Job now wants to show his contemptuous friends that he knows all about the inscrutable power of God that Zophar had just described. So, in Job 12:7–25 he offers his own soliloquy on the subject.

All creation attests, says Job, that:

In his hand is every living soul
And the breath of all mankind. (Job 12:10)

For Job, however, God's sovereign power over all flesh is exhibited mainly through destruction.[9] God tears down and imprisons (v. 14), withholds water and then overwhelms with water (v. 15), brings down counselors, judges, kings, priests, elders, princes (vv. 17–21), shuts down one's power of speech and another's mental capacity (vv. 20, 24), and lifts nations up only to destroy them (v. 23). Job's recitation of God's power is satirical, as if he is taking biblical piety about God's wisdom and authority (cf. Prov 8:14–16) and turning it upside down.[10] C. L. Seow, in his commentary on Job, calls this an "antidoxology."[11]

Job's protest is not that there is no God or that God is uninvolved with human life, but instead that God is an inscrutable wrathful force who appears to glory in destruction. It is God's creative goodness and God's justice, not God's power, that Job denies.[12] And Job has no patience for those who would want to blame the victims of God's indiscriminate destructive power for their own suffering.

20

Do Not Testify Falsely—Not Even on God's Behalf (Job 13–14)

I would speak to the Almighty;
I insist on arguing with God.
But you invent lies.

Hear now my arguments,
Listen to my pleading.
Will you speak unjustly on God's behalf?
Will you speak deceitfully for Him?
Will you be partial to Him?
Will you plead God's cause?
Will it go well with you when He examines you?
Will you fool Him as one fools men? (Job 13:3–4a, 6–9)

Job Has Prepared His Case against God

Job's long speech in response to Zophar continues into chapter 13. As the chapter opens he reiterates that his friends know nothing that he himself does not know; they are not his teachers, and he is not their "inferior" (13:2 NRSVue). Their position of ease compared to Job's misery has not made them more knowledgeable of the tradition, nor more wise. Indeed, they are "plasterers of lies" and "worthless physicians" (13:4), defending God by being unjust to Job.

This line—"I am not inferior to you"—reminds me of times in which spiritual exiles have made intellectual moves based on hard experience, human relationships, or fresh biblical study, only to be met with repeated elementary instruction from traditionalist "friends" who shout the old verities just a little bit louder as though that will make us suddenly realize the error of our ways.

The idea that Job wants to go to trial with God is indisputable in the verses that follow.[1] "I desire to argue my case with God" (13:3 NRSVue). Indeed, it is possible to read these verses as if Job has already initiated the trial. "I have prepared my case," says Job (13:18a). He goes on to say, very boldly, "I know that I will win it" (13:18b). The only thing missing is Job's adversary—God. It is as if Job has subpoenaed God and is waiting to see whether God will show up.

Job knows how brazen it seems even talking about putting God on trial. He acknowledges that he is risking his life:[2]

> *I will take my flesh in my teeth,*
> *My life in my hands.*
> *He may well slay me; I may have no hope;*
> *Yet I will argue my case before Him.* (Job 13:14–15)

Many translations have butchered 13:15a into the following pious memory verse: "Though he slay me, yet will I trust in him" (cf. NASB, NIV). That line survives as an alternate reading in the NRSVue, but it is not a good translation and totally obscures what is going on in this section.[3]

It is certainly impudent to prepare a case against God, and Job knows it. But he appears to be arguing at the end of this section that no human, and perhaps not even God, can "challenge" him (13:19a). In other words, his experience is what it is; he has testimony to give that cannot be impeached; he demands to be heard; he is "completely innocent and ought to be vindicated publicly."[4]

Then Job simply says, "I would then keep silent and expire" (13:19b). Either this means that having courageously confronted God, Job "is ready to hear God's answer and to die at God's hands,"[5] or that not being able to tell his story, to make his case, would also be a path to death—in this case, the silent death of despair.[6]

Again I am reminded of Elie Wiesel's decision as a teenager first to keep silent for ten years about what he had witnessed at Auschwitz and Buchenwald, but then to spend the rest of his life bearing witness, giving testimony, telling his lacerating story.[7] Sometimes silence is the only proper response to horror and trauma; but there comes a time when silence is itself unbearable, deadly to the human spirit. For Job, *now* is that time. He *may* die if God responds to him in anger; he *will* die if required to remain silent now.

God Demands Truthful Witness and Impartiality —Even for God!

The most fascinating thing about Job 13 still awaits our attention. Job accuses his friends of two clear offenses against law—giving false testimony and showing partiality (13:7–8). Bearing false witness is important enough to be among the Ten Commandments (Exod 20:16), and in a court of law lying under oath is explicitly forbidden as well (Deut 19:16–19). Torah also repeatedly forbids showing partiality to anyone in court (cf. Exod 23:3, 6; Lev 19:15, etc.). All such acts are banned in any just legal system.

Those serving within the judicial system must follow the law and the facts without fear or favor in relation to individuals they represent or judge. Justice is blind in this sense—at its best, the justice system is meant to disregard the power, status, or wealth of those in litigation.

The way Job formulates his language here (vv. 7–12) clarifies that he is indeed intending to put God on trial for God's abusive mistreatment of him. Eliphaz, Bildad, and Zophar have been called as witnesses. Their initial speeches are being treated as something like trial testimony.

After just one round of speeches, Job is clearly accusing his friends of bearing unjust, false, and deceitful witness on God's behalf and as showing partiality toward God (vv. 7–8). He moves on to warn them about the dire consequences of doing this. God sees, God cannot be deceived, and God will "surely reprove you / If in your heart you are partial to Him" (vv. 9–10).

All they are offering are "empty platitudes" (v. 12)—or in the memorable words of the NRSVue translation, "proverbs of ashes." That is, "their maxims may be time-honored, but their time has passed. They bear witness to old sayings that Job's reality has reduced" to ashes.[8] This means that they are false testimony. Something remarkably interesting that we will see in the epilogue of the book of Job is that this negative judgment of the friends' testimony is confirmed by God (Job 42:7).

Hardly any part of the book of Job feels more Jewish than this. I mean that as the highest compliment. That is, hardly any part of the book of Job is more paradoxical. Job accuses his friends of violating God's justice in the very fact of defending God's justice.

Job treats the legal norms of truthful witness and impartiality as sacred, and certainly as norms for which everyone is accountable to God. Job treats God as vigilant in examining the hearts and behaviors of all who go to law to resolve disputes.

But here the accused is God. Job's friends have risen to the defense of God. What could be a higher cause than that? Surely the Holy One, the Creator, the Judge, the Sovereign God, deserves to be defended against such an impudent fellow as Job, who dares to take God to court!

But Job's answer is this: If God is to be arraigned, as Job is attempting, even God can and must be defended in a manner congruent with the terms of a just legal system—a system which, if we are thinking in terms of the Hebrew Bible, God Himself has established in detail in the Torah.

If the legal norm commanded by God is always truthful witness, then that norm applies even when God is on trial. And if that legal norm commanded by God is strict impartiality, then that norm also applies even when God is on trial. As Abraham Joshua Heschel writes, "Suffering can be accepted. . . . Falsehood, however, cannot."[9]

J. Gerald Janzen writes, "In . . . a strange way, Job witnesses to the covenant still alive between him and God."[10] Newsom also emphasizes that Job's relentless demand for truth, and his own truthful speech—at high risk—"bear[s] witness [as] an act of faith. . . . Job's act of faith is that God is fundamentally a God of justice who will yet respond."[11]

This is how even God can be put on trial—because the standard of justice, which God has established, applies even to God. This is true if God is being arraigned by Job, and also true if Job is being arraigned by God (cf. 13:22).

Buber writes, "Job knows of justice only as a human activity, willed by God, but opposed by His acts. The truth of being just and the reality caused by the unjust acts of God are irreconcilable. Job cannot forgo either his own truth or God."[12] In these verses, Job is demanding that God find a way to bring reconciliation precisely at this crucial point.

What greater demonstration could there be of the sacred principle of equality before the law, of impartiality in court, of the absolute requirement to bear only truthful witness? It applies even to God.

Slandered in the Name of God

Many of us on the other side of traditionalist religion will be able to identify with Job's bitter frustration with his friends. When, as spiritual exiles, we, for example, decided we were called to stand in solidarity with LGBTQ+ people—or to identify as such—many of us experienced every kind of slander in the name of God. Every kind of false witness. Every kind of partiality.

The accusation of traditionalist friends may go like this: *You must not have really been a Christian, ever. Your conversion was an illusion. Your call to ministry was a deception. Your prayers were never real and never heard. Any good fruit your life or ministry was once seen to bear was illusory. Because you were never a real Christian, anything you ever did or said that we once respected we now reject.* The logic isn't one of a just trial, but of cancelling a just trial based on an assumption of guilt.

Job's stringent demand of his friends to not speak falsely about him or God, to not show partiality to anyone, not him and not God, ought to encourage those of us in such a position to cry out in a comparable way, saying something like this: *Make whatever fair argument you want against us, against what we believe and what we do, but we will not permit you to bear false witness or show unfair partiality about our lives. About that, we will always protest.*

Janzen writes that Job "levels a devastating critique against religion and its custodians in their attempts to absolve God of implication in the pain and darkness of the world."[13] There is also a parallel lesson to draw: Job levels a devastating critique against religion and its custodians when they bear false witness against dissenters in the name of God.

Job's Despondent Closing Prayer about Human Mortality

Most biblical scholars believe that Job 13:20–14:22 is one long, despondent prayer. Job switches from bold accuser of God to sad supplicant before God. It is a more familiar voice. It might seem like a contradictory voice, but by now we can understand a Job who at times rises in defiance against God and at other times falls on his knees before God. As Gordis writes, "Job flees from God to God."[14]

In this long prayer Job asks God to relent from attacking and terrifying him (13:21). He requests that God let him know (at last) what he has done to deserve God turning on him like Job is his enemy (13:23–24). Job complains that God is punishing him dreadfully and publicly, hemming him in, making him waste away like a moth-eaten garment (13:27–28). This then provokes further thoughts on the hopeless condition of humans. Life is short and full of trouble for a human being (14:1–2). Humans are unclean (14:4). We die quickly without any hope of rebirth (14:5–12).

Job briefly toys with the idea of postmortem life (14:13–17). He creatively imagines it as a time of waiting for God's wrath to pass, a time of hiding in Sheol, after which all would be forgiven, and God and Job would enter into restored relationship. Samuel Balentine writes, "What is most striking about Job's vision is not that he contemplates life after death . . . [it is] that the purpose of his time in Sheol is not so much to give *him* an opportunity to change as to give *God* the chance to change."[15]

But this hope passes. Job returns to the cruelty of the aging process. Our bodies, appearance, and hope are worn away, like water wears away mountain and stones (14:18–19). We die in pain, mourning only for ourselves; humanity no longer has the joy of even knowing what happens to our beloved children who live after us (14:21–22). Gordis notes that this painful truth marks a "reject[ion] even [of] the vicarious immortality of children."[16] In the end, God always prevails against us; death always wins (14:20). How can such pitiful creatures be held to strict account by God? It would be fairer simply to make us and leave us alone to enjoy our few pleasures (14:3, 5, 6).

We return to faces and facing God (Heb: *panim*) in Job 13–14, some of it obscured in translation. Job's accusation of his friends' lack of partiality in 13:8, 10 literally reads "lift God's face."[17] Job is ready to argue his case to God's face (13:15) and says, "No godless person would dare come before God's face (13:16).[18] He wonders why God hides His face (13:24). Job says that if God would let up, Job would not hide his face from God (13:20). And Job speaks sadly of the worn away, altered "visage" (14:20) of the aged human face.

All this time, Job awaits a face-to-face encounter with God. He may not have much of a face left to look at, but with the face that he has, he wants to see God.

III

The Second Cycle of Speeches (Job 15–21)

21

You Subvert Piety and Restrain Prayer (Job 15)

You subvert piety
And restrain prayer to God.
Your sinfulness dictates your speech,
So you choose crafty language.
Your own mouth condemns you—not I;
Your lips testify against you.

—Job 15:4–6

Job as Enemy of Religion?

As the second cycle of speeches begins, the tone darkens even further. Eliphaz moves directly into insulting Job, whose anguished speeches are dismissed as "windy," (15:1), "useless talk," and "words that are of no worth" (15:2).

But now the insults take a turn. The man once described (by God!) as "a blameless and upright man who fears God and shuns evil" (1:8) is now accused of "undermining religion" and "crippling faith in God"[1]—or in the NJPS above, of "subverting piety" and "restraining prayer." The Hebrew word translated piety in NJPS (v. 4) is *yir'ah*, literally, "fear" (of God), related to the corresponding verb *yare'* in 1:8. The one who once feared God is now hindering such fear (reverence, awe, piety, devotion), which is the core instinct, at least of this version of religion.

Job's anguished protests are no longer a matter of mere personal concern, and his friends are no longer merely his personal counselors. Job's friends—at this point let's call them ex-friends—have begun to see Job, that former paragon of piety, as an active threat to the religion of the community. Regular people's faith is being damaged by the things that Job is saying. Community members are being hindered (Heb: *gara'*) from praying. The sense of the Hebrew is that he is "taking away" people's motivation to pray—stealing prayers from God, as it were.

The Community Gathers Round

If Job can be described as restraining prayer to God and subverting the piety of the community, this may mean that the conversation has graduated beyond Job and his three ex-friends. By now, fifteen chapters into the book and entering the second round of dialogue, other people must be listening, seemingly confirmed by this line (v. 10):

> *Among us are gray-haired old men,*
> *Older by far than your father.*

It is possible that the Hebrew word *banu* simply means "on our side" or "in our [little] group," and may just refer to Eliphaz, Bildad, and Zophar. (It is in fact translated as "on our side" by NIV.) But most translations opt for phrases like "among us" (NJPS, ESB, NASB) or "with us" (JPS). The word seems to imply more than three people.

If Eliphaz says Job is undermining religion and stealing the motivation for people to pray, and if he then says that "among us are gray-haired old men," it's probable that the lengthening disputation between Job and his three long-distance ex-friends—perhaps still gathered on the dunghill—has now attracted the attention of the broader community.

I picture Job surrounded by a significant number of at least the men of this (patriarchally organized) community. Crowds gather near crime scenes and yellow police tape, and Job's life is a crime scene. Given his prominence in the community, perhaps it would be inevitable that a crowd would gather at the scene of his ruined face, listening as he cries out his anguished protests to God.

The gathered men are quite concerned because Job is raising questions about matters settled by the ancient wisdom of the community's tradition long before he was born.[2] Job was, indeed, *not* "the first man born" (v. 7). Job was, indeed, *not* created before the hills, *not* present at "the council of God" (v. 8). Picture Eliphaz gesturing to the gathered crowd and pointing out the numerous aged elders listening in, as he says (15:9–10),

What do you know that we do not know,
Or understand that we do not?
Among us are gray-haired old men,
Older by far than your father.

Incidentally, these verses may help to fix Job's age as something like forty-five to fifty-five, with his grown children in their twenties, and the elders in the community gathered around him being as much as a full generation older. The elders are saying to Job: *You have gone too far in your complaints. Together we attest that the tradition has an answer to which you must submit, as we have done in our own times of woe, and as our fathers did before we ever came along.*

Verse 10 might also suggest that Job still has a living father! Where is he at this moment? How is he processing the loss of his own grandchildren (and perhaps great-grandchildren) and the ruin of his son? Is he suffering along with his son, worried about his son? Is he joining in the aged ones' forceful rejection of the way his son is articulating his protest against God? Or is he too miserable to speak? Father of Job, where are you in this story?

Three Explanations for Where Job Has Gone Wrong

Eliphaz categorically reaffirms that no human being can be innocent before God (vv. 14–16). Perhaps correcting Job's sarcastic riff on Psalm 8 in Job 7:17, and in a sense agreeing with Job's despairing cry in 14:4, Eliphaz says,

What is man that he can be cleared of guilt,
One born of woman, that he be in the right?

Eliphaz then quotes himself (from 4:18), suggesting that even the angels and the heavens are "not guiltless" in God's sight, following up with a "how much more" argument about the patent sinfulness of "loathsome and foul" human beings who "drink wrongdoing like water"

(15:z16). This may just be a slap at Job, but overall, it seems that Eliphaz and John Calvin would be friends in their comprehensive doctrine of creaturely depravity.

Since this is true, argues Eliphaz, and since the tradition and the gray-haired elders all affirm it, Job is clearly in the wrong in arguing for his innocence, to such a degree that he is framing his innocence within a lawsuit against God that also threatens to undermine religious commitment in the community.

Eliphaz gropes for an explanation as to why Job could have gone so wrong. He responds in a brief section, offering three possible reasons.

Emotions/Mind. Eliphaz's first and gentlest explanations is that Job's "heart" has "carried" him away (15:12a). We tend to assume "heart" means emotion, though in Israelite psychology, the heart does not indicate so much the emotions as the mind (though emotions can be so indicated). Emphasis on emotions is more often expressed by terms referring to the intestines (*me'ah*, Job 30:27) and kidneys (*kilyah*, Job 19:27). Whether it is his thinking or his emotions at fault, by now Job's words are having negative public impact, and according to Eliphaz, Job needs to get control of himself.

Pride. Eliphaz concludes the couplet beginning his reasoning by saying something that the NJPS renders as tentative (15:12b):

How your eyes have failed you.

The verb translated "failed" here (Heb: *razam*) is a *hapax legomenon.* The word can be translated with a range of possibilities that include "stir," "dart," "wink," "flash," and so on. Probably, given the characteristic pattern of Hebrew poetic parallelism, Eliphaz is simply illustrating his first point with a physical example, to wit: *I see your anger in your eyes.*

The idea may be that Job's pride is getting the better of him. He had been a man in full, at the very top of his community. He had perhaps become quite proud of himself, his achievements, his place in society. Now his pride is wounded; indeed, it is shattered, as he sits with shaved head and beard publicly scraping his scabs with pottery shards.

In talking over passages from the book of Job with some serious Christians who know the book well, I have heard the suggestion that Job's defiant posture toward God in these middle chapters does exhibit an unwholesome pridefulness. He seems not just wounded but angry, and not just regular-angry but prideful-angry, the way that entitled, proud people get angry when they don't get what they believe they deserve. That idea may support this second explanation. Job is not just overcome by emotion; he is overcome by wounded pride.

Wickedness. Eliphaz offers a nastier explanation for Job's missteps when he says, as we quoted above (15:5–6):

> *Your sinfulness dictates your speech,*
> *So you choose crafty language.*
> *Your own mouth condemns you—not I;*
> *Your lips testify against you.*

All translations of Job 15:5 agree on the basic idea: Eliphaz claims that Job's sin, or sinfulness, is shaping what he is saying. Job is choosing language in a calculated fashion to be crafty (Heb: *ʿarumim*)—that is, to be deceptive, cunning, wily, or manipulative. It is the same Hebrew word used of the serpent in Gen 3:1. Eliphaz goes on to say in 15:6 that Job's words are so wrong that he is condemning himself, perhaps a reference to Job's desire for a trial with God. The idea is that Job is a wicked person who, motivated by his sins, is actively manipulating his public words to do real harm to religion and to the practice of piety in his community.

This cruel accusation is not made any better by the more sympathetic explanatory options Eliphaz later explores. It suggests that at least some of Job's listeners have not only turned decisively against him but also have come to believe that he is a threat to the piety of the community.

This is a serious assertion. After all, in the ancient world, to be accused of subverting worship of God or the gods could get you killed. Just ask Socrates.

Just-World Theology Again Reaffirmed

The final part of Job 15 (vv. 17–35) is a long recitation of the just-world theology that Eliphaz feels the need to affirm once again: *The tradition tells us that the wicked will be brought low eventually.* If we feel a bit bored with the repetition of this theology by now—*just-world theology blah*

blah—imagine how Job felt hearing the same standard response to his pain.

The only remotely interesting thing about this specific accusation is that Eliphaz seems to be including Job himself in his recitation of all the bad things that happen to the wicked. The references to destruction of prosperity (v. 21), defiance against God (v. 25), and an implied reference to the loss of progeny to death (v. 30) support the suggestion. This would mean that just-world theology is no longer being used to comfort Job with the idea that if he is truly just and pious all things will turn out fine for him, but instead to prove to him the reason all the events have turned out so terrible for him: his increasingly obvious sinfulness.

Seeing through Eyes That Have Cried

In chapter 15, Job becomes an even deeper friend to spiritual exiles, to those in posttraditionalist spaces whose theology has been changed, who see the world through tears. Who see the hungry eyes of the poor, the haunted eyes of rejected LGBTQ+ teenagers, the frightened eyes of undocumented immigrants. And I note that Job for the first and only time will soon mention his own tears (16:16): "My face is red with weeping."

More than a few of us have been accused of letting our emotions carry us away, of sacrificing the ancient wisdom of tradition to the passing feelings of the moment. Many of us have been condemned as undermining (true) religion, of being a bad influence on the next generation of believers, skeptics, and onlookers. Basically, we have been accused of undermining religion and hindering people's prayers. Along with our brother Job, we reject that accusation.

Yet, the power of the book of Job is most keenly felt by those who do not simply dismiss the concern of Eliphaz and those he represents regarding the destabilizing of religious tradition understood as anchoring the piety and morality of a community. For those who also care about whether the elders are passing along to the ones behind us an adequately sturdy foundation for living, we wrestle with dilemmas that never go away.

Among these are four I'd like to address:

- Where the traditionalist side worries about what happens when a religious community's most ancient doctrines are challenged, spiritual exiles worry about the harm that certain aspects of our religious tradition do to the most vulnerable in our faith communities.
- Where religious traditionalists accuse spiritual exiles of acting as though they were the first to run into a problem that tempts believers to depart from tradition, demanding the exiles return to the ways of the tradition, spiritual exiles respond with the momentous claim that, yes, in this case the ancient tradition may be mistaken and so falling back into line would also be problematic.
- Where religious traditionalists say that the only way one "knows" what is right is by reference to sacred and ancient tradition, its revered textual sources, and its wisest community interpreters, spiritual exiles respond, saying people can and do "know" at least some things through experience, through pain, grief, and joy, and through our embodied lives and emotions, including our tears.
- Where traditionalists say that the community of spiritual exiles is subverting piety and hindering prayer, spiritual exiles say that often unbending religious tradition is responsible for people's loss of faith and their turn away from God.

And so, our engagement with the book of Job continues, with its endless fecundity and Job's own insistence on engaging God and responding to the community of faith that has all but left him, shunning him in an embrace of tradition at all costs.

22

Attacked by God and Men (Job 16:1–17)

Now He has truly worn me out;
You have destroyed my whole community.
You have shriveled me;
My gauntness serves as a witness,
And testifies against me.
In His anger He tears and persecutes me,
He gnashes His teeth at me;
My foe stabs me with his eyes.
They open wide their mouths at me;
Reviling me, they strike my cheeks;
They inflame themselves against me.

—Job 16:7–10

If You Were in My Place

Job has just suffered a grievous public attack on his character, and his community has turned against him. He responds with a speech that exhibits a level of isolation and despair that goes beyond anything we have seen thus far.

Job feels attacked by both God and men. To be exact, Job feels attacked first by God, and then by his community. For Job, God is like the playground bully, while the community is like the bully's gang, free to finish off what the bully started.

Job's third speech, and second in dialogue with his (ex-)friends, begins with a now familiar dismissal of the "windy words" (v. 3) offered by his "sorry comforters" (v. 2, NASB).

As this speech opens, Job reasserts the idea that his friends simply cannot or will not enter his experience with him, and thus they have only their familiar truisms to offer. Job returns to the same theme we saw in 12:5—the complacent contempt for calamity on the part of those spared such calamity. The sorry comforters are unable to move from their complacent judgmental "above"-Job stance to empathic co-suffering "with" Job. And thus, Job finds their "windy words" worthless.

There is an interesting English translation decision to be made in Job 16:4. Compare the NJPS and NRSVue here, looking at the words "would" and "could."

NJPS	NRSVue
I would also talk like you *If you were in my place;* *I would barrage you with words;* *I would wag my head over you.*	*I also could talk as you do,* *if you were in my place;* *I could join words together against you* *and shake my head at you.*

While the Hebrew is open to reading either "would" or "could" here, in English the meanings present as very different. Job may be saying that, if he had not had this horrible experience, he also would offer complacent truisms from above, along with lots of lacerating judgment. This reading would reflect Job recognizing that there is an infinite experiential gulf between those crushed by affliction and the more comfortable ones around them. That seems to be the implication of the NJPS reading.

But Job might also be saying that if their roles were reversed, he *could* act the awful way the friends are acting—but he *would not do so*! One way to understand this approach is by combining the NRSVue for v. 4 with the NJPS for v. 5:

I also could talk as you do,
if you were in my place;
I could join words together against you
and shake my head at you.
[But]
I would encourage you with words,
My moving lips would bring relief.

This reading (very similar to what the NIV offers) makes the most sense in terms of Job's immense frustration with the failure of his (ex-)friends. They have defaulted to complacent judgmentalism based on old-school, just-world theology. That is easy enough to do. But Job appears to be saying that if he were in their place, and they were in his place, he would not offer complacent judgmentalism. Instead, he would use his words to bring encouragement and relief. This they have singularly failed to do, and thus they have added greatly to his suffering and his sense of isolation.

Attacked by God, Finished Off by Men

Immersion into the book of Job begins to yield a sense of the flow of Job's thoughts and emotions, of the pauses, as well as the words.

As we turn now to Job 16:6, I invite you to sense pauses in the text, both before and after.

Before: Job has just finished saying that if the positions were reversed, Job would indeed be an encouraging friend—unlike the way his sorry comforters have been. This is how he wraps up his response to Eliphaz.

Then, a pause.

Next (v. 6, NRSVue):

If I speak, my pain will not be assuaged,
And if I refrain—how much of it leaves me?

Which is to say, I can't bear either to speak or to remain silent. Nothing eases the pain.

Now, picture Job pausing again before summoning the energy to say the lines quoted as epigraph to this chapter (Job 16:7–10, emphasis added):

Now ***He*** *has truly worn me out;*
You *have destroyed my whole community.*
You *have shriveled me;*
My gauntness serves as a witness,
And testifies against me.

In His anger **He** *tears and persecutes me,*
He *gnashes His teeth at me;*
My foe stabs me with his eyes.
They *open wide their mouths at me;*
Reviling me, ***they*** *strike my cheeks;*
They *inflame themselves against me.*

For readers taking time to read the whole section, running through v. 14, what we find is a devastating depiction of God directly attacking Job. God has worn Job out, shriveled him, torn and persecuted him, gnashed his teeth at him, handed him over to evil men, broken him into pieces, taken him by the scruff of the neck and shattered him, set him up as a target for archers, pierced his kidneys with arrows, spilled his bile on the ground, breached (attacked) him again and again, and rushed at him like a warrior. God the Warrior (a hoary biblical motif) has turned on a man, "for no injustice on my part / And for the purity of my prayer!" (16:17).

Job then says that God's attack has set him up to be entirely rejected by his community. A key translation decision must be made here in v. 7: "You have destroyed my whole community" (NJPS).

The term translated "my whole community" (Heb: *kol ʿadati*) could refer to his "company" (NRSVue, NASB), that is, his family and household. But in the context of Job 15:10—"among us are gray-haired old men"—and considering the immediate next verse—"My gauntness serves as a witness, and testifies against me"—the sense seems to be that God's attack on Job, visible in Job's shockingly changed physical appearance, has been taken by his community as evidence of his sinfulness. That's because in the terms of just-world theology, sin is punished by God, immediately, or eventually, or in the next life, if there is one.

The community's conclusion is that only someone who has gravely sinned could be transformed from "a man in full" to this disgusting, worm-riddled, shriveled, gaunt guy sitting on the ashes outside town.

Ambiguity in the Hebrew makes it difficult to determine who the subject is when Job describes the attacks on him. There are abundant references to "he" and "you" and even a crucial "they" in 16:10. I have put all the pronouns in bold to highlight this point. Most translations follow the sense that all or almost all the he's and all the you's refer to God—NJPS makes the decision to render pronouns for God in upper-case, which helps the reader—and it is indisputable that Job is placing ultimate responsibility on God as his attacker. (Notice again that the role of the Adversary who first presented a challenge to God remains completely invisible here.)

But Job also may be speaking in layers. The idea would be that while God is the ultimate adversary to Job, his attack on Job has authorized the onslaughts made by others (v. 11). This would refer not just to the original devastating blows against Job's family, household, and health, but also the attacks that follow, now coming from Job's erstwhile friends and his community.

By now, it is not only God but his entire community that is gnashing its teeth at him, stabbing him with their eyes, opening wide their mouths to revile Job, and (only metaphorically, one hopes), striking Job's cheeks (vv. 9–10). It is God whose attacks have rendered Job defenseless, but the "bowmen" who have "surrounded" him (v. 13) and are now firing arrows into him are his community busily finishing him off.

The Cain and Abel (Gen 4) reference Job makes in v. 18—"Earth, do not cover my blood"—must make readers wonder whether he fears the community is about to murder him in cold blood as a threat to piety and religion. It would not be the first time a person was killed by his or her community as an enemy of religion. Whatever Job's community is doing or might do, they do so freely and unreservedly because they feel fully authorized by God, the One who initiated the attack on Job.

More than any other author on the book of Job that I've read, French philosopher René Girard zeroes in on this dynamic of Job being scapegoated by his community. With reference to 16:18, Girard writes, "Some would say that Job's life is not really threatened, and that there is no question of killing him. He is protected by his friends. This is absolutely false. Job thinks they are after his life. . . . He expects to die soon and not from the illness. . . . He thinks he is going to die a violent death: he imagines the shedding of his own blood."[1]

Job and Jesus

Christian readers will likely notice the striking resonances between Job 16, Suffering Servant texts like Isaiah 53, the majestic/miserable Psalm 22, and the scene at the Cross. Here is Job the innocent, righteous Jesus-figure, despised and rejected by people, in the clutches of the wicked (Job 16:11), surrounded by enemies who revile, strike, and (threaten to) murder his defenseless self. No less a figure than Swiss theologian Karl Barth ends his brief excursus on Job in the *Church Dogmatics* by noting several interesting parallels between Job and Jesus, saying, "with suitable qualifications Job may thus be called a type of Jesus Christ, a witness to the true Witness."[2]

Yet of any figure and any text we find in the Bible, Job offers the most lacerating attack on the goodness of God, the character of God. It is genuinely shocking.[3] This Jesus did not do, even as he cried the tears of the abandoned, "My God, my God, why have you forsaken me?" (Matt 27:46; Mark 15:34).

23

Surely Now My Witness Is in Heaven (Job 16:18–17:16)

Earth, do not cover my blood;
Let there be no resting place for my outcry.
Surely now my witness is in heaven;
He who can testify for me is on high.
O my advocates, my fellows,
Before God my eyes shed tears;
Let Him arbitrate between a man and God
As between a man and his fellow. –Job 16:18–21

Appealing to God against God and Neighbor

As my mind searches for contemporary parallels to Job's utter bereftness, only one readily comes to mind. Religious traditionalists often take aim at LGBTQ+ people within their faith communities, adding their quite near-at-hand interpersonal rejection to the sense of transcendent divine rejection that such believers have often internalized.

Sometimes LGBTQ+ people have accepted the traditionalist framework of their own divine rejection and community rejection, as waves of accusation in the name of Scripture, tradition, and God relentlessly victimize them, driving home that perspective. Only those LGBTQ+ people able to work their way to religious self-acceptance through abandonment of the belief that they somehow rightly have been rejected by both God and people can come to see themselves as innocent before God—and their accusers and the tradition itself as having been the source of wrong and harm.

It is only after this very hard work has been done that brave postrejectionist LGBTQ+ people are able to call on the name of God again, realizing that God has not been their enemy, only the tradition that cites God's authority to harm them. Now able to distinguish between a false God who rejects them and the true God who welcomes them, they become able to call on God in heaven as their witness against the traditionalists' God who has hurt them so.

Who Is This Divine Witness?

These reflections may help us understand the last dramatic move in Job's second response to Eliphaz, and one of the most remarked-upon passages in the entire book of Job—especially for Christians.

"Surely now my witness is in heaven," says Job within the lines quoted above from Job 16:19–21.

Seven chapters earlier, in Job 9:33, Job had lamented that there is no arbiter, no mediator (Heb: *mokiaḥ*), to umpire the dispute between himself and God. But here, Job appears to utter something more like a hope that he might find in heaven a witness (Heb: *edi*) to testify on his behalf, someone indeed to "arbitrate" (v. 21, Heb: *yakaḥ*) between him and God.

There are three options as to who this witness or arbiter could be: (1) God, (2) an angel/member of the divine council (cf. Job 1–2), or (3) the Messiah (for Christians, this would be understood to be the future Messiah, Jesus).

The latter is a tantalizing option for Christians. (And we have Handel's *Messiah* that brings the testaments together, suggesting that the "redeemer" in Job 19:25, the next place where Job utters such a hope, is Jesus.) We have biblical warrant to think of Jesus as the mediator between God and humanity (1 Tim 2:5). As a general principle of biblical interpretation, however, it seems best not to retrofit Christian theology onto a Jewish text that shows no evidence of having a messianic bent. Also, a splitting of the character of God in this way is disturbing; if we need the merciful Son to placate the capricious, cruel Father, what kind of God/gods do we really believe in? Not only because it's problematic, but because the text itself does not suggest this connection, let's set that option aside for now.

As for the idea that Job may be thinking of an angel or a member of the divine council, Job himself is relentlessly monotheistic, centered on the one God. He never references any divine being other than God. While feeling under attack from God, Job may be *longing* for a different divine advocate, but he still does not appear to believe in—or desire to appeal to—such a being.

Appealing to God against a Cruel Idea of God

My tentative proposal given the options is this: Under cruel attack from his friends who evoke the name of God, Job has a moment of turning to God to stand up for him against the (idea of a) God who has treated him unjustly. And Job is asking God to stand up for him against a hostile community that evokes a God who is not just, and against friends who are no longer his advocates but instead his "scornful" (16:20 NRSVue) adversaries, who have made him a "byword" (17:6) of shame and mockery (17:2).

Of course, the idea that Job is asking God to witness for him to God is paradoxical, but paradox is not unusual in the book of Job. Consider for a moment how Job has been sure that God is unjustly attacking him. Now he is further embittered that his friends are joining in with their "windy" diatribes, asserting and reasserting the idea that God is justly punishing him for his supposed sins.

Freedom and an end to despair only come when the attacks of the believing community in the name of God are repudiated by the target of those attacks in the name of a more just and loving God.

That is, freedom and hope happen when the assertions about God of the believing community and the faith tradition they claim to represent are *repudiated in the name of a revised understanding of God and a challenge to the tradition*. Only the idea of a better God, a more just God, can end the torture of believing that a capricious version of God and a damning community could be signs of justice.

What if Job, terribly stung by the awful attacks that he is receiving from his pious friends, has a moment of turning back to the God whom heretofore he has believed is attacking him, and is asking that God to now come to his aid?

And/or, what if Job is getting the seedling of an idea that the real God is not his enemy? He may be surmising that the problem is the *idea of God* that he has been carrying around and torturing himself with—and the very similar idea of God that his friends have been asserting.

Job thinks God has been attacking him, unjustly.

His community thinks God has been punishing him, justly.

But what if neither is the best interpretation of God's ways with Job and the world?

What if there actually exists, in the heavens, a God of compassion who sees how Job "sheds tears" (16:20), who sees Job's face "red with weeping" (16:16), who sees a man losing all hope (17:15), who in mercy will turn to this suffering man? One might say that this is the God of whom Job catches just a glimpse, for just a moment.

Surely now my witness is in heaven;
He who can testify for me is on high.
O my advocates, my fellows,
Before God my eyes shed tears;
Let Him arbitrate between a man and God. (Job 16:19–21)

24

Will Earth's Order Be Disrupted for Your Sake? (Job 18)

You who tear yourself to pieces in anger—
Will earth's order be disrupted for your sake?
Will rocks be dislodged from their place?
Indeed, the light of the wicked fails;
The flame of his fire does not shine . . .
Generations to come will be appalled at his fate,
As the previous ones are seized with horror.
—Job 18:4–5, 20

You Tear Yourself to Pieces in Anger

As the erstwhile friends are growing weary of Job's talk, Bildad's second speech begins with yet another reminder that they feel offended by his challenges to their theology, as though Job were challenging their basic intelligence (18:2–3).

In Bildad's speech, there is only one verse that seems to offer anything new or of much interest. Look at v. 4, cited above:

You who tear yourself to pieces in anger—
Will earth's order be disrupted for your sake?
Will rocks be dislodged from their place?

Bildad is correctly noting that Job is not just sad but enraged (v. 4, Heb: *ʾap*). Sadness might signal defeated surrender to grief, but Job has not gotten there—though some moments read like it. Instead, Job is primarily angry—an anger that does not suggest surrender nor acceptance of what has happened to him and his family. Because at the core of that lack of surrender is Job's vivid sense that his suffering is unjust and must be protested.

Again, it seems appropriate to note that Job's earlier life was not like those whose entire existence consists of being ground into the dust by more powerful people and forces. Job was accustomed to being empowered and having his rights respected by God and neighbor. Job's plight is the existential situation of the privileged rights-bearing member of a community who suddenly finds all such rights and privileges taken away. *I deserve to be treated better than this!* The reaction to such an affront is not primarily sadness but blazing anger.

Bildad says to Job: in your rage—which Bildad clearly thinks is not appropriate—"you are tearing yourself into pieces." The Hebrew word translated "yourself" is *napšo* (lit. "his life"), a form of the familiar term *nepeš*, which means one's life/soul/self. *You are tearing your soul into pieces* would be an apt translation. But, of course, this is a misdiagnosis: Job's life has been torn into pieces by the suffering that God has authorized to be inflicted upon him. Job's anger is his response. And Bildad makes a classic blame-the-victim move, where the expression of hurt or anger on the part of the victimized Job gets defined as the problem.

The Essential Idea of the Moral Order of the World

The central theme that must be addressed from Job 18 is Bildad's picturesque reiteration of what is to him an essential idea—the moral order of the world or, as I termed it earlier, just-world theology.

It is easy to miss the heart of Bildad's concern if Job 18:4 is translated too woodenly. Take a look at these two translations of the verse:

NRSV	You who tear yourself in your anger— shall the earth be forsaken because of you or the rock be removed out of its place?
NASB	You who tear yourself in your anger— Should the earth be abandoned for your sake, Or the rock removed from its place?

Now compare these to what the NJPS does:

NJPS	You who tear yourself to pieces in anger— Will earth's order be disrupted for your sake? Will rocks be dislodged from their place?

In its marginal notes, the NJPS acknowledges that this is not a literal rendering, which suggests that in this case the translators are attempting to communicate the sense of the line. That is why they go with the subtly metaphorical "Will earth's order be disrupted for your sake?"

To take the literal reading and suggest that Job is calling for the earth to be abandoned/forsaken makes no sense. Where would one go?

No, the idea, especially when taken in tandem with its next line (in keeping with Hebrew poetic parallelism), is that from his ex-friend's perspective, Job is offering a terrifying challenge to the moral order of the world. If Job's critique is accepted, the moral order as taught by generations will suffer something like an earthquake or a rockslide. Job is challenging the very bedrock of the historic moral and religious imagination of his community

Dietrich Bonhoeffer once said of his own morally confused culture during the Nazi era that people no longer had "solid ground under their feet." It is hard to "stand fast"—another Bonhoeffer phrase—when the ground is shifting under one's feet. We rely on solid ground, earth that does not move, both literally and metaphorically. Here, what Bildad is saying is that Job is challenging the moral solid ground of his culture in such a dramatic way that he must be stopped.

The following diagram may help in visualizing the problem. I have used it in books since my book *Kingdom Ethics* was published.[1]

Human moral reasoning has a discernible multilevel structure that we can recognize from this image. Working from the top down, the chart suggests that people make "particular judgments" in specific situations (we do this all the time), and that if you ask someone why they chose to act as they did, they could perhaps cite a moral rule as the basis. Then, if you ask, again, what is the basis of that rule, they might be able to cite a broader principle that grounds the rule. Then, finally, if you ask them why they care about that principle, they might be able to reach one level

Levels of moral norms

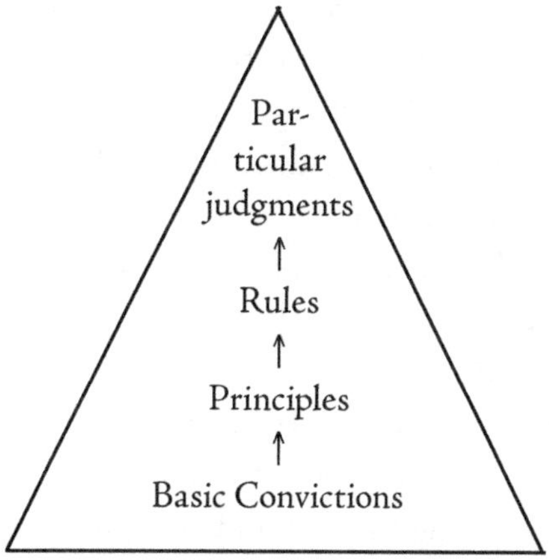

deeper and tell you about a "basic conviction" that sits at the bedrock of all their moral reasoning.

For example: From a distance, I see a little old lady laboriously walking across a busy street trying to push a shopping cart. However, she is too slow, so she is caught in the middle of the crosswalk as the light changes. So, at that moment I jump out of my seat at the coffee shop and rush to the old lady, waving my arms frantically at the traffic to stop for her. I then walk her across the street.

Why do I make this "particular judgment"? Probably because I am working out of a rule I was once taught—go to the assistance of people who need help. If asked for the principle underneath that rule, it would be that any decent person should give help to those in need, especially in specific vulnerable cases, especially when the situation might be life-threatening. If asked, finally, what is the basis for my commitment to that principle, it would be something like the sacred worth of every life in God's sight. What makes this a basic conviction is that it is moral bedrock. I can't get lower or more basic than this level. If you ask me why I believe life is sacred, I will say that it is a central conviction of my faith. Period.

In the same way we discovered my moral bedrock for the decision I made to help the elder woman across the street, you can see how a just-world theology would function in this chart, as a *basic conviction* for Job's interlocutors and community.

Let's set it up this way. Job's friends are rejecting Job's good character and his place in their community and offering statements of negative moral evaluation of him. That is their particular judgment.

The rule underneath that judgment could be rendered as: Always act to reinforce community adherence to the God-given moral order of the world, using positive or negative reinforcement as appropriate.

The principle underneath that rule could be articulated as follows: It is essential for social morality for people to live according to the moral order of the world.

The basic conviction undergirding that principle might be something like this: The one sovereign God is the just creator of a morally ordered world and rightly demands that humans live according to the moral order He has created.[2]

The threat that Job poses, then, is that he is rejecting not only the particular (negative) judgment that his friends are inflicting upon him. The deeper problem is that his rejection goes all the way down to the basic conviction level—he is articulating explicit rejection of the theological and moral bedrock of their worldview. If God is not in fact just, not in fact the creator of a morally ordered world, God cannot rightly demand that people live according to this (apparently nonexistent) moral order. Therefore, the principle, the rule, and the particular judgment articulated by his community are baseless.

If Job is right, it means that his community has no moral foundation anymore. Earth's order has been disrupted for Job's sake. The ground is no longer steady. Everyone is flying about in midair. And this is intolerable. According to Bildad, this is a trainwreck of religious principles. Job must be pummeled into submission or else all moral order will fall.

But what if Job simply refuses to submit? What if his newly learned basic conviction now makes it impossible for him to submit?

But We So Need the Hitlers of the World to Be Destroyed

Bildad follows his warning to Job about disrupting the moral order of the world with yet another lengthy discourse on all the bad things that happen to the wicked. Is this just another round of *just-world-theology blah blah?*

Yes and no. Yes, in the sense that the basic argument is the same—the wicked will be brought low, in this life, in a decisive, unmistakable way that everyone can see.

No, in the sense that Bildad's description of the downfall of the wicked is unusually picturesque, thorough, and devastating (18:5–19), ending with:

Generations to come will be appalled at his fate,
As the previous ones are seized with horror.

This vivid depiction of the ruination of the truly wicked person reminds me of the trajectory of Adolf Hitler's life. For about twenty years (1925–1945) he was a household name, the ruler of Germany for twelve years (1933–1945), and arguably the center of world politics for ten years (1935–1945). To read the newspapers and political commentary from this period was to see Hitler omnipresent, the dominant figure almost every day.

But his ominous dark light failed. He walked into traps that he himself unwittingly set. Disaster finally came to him. In 1944, he was nearly killed in an assassination attempt that harmed his mental and physical health. In late April 1945, surrounded by enemies on all sides, he killed his new wife and himself. On his orders, his body was turned to ashes in a Berlin bunker. He had no progeny. Future generations were and are appalled at his deeds and his fate. He is understood by all decent people to have fully deserved his premature death and eternal infamy.

So, Brother Bildad, we grant you this: We human beings very much want and need the Hitlers of the world to be destroyed in the comprehensive way you describe here. We need their wickedness to be so completely repudiated, their reputations to be so completely destroyed, that generations to come will be reminded that there is right and there is wrong, and there are consequences for human actions. Just as we need evidence that the truly good life is rewarded, so also we need evidence that the truly wicked life is punished. Especially do we elders feel the need for such moral clarity to be communicated to the young ones, that they might rightly direct their paths and might preserve a world worth living in.

The Essential Myth of a Just World

The book of Job may be teaching (and is certainly voicing the idea) that the ancient idea of earth as a morally ordered world in which the good are visibly rewarded and the wicked are visibly ruined is a myth. One way we can know it to be a myth is because, sometimes, horrible suffering comes upon the innocent—like the character named Job.

But the culture that produced the book of Job—and not only that culture—also knew that just-world theology, even if it is a myth, is a useful—even an essential—myth, in motivating good and just behavior by real people in real time.

In the book of Job, Job's friends and apparently his entire community are so committed to the essential myth of a just world that they are willing to sacrifice him on that myth's altar. But the very fact of the grave suffering of such a good man threatens the myth, and his vocal protests turn that threat into a communal religious crisis. Job must be destroyed, scapegoat to the myth of a just world.

As René Girard writes, "Job clearly articulates the cause of his suffering—the fact that he is ostracized and persecuted by the people around him. He has done no harm, yet everyone turns away from him and is dead set against him. He is the scapegoat of his community."[3]

Quite independently of discovering Girard's treatment of Job, I had earlier concluded that Job's misery was at least compounded by, if not centered in, his rejection by his community, made even more intense because he had once been, as Girard says, the "idol" of that same community.

Girard emphasizes that a scapegoating mob relies on unanimity of accusation and often gets the innocent victim to join in on the accusation by pleading guilty despite their own innocence. This is what Job refuses to do, which enrages the mob even more, placing him in even more danger.

25

He Has Stripped Me of My Glory (Job 19)

He has stripped me of my glory,
Removed the crown from my head.
He tears down every part of me; I perish;
He uproots my hope like a tree . . .
My dependents and maidservants regard me as a stranger;
I am an outsider to them.
I summon my servant but he does not respond;
I must myself entreat him.

—Job 19:9–10, 15–16

You Magnify Yourselves against Me

Job begins his response to Bildad's second speech by renewing his lament that his friends have "time and again" added their grievous, crushing, and abusive insults (vv. 2–3) onto God's terrible assault on him. Again, Job attributes the primary wrong to God (vv. 6, 8–12), but God is not speaking to him, while his friends continue to do so through various attacks on his character and piety.

For Job, the main story remains the injustice God has inflicted on him and God's silence in response to his complaints (v. 7):

I cry, "Violence!" but am not answered;
I shout, but can get no justice.

But Job is increasingly angry about his growing humiliation (v. 5, NRSVue):

You magnify yourselves against me
And make my humiliation an argument against me.

From Job's perspective, it is (obviously) bad enough that God has assaulted Job as He has. The fact that his former friends have felt the need to pile on has astounded and enraged him. His analysis is that they have responded to his humiliation not by empathetic identification but by prideful distancing. They have "magnified" themselves (NASB: "vaunted") against him. That is, they have looked at Job's oozing sores and ruined life and, rather than entering into his suffering, have used it as an argument against him. Only someone whom God is judging could possibly look like Job does! That is the move they have made, and Job sputters with outrage about it.

The idea that Job's humiliating physical and material condition is being taken as evidence of his moral degradation holds similarities to how the Nazi regime set up massive, overcrowded Jewish ghettos in major cities in Poland, and their cameramen filmed images of the starving, overcrowded, often diseased Jewish residents of these ghettos as evidence of their worthiness of suffering in this way. Nazis incorporated these revolting images into propaganda pieces for their military and civilians in order to deepen disgust at "the Jews"—who had been subject to years of dehumanizing treatment and Nazi rhetoric already. These filmed images made it all the easier to take the next step against them—extermination. To borrow Job's words, the Nazis were "magnifying" themselves by using the Jewish suffering that they had created as evidence that their victims deserved it.

If Indeed I Have Erred

And here in the text we discover a pivotal, elusive little verse at the opening of this chapter (v. 4):

If indeed I have erred,
My error remains with me.

Job does not concede that he has sinned. But for the sake of argument, he presents the "if" idea (Heb: *šagah*). Even so, Job says, "my error remains with me" (Heb: *ʾitti talin mešugati*).

This line is a subtle expression of moral agency and dignity on the part of Job. Job's friends—whom Job did not invite to come see him, whom Job especially did *not* invite to make moral commentary on his life—have crossed a line related to Job's moral dignity. Job is telling them to back off from their prideful moral judgments against him, because if indeed he is being punished by God—an idea he does not concede—his misdeeds and his punishment are between him and God.

Job is quite explicitly saying that he never invited his friends into such an unbalanced relationship. Job's sense of personal moral agency and dignity are offended. *Back off, old friends. I never asked you to make yourselves judges over me. You came to offer me comfort. Maybe do some of that.*

Job Has Lost Power, Respect, Community

Sometimes it is the odd, overlooked little verse that best illuminates what is really going on in a passage. That is the case, I believe, with Job 19:16:

> *I summon my servant but he does not respond;*
> *I must myself entreat him.*

On first appearance it might seem this line is far less important than those that surround it, all of which point to Job's profound sense of isolation.

In vv. 13 and 14 Job describes how he has been abandoned both by his relatives and his friends. In v. 15 he laments that he has become a stranger to his dependents and maidservants. In v. 17 he says that even his odor is repulsive to his wife and family members. In v. 18, Job laments that even youngsters, or young children,[1] "disdain" and speak against him. "Those I love have turned against me" (v. 19a) summarizes his overall situation of complete isolation. Job has become a byword, a pariah, alienated from his most intimate relations all the way through to his entire community.

What is so striking about v. 16 is Job's loss of the *power to command* even in his own household. Notice that he still has servants, likely slaves, whom he was certainly accustomed to commanding. This one detail helps illuminate the fact that Job's community has coalesced around an interpretation of his plight that has robbed him not just of relationships but of the communal respect he once enjoyed as "the greatest man in the East." Job has been "stripped of [his] glory," the "crown" has been "removed from [his] head" (v. 9). This is how he himself describes what has happened to him.

Bible professor Laura Quick, in her study of the metaphorical use of images related to clothing and unclothing, dressing and stripping, in the biblical world, shows that loss of clothing and thus nakedness, especially for men, is often associated with shame and with weakness.[2] Before the world, Job has been stripped naked, in a scene that would be hard for Christians to read without thinking of Jesus, stripped naked and raised on a Roman cross.

This is a reminder that Job's suffering is of a particular type tied to his social location. He was *not* one of the wretched of the earth who was always beaten down and who had learned never to expect any better. He was a leader, a wealthy, respected man with a large household and a dominant place in his community, "clothed" in honor. It is this kind of man who has now lost not just his children, his wife's affection, and his wealth but his social status and the honor that went with it.[3] This loss is signaled by the fact that when he sends someone to summon one of his household servants, the latter doesn't bother to respond without personal entreaty. O how the mighty have fallen!

This may not seem like it matters all that much—but honor and respect and status do matter. It is why Jesus taught so much about these issues, teaching his disciples to train themselves out of seeking them. He said, Go to the lowest place at the banquet rather than the head table (Luke 14:7–11). Do not invite the rich and powerful to your parties but instead those who can't repay you (Luke 14:12–14). Be a humble servant rather than an exalted lord (Matt 23:12; Luke 14:11).

After I wrote *Changing Our Mind* in 2014, I lost relationships with some close friends and colleagues. That hurt, for sure. But the loss of professional and especially religious honor and respect stung with surprising force. *We withdraw our lecture invitation to you. We cancel the award we were about to give you.*

Humans are social animals. For millennia we have depended on our communities not just for a place to live and a sense of security but for the intangible yet very real experience of being valued, honored, and respected. Those of us who have experienced the intoxicants of high status, high honor, high respect, and high power find it shocking and terrible to lose them and to descend, descend, descend to the depths of our communities—or to be pushed outside the gates altogether.

As the book of Job continues to reveal, Job's former life was one of unimpeachable piety and integrity *within a certain social stratum*—the very highest of his world. He had some things to learn about what piety and integrity look like when a person is forced into social descent, humiliation, and powerlessness, when joining the wretched of the earth. And he *is* learning some of those things. And it hurts to learn them.

I Know That My Redeemer Lives

And as for me, I know that my Redeemer lives,
And at the last He will take His stand on the earth.
Even after my skin is destroyed,
Yet from my flesh I shall see God;
Whom I myself shall behold,
And whom my eyes shall see and not another.
My heart faints within me.

—Job 19:25–27 NASB

Historically, Christians have thrilled to the surprisingly hopeful notes occasionally struck by our miserable brother Job. We saw in Job's last speech (16:18–21) his hope-against-hope of a "witness" in heaven to testify on his behalf, someone, or Someone, to "arbitrate" between Job and God.

Here Job again returns to the theme of a Redeemer, in verses that have inspired many a Christian musician and homilist. In this text Job introduces a term familiar in the Hebrew Bible, but a new one for Job in this story: Job seeks a *go'el*—a vindicator, redeemer, rescuer.

In its use in Scripture, this term most often refers to a kinsman who acts to vindicate the rights or avenge the wrongs done to a fellow family member. In Leviticus 25, the kinsman is required to redeem property lost due to poverty and to reclaim a family member sold into slavery. In Numbers 35, the task of the kinsman-redeemer is to avenge the blood of a murdered family member. In Ruth 2–4, Boaz functions as *go'el* to Naomi and Ruth by protecting Ruth, redeeming family land, and ultimately marrying Ruth to fulfill the levirate function. Perhaps most relevant to Job 19 is the word's use in four passages late in Isaiah (41:14; 43:1; 44:6; 63:16), where God is described as *go'el*—usually translated "redeemer"—of Israel.

We have considered the occasionally irresistible idea (to Christians) that this mediator/arbitrator and now vindicator/redeemer is Jesus Christ. This passage in Job is the one that has given rise to the most intense messianic readings (see Matt 24:30; John 14:3; Acts 1:11; 1 Thess 4:16–17; Rev 22:12). Christians confess that the risen Jesus will return to earth at the last day. He will raise the dead as he was raised from the dead. This would mean for Job, as for us, even after his "skin is destroyed," Job will see God with his own eyes (v. 27).

On this reading, the character Job is uttering a misery-inspired prophetic word that goes beyond what his tradition would have produced. Even assuming a late date for the composition of the book of Job, if this is an explicit statement of resurrection hope, this is an innovation. And if this is a turn to the idea that because there is no reliable justice in this life, on this earth, there must be justice (and mercy, and rescue, and vindication) on the other side, in another realm after death, then we glimpse here the seedling of an idea that came to occupy a very important place in Christianity—and a somewhat more contested place in Judaism. Because, after all, it is one solution to the problem of persistent injustice and evil in this world: Justice will come in the next one.

The NJPS translation subtly signals a very different kind of reading:

But I know that my Vindicator lives;
In the end He will testify on earth—
This, after my skin will have been peeled off.
But I would behold God while still in my flesh,
I myself, not another, would behold Him;
Would see with my own eyes:
My heart pines within me.

By translating *go'el* as (capital-V) "vindicator" rather than "redeemer," NJPS subtly signals a this-worldly vindication for Job. Reading "testify on earth" rather than "take his stand on earth" far more clearly connotes a legal metaphor rather than some kind of spiritual redemption. This is a vision of a vindicator—God—who finally answers Job's summons and testifies on his behalf, right here on earth. If we take 19:26 to read Job's skin as "peeled off" rather than "destroyed," it could easily speak to the further degradation of Job's skin condition rather than his bodily death, though it may indicate his death and his chagrin that such vindication won't happen while he is alive even as he wishes it to.[4]

From my reading, this idea is that God will at last show up for even the physically ruined Job, not a moment too soon, finally to testify to his piety and integrity and to refute the iniquitously false testimony (19:29) of his friends and community. In this way, God will "redeem" Job, not by restoring all that he has lost but by restoring the one thing Job seems to care about most—his ruined moral and spiritual reputation. Is this what God does at the end of the book of Job?

Notice that in both Job 16:19–21 and here in Job 19:25–27 Job makes a desperate turn to God as arbitrator, as vindicator, as redeemer—as *justice-maker*—in the teeth of the cruel misjudgments being inflicted upon him by his (ex-)friends and formerly respectful community.

The pattern is similar in both chapters: Job views God as the initial assailant, then the community has joined in with its gratuitously cruel, unwanted rejection, and finally Job turns back to God for rescue and vindication. This at least raises the possibility that Job is reconsidering the idea that God is his assailant; it certainly reflects a desperate hope that God's mercy, and perhaps even God's justice, will finally prevail.

In the face of human cruelty, Job turns back to a God whose character he is reconsidering with a glimmer of hope. He will not "give in to overwhelming pressures and sink into passivity and disintegration." Instead, he has found "the will to fight."[5] He does so by once again making his case to God.

This may be a reminder that while our theories about what an invisible God is doing to us in a bad situation are based on disputable theological theories, what our kin, friends, and community do to us in a bad situation is not theoretical or theological. It is flesh-and-blood, this-worldly reality. Those who have tasted comprehensive rejection by kin, friends, and community know this.

26

The Wicked Are Punished, or Not (Job 20–21)

Heaven will expose his iniquity; *Earth will rise up against him.* *His household will be cast forth by a flood,* *Spilled out on the day of His wrath.* *This is the wicked man's portion from God,* *The lot God has ordained for him.* —*Job 20:27–29*	*Why do the wicked live on,* *Prosper and grow wealthy?* *Their children are with them always,* *And they see their children's children.* *Their homes are secure, without fear;* *They do not feel the rod of God.* —*Job 21:7–9*

Completely Contradictory Texts

In Job 20, Zophar claims in a long and picturesque soliloquy that the wicked are punished in this life, in the end coming to complete ruin. This claim is quickly refuted in Job 21, as Job claims that the wicked are not punished in this life but instead prosper and live at ease until their peaceful deaths.

One translation, the New American Standard Bible (NASB), a favorite among evangelicals, seems to be protecting the tender sensitivity of its readership, with translator acrobatics that avoid communicating the idea that Job 20 and 21 directly contradict each other. But in so doing, these translations misdirect the reader of the text.

While the subheading for Job 21 has the NASB rendering as "Job says God will deal with the wicked," NJPS as usual is comfortable rendering contrary texts as simply contrary, reading, "For the evil man is spared on the day of calamity." The Hebrew verb there is *ḥaśak*. While it can mean "withheld" or "reserved" rather than "spared," no major modern translation other than NASB uses "reserved," and it makes little sense in context.[1] I bring this up to remind the reader that translations really do involve choices, and those choices matter.

A Point–Counterpoint Debate

Close study of these two chapters yields the conclusion that these texts are a matched set, an intentionally contradictory pair, a point–counterpoint debate familiarly used in Hebrew texts and deployed here to end the second cycle of speeches. Every point Zophar asserts in Job 20 is rebutted by Job in Job 21. To give you a sense of this point-counterpoint approach, here are five crucial examples:

1. Zophar claims that "since man was set on earth, the joy of the wicked has been brief" (20:4–5).

Job rebuts this by saying that if one had "consulted the wayfarers" (21:29–30), they could offer plenty of "evidence" to the contrary. Experienced observers can easily report that instead of being punished, "the evil man is spared on the day of calamity." Zophar, Job suggests, could use less doctrine and more observation.

2. Zophar claims that while the wicked man "grows as high as the sky," soon enough he perishes so completely that he disappears like a dream (20:6–9).

Job rebuts this by saying that "the wicked live on" (and on, and on), and you can easily find them at their homes enjoying their enviable prosperity (21:7–9).

3. Zophar claims that the children of the wicked also are ruined, as their father's loss of prosperity falls on them as well (20:10, 19–21, 26, 28).

Job rebuts this by saying that the children and children's children of the wicked continue on, the little ones frolicking and playing on the family estate, skipping about and singing, enjoying the good life that the wicked patriarch made available to them (21:8, 11–12).

4. Zophar uses an extended food metaphor—"though evil is sweet to his taste"—to suggest that the ill-gotten happy lifestyle of eating and drinking and merrymaking of the wicked will soon enough turn to poison in their bellies (20:12–17, 23).

Job rebuts this with a similar metaphor but an entirely different meaning: "His pails are full of milk/The marrow of his bones is juicy" (21:24). The wicked die fat and sassy. The poison never comes.

5. Zophar claims that "because he crushed and tortured the poor," the wicked will have to "give back the goods unswallowed" (20:19).

Once again Job rebuts this by lamenting "how seldom does the lamp of the wicked fail" (21:17) and how "they spend their days in happiness and go down to Sheol in peace" (21:13). In addition, the wicked also mock at God and refuse to learn God's ways, yet without any adverse happenings affecting them (21:14–15).

The book of Job offers these arguments as readers field the logic for themselves, comparing the words of Zophar or Job to determine where they themselves land in the point-counterpoint assessment of the wicked.

The Current Climate

The point-counterpoint of Job 20–21 resonates deeply in our present political climate that favors the power of the 1 percent. We watch as the millionaire and billionaire class grow their estates, their children flourishing; evil has not turned to poison in their mouths. They have plenty of survivors to enjoy (or fight over) their ill-gained financial legacies, while those on the financial margins suffer.

Job observes what is in front of him with accuracy: "The wicked live on, prosper, and grow wealthy" (21:7). As Zophar offers the perspective of how tradition would respond to the wicked, Job observes, without magical thinking, that the wicked are secure and unpunished either by humans or by the "rod of God" (21:9). The "calamity" that Zophar and his friends believe is fully deserved by the wicked is actually the fate of the man Job, who though declared righteous by God suffers greatly, while for the wicked, "his pails are full of milk," his estates full of guests, his bank accounts full of money (cf. 21:20–25).

Maybe We Cannot Agree on Who Is Wicked

Zophar says the wicked are brought low. Job says they are not. This might seem like an empirically solvable argument. In theory, all one must do is undertake a count of wicked people and look what happens to them.

But that would require being able to agree not just on what is wickedness (and what is goodness) but also on an assessment of who falls within those categories. In our morally divided societies today, we are experiencing very great difficulty doing precisely this. One group's hero is another group's villain.[2]

Later in the book of Job, our hero will conclude his defense of his life with three chapters (Job 29–31) describing in magnificent detail the virtuous life he sought to live prior to the unjust ruin that fell upon him. Surely, he will not offer such a defense without believing that his community will agree on what qualifies as virtuous behavior. *The question for Job is not what he and his community believe is virtuous but whether he has been virtuous.*

Here in the twenty-first century, in the United States at least, we do not agree on what is virtuous, and perhaps this is why we cannot agree on who is virtuous. In terms of social cohesion over the long term, we may be far worse off than the community that surrounds the unfortunate man named Job.

Job's community needs to interpret Job as wicked to make moral sense of his ruination. We, however, don't know how to make moral sense at all. This leaves terrifyingly open the question of whether we can find sufficient moral agreement to survive as a community.

IV

The Third Cycle of Speeches (Job 22–27)

27

Eliphaz Throws Everything He Has at Job (Job 22)

Can a man be of use to God,
A wise man benefit him?

Is it because of your piety that He arraigns you?
You know that your wickedness is great.

Therefore snares are all around you,
And sudden terrors frighten you.

You say, "What can God know?
Can He govern through the dense cloud?"

Have you observed the immemorial path
That evil men have trodden;
How they were shriveled up before their time
And their foundation poured out like a river?

If you return to Shaddai you will be restored.
—Job 22:2, 4a, 5, 10, 13, 15–16, 23a

The Third Cycle Is More Like a Unicycle

Traditionally, Job 22–27 is described as the "third cycle" or "third round" of speeches between Job and his erstwhile friends. But when you look at it closely, it is more like a unicycle. Eliphaz returns to offer the last full "friend" speech in the entire book of Job. Job follows with a long response (Job 23–24) that, for reasons I will propose, does not address Eliphaz directly. This is no point-counterpoint exchange here.

In Job 25, "friend" number 2, Bildad, sputters into the text, with a puny miniresponse. And Job responds to the three one last time from 26:1 to 27:6 or 27:7. One speaker shows up in the rest of chapter 27, but who that speaker is, is unclear. Zophar is not credited with a final speech. And after that the dialogue between Job and his friends limps toward a conclusion.

Viewed from this perspective, Job 22 looks especially important. It is the last full-length speech clearly uttered by one of Job's three friends. It is certainly the last word that the first and presumably most distinguished friend, Eliphaz, offers in the book.

Given the context, though, the content of the speech is especially disappointing. The speech is incoherent. The best that can be said of it is that Eliphaz throws everything he has at Job, without effort anymore to offer a sustained and logical argument. It's like he's throwing spaghetti at the wall and seeing what sticks.

That is instructive, of course, suggesting it's more important to Eliphaz to hit Job with every possible attack he can muster than for any argument to make sense—or for ideas to cohere with one another. Perhaps you have had the misfortune of finding yourself in an angry, bitter argument in which you realize that hurting the other person through words, rather than communicating information, has become the point of the exchange. That, it seems to me, is what Eliphaz is doing in Job 22.

Job 22 in Seven Moves

Here's what I observe in Eliphaz's last speech. He makes seven moves:

1. Job 22:2–3: "Does Shaddai gain if you are righteous?"

Eliphaz begins his third speech by raising four questions that can be summarized by one question: Does God need us? God is so majestic, elevated, and self-sufficient, the logic goes, that puny human efforts at righteous living and integrity don't really matter to God. If a person were to make a case for a God utterly removed from human affairs, a God whose transcendence amounts to indifference to worldly events, this argument might work.

But the just-world theology that Eliphaz and his peers have been asserting goes in exactly the opposite direction. God, who created the world, is so attentive to human affairs that He carefully punishes the wicked and rewards the good, in this life. That's why this opening gambit in Job 22 feels like spaghetti thrown against the wall. It is not coherent with the rest of the argument that the friends make—not just incoherent with the entire book of Job and their previous arguments but also with the very next verse.

2. Job 22:4–9: "You know that your wickedness is great."

The most appalling thing that Eliphaz does in this discourse is to move into a direct attack on Job's supposed wickedness. He begins by accepting Job's courtroom metaphor (v. 4) and then uses it to spell out his indictment against Job. The indictment amounts to violations of moral obligations that the privileged owe to the poor and vulnerable, in the Jewish context, moral obligations clearly codified in Torah.

For example, Job is falsely accused of exacting pledges (Heb: *ḥabol*) from his "fellows" or "brothers" (Heb: *ʾaḥeka*) for no good reason. This means that Job as creditor has required of his debtors (NRSVue takes the debtors to be his own family members, making the offense worse) a form of security on a loan that is both cruel and gratuitous. From the second half of the verse, it is clear that the pledge he has taken is the very garment that keeps the poor person from being naked. He who has so many clothes takes the one remaining garment of the poor as collateral, a practice explicitly banned in Exod 22:25–27 and Deut 24:10–13![1]

Eliphaz goes on to accuse Job (again falsely) of failing to provide food for the hungry, drink to the thirsty, and assistance to the widow and the orphan. Overall, the suggestion is that Job has acted like an indifferent "privileged" person who possessed land and enjoyed its benefits with profound indifference to the needs of the less privileged. Job, stung by this brutal accusation, then defends himself in detail precisely on these points in his final moral self-defense (Job 29–31). Eliphaz, in his last speech, has gratuitously and falsely attacked Job on matters central to Job's own moral code as well as the core moral obligations Job has to his religious community.[2] Soon Job will demonstrate proper outrage at such accusations. Wait for it.

3. Job 22:10–11: "Therefore snares are all around you."

Moving from false accusations of Job, Eliphaz then makes the inevitable move into now-you-are-being-judged. You are trapped, terrified, blinded, drowning (vv. 10–11) as punishment for your sins. *Just-world-theology blah blah.*

4. Job 22:12: "God is in the heavenly heights."

Eliphaz next uses a vertical image, so common to the ancients and to many today, of God being up-up-up, high in the heavens, above the lofty stars. God is the majestic, awe-inspiring Creator, high above us all. The implication is that lowly earth-treading humans are in no position to question Him.

5. Job 22:13–14: "You say, 'What can God know?'"

Here Eliphaz falsely accuses Job of denying God's knowledge of human affairs because—get this—God can't "govern through the dense cloud," clouds which "screen Him so He cannot see." Job has never argued that God is unable to see what happens on earth. Job would never make such a puerile claim. Job's claim is that God not only knows but has orchestrated Job's suffering, and moreover that God knows about other instances of injustice in the world and does nothing to stop it. The issue for Job is not God's knowledge or awareness but God's justice and goodness.

6. Job 22:15–20: "Have you observed the immemorial path that evil men have trodden?"

Eliphaz returns to the evil-men-are-punished theme with a picturesque mini-narrative of the ephemeral rise and great public fall of those who mock God, do great wrong, and are publicly ruined.

7. Job 22:21–30: "If you return to Shaddai you will be restored."

In the final movement of Job 22, Eliphaz makes what sounds like a rather gentle appeal to repentance. All will go well for Job if he just repents. Come close to God with a whole heart. Accept God's instruction. Banish iniquity. Renounce greed. Seek God's favor. Pray to God. If Job does this, all will at last be well with him. The problem, of course, is that Job does not grant the basic premise of Eliphaz's argument that the reason for his suffering is that he has sinned. There is nothing quite as offensive as being called to repent for sins one has not committed.

Nothing More to Talk About

So, Eliphaz, having thrown everything he has at Job, hopes something will stick. His final speech, and the last major speech of any of the three erstwhile friends, is mainly but not exclusively a reiteration of their familiar claim that Job must have sinned and is being punished.

In a speech notable for including several obviously false and even ridiculous accusations, Eliphaz makes his accusations this time even more offensive and hurtful. Frustrated with Job's unwillingness to submit to theologically based character assassination, Eliphaz doesn't even pretend to be in conversation. This is anger and alienation incarnated in speech. And because it isn't a reasoned or dialogic approach, Job won't glorify the spew by bothering to respond directly to this speech and Eliphaz's "arguments."

28

Evil Triumphs, Innocents Suffer, God Hides (Job 23–24)

They pass the night naked for lack of clothing,
They have no covering against the cold;
They are drenched by the mountain rains,
And huddle against the rock for lack of shelter.
They snatch the fatherless infant from the breast,
And seize the child of the poor as a pledge . . .
Men groan in the city;
The souls of the dying cry out;
Yet God does not regard it as a reproach.
—Job 24:7–9, 12

Job 23: No Trial before a Hidden God

As Job responds in Job 23, we see he does not in fact respond to Eliphaz. That indiscriminate attack was not worthy of a response.

Instead, Job returns to a kind of lonely soliloquy. In this speech, Job renews his complaint against God in three familiar moves.

First, Job laments the absence or hiddenness of God (vv. 8–9), with a kind of inverse of Ps 139:7–12:

But if I go East—He is not there;
West—I still do not perceive Him;
North—since he is concealed, I do not behold Him;
South—He is hidden, and I cannot see Him.

Job seeks encounter with God. The primary form of encounter that he mentions is a kind of legal arraignment, as we will again see in a moment. But above all, courtroom or not, Job seeks primarily an encounter—some encounter, any encounter—with God.

Consider the difference between *absence*, on the one hand, and *hiddenness* or *concealment*, on the other. When someone we love or need is simply absent, that means they are not present—dead, missing, disappeared, far away. There are times when Job has lamented God's absence. But here, he quickly moves on to refine his claim to the idea that God is concealing Himself from Job's sight. The difference between someone appearing to be hiding and someone intentionally absent is crucial.

What makes matters worse is that Job is convinced God is misusing His vast powers to continually inflict harm on Job—even while hiding from him (vv. 13b-15):

Whatever He desires, He does.
For He will bring my term to an end,
But He has many more such at His disposal.
Therefore I am terrified at His presence;
When I consider, I dread Him.

Here we come to Job's second familiar move: Job squarely attributes his suffering to God. Quite unlike what Eliphaz accused Job of believing (22:13–14), Job is confident not just that God sees what is happening to him but that God is also orchestrating it. God is Job's hidden enemy, making Him even more dangerous. After all, it is far harder to fight a hidden enemy than a visible one.

These verses clarify still further that Job never stopped believing in God, or in God's presence, or in God's great power—but that Job has lost confidence in God's *goodness*. "Whatever He desires, He does," without regard to justice or mercy, is a statement about capricious divine power. God is like an autocrat who arbitrarily picks this one for favor and that one for banishment, just because He can, just because He wants to demonstrate the full extent of His power.

In Job's third familiar move he imagines a legal arraignment (vv. 3–7) which, if it were fair, would yield his vindication (vv. 10–12). If only God would allow Job to "set out [his] case before Him" (v. 4); if only God would reason with Job using arguments (v. 5); if only God would render justice based on the evidence presented by the way he has conducted himself his whole life (vv. 7, 10–12), then Job would be acquitted. Indeed, he says confidently, "I should emerge as gold" (v. 10b).

Recall how the book opened with Job described—by the narrator, and by God—as blameless and upright, fearing God and shunning evil. In addition, everything the reader is presented about Job's thoughts, words, and actions in Job 1–2 confirms that assessment.

Despite being barraged by attacks both from God (e.g., allowed and authorized by God), his three (ex-)friends, and his community, Job returns to this baseline. His self-description in 23:10–12 is not just that he has refrained from wrongdoing but that he has lived with heartfelt piety and love for God's word and God's commands (v. 12).

But God has unjustly hidden from Job, attacked Job, refused to go to trial with Job, authorizing such obvious, manifest suffering upon Job that the just-world theology of his entire community has been activated in such a way as to socially annihilate him. Job will never, ever, stop protesting this, and he will never, ever, accept that he has done anything to deserve it. Job wants legal vindication and lives in anxiety, dread, even terror (vv. 13–17) about that prospective encounter with God.[1]

Job 24: Job's Empathetic Lament over Human Misery

In chapter 8, we looked at how Job's unmerited suffering was having one salutary effect—he was now noticing the misery of the wretched of the earth in a way that seemed likely to be new for him. Having his privilege shattered, moving from the penthouse to the dunghill outside of town, Job was now viewing life from below rather than above. Things look different from the city dump, where the destitute gather, than from the city gate, where the leaders rule.

In Job 24, Job again demonstrates in a profound way his empathetic engagement with the suffering of the most destitute and powerless of this world. His lament over their misery is mixed with condemnation of the unjust actions of those who create such misery. Gustavo Gutiérrez, in *On Job: God-Talk and the Suffering of the Innocent*, describes the text of Job 24 as "the most radical and cruel description of the wretchedness of the poor that is to be found in the Bible. . . . The description is full of detail and shows careful attention to the concrete situation of the poor."[2] Carol Newsom strongly concurs, adding, "There is no stronger indictment of God in the book of Job than the depiction in chap. 24 of divine indifference in the face of the pervasive misery, abuse, and injustice endured by the most vulnerable people."[3]

Job 24 begins with a kind of topic sentence (24:1): "Why are times for judgment not reserved by Shaddai?" He then spends most of the rest of the chapter describing so many human actions worthy of negative divine judgment, along with so many miserable human sufferers worthy of divine justice-making.

Job attacks those who remove boundary stones, carry off flocks and the donkeys of orphans, and take "the widow's bull as a pledge" (24:2–3). He critiques powerful people here who seize on the vulnerability of widows and orphans to seize land and animals and exploit the debt that they themselves are likely creating. This is a clear and obvious violation of justice and is explicitly addressed in the Hebrew Bible.

Then, as a logical next step, Job describes the plight of those who have lost their homes. They are now "the needy" who wander about on "the roads" looking for food in people's fields (vv. 4–6). But because housed and prosperous people don't like to see unhoused hungry people—then or now—Job describes how the needy are "chased" off the roads and driven into hiding. They now live like wild animals, attempting to "scavenge" (24:5 NRSVue) for food in the wilderness and to glean a few grapes from "the vineyards of the wicked."

But they don't even have clothes (v. 7). They shiver at night in the fields, and when the rains come, they have no covering. They "huddle against the rock for lack of shelter" (v. 8). They may be hired as day laborers in the fields or vineyards (vv. 10–11), hungry as they harvest wheat, thirsty as they "tread the winepresses" (vv. 10–11). Exhaustedly working to earn a few pennies, the poor are slowly dying, sometimes losing even their children, sold to pay off their growing debts (v. 9).

Groaning under their fate, the poor are slowly dying in the streets of the city, crying out to God and neighbor for help that is not forthcoming, while those more fortunate go about their daily business and God Himself does not appear to be troubled by what is going on (24:12).

This very powerful statement is enough to condemn all of us complacently housed, fed, clothed humans.

But Job is not done. He goes on to condemn murderers, thieves, and adulterers, especially those preying on the poor (vv. 13–17). Job sounds like his friends now as he offers imprecations against such wicked ones, calling down justice upon those who do injustice (vv. 18–22). But unlike his friends, Job does not see that justice is actually taking place (24:23, 25):

Yet [God] gives him the security on which he relies,
And keeps watch over his affairs . . .

Surely no one can confute me,
Or prove that I am wrong.

NJPS chooses to render the relatively ambiguous Hebrew of 24:23 as an indictment of God. The Hebrew "he" in v. 23a is rendered "God" (though within brackets, indicating the question mark). This is followed by v. 23b, which is subtly rendered in English as a kind of indictment of God's protection of the wicked—God "keeps watch over his affairs"—rather than as a warning of coming divine judgment, as in NRSVue—"his eyes are upon their ways."

NJPS also renders the verse that follows, v. 24, as an imprecation that the wicked *should* be brought low, whereas NRSVue (also NASB) renders it as a fact claim (from just-world theology) that the wicked *are* bought low:

NJPS	NRSVue
Exalted for a while, let them be gone;	*They are exalted a little while and then they are gone;*
Be brought low, and shrivel like mallows,	
And wither like the heads of grain	*they wither and fade like the mallow;*
	They are cut off like the heads of grain.

Once again the NJPS is willing to take the most provocative approach in its translation. It also makes the most sense for this book of protest theology, Job.[4]

In chapter 23 Job laments the injustice of his personal fate and asks for a fair hearing from a hidden God.

In Job 24 our hero widens his gaze (again) to offer in compact brilliance a concrete lament over the suffering of those who are made poor by the unjust actions of their neighbors.

Job is not just saying, Isn't it too bad that some people are unhoused, naked, hungry, wet, cold, scrounging for food and working to exhaustion and dying too soon and losing their children and groaning to early deaths in indifferent countrysides and cities. He is instead saying that because some people misuse their power to drive other people out of their homes and to strip them of their productive capital through theft and usury, these other humans are made into homeless, hungry, thirsty, naked, cold, miserable, groaning, dying ones. And God lets it happen, over and over again. That is Job's real complaint. And the fact that he can lift his gaze from his own suffering to that of so many others is a sign not just of his integrity but perhaps also of his growth. He has seen life from the dunghill for a while now.

29

No One Is Denying God's Power—and Thus I Protest (Job 25–27)

Bildad:

Dominion and dread are His;
He imposes peace in His heights.
Can His troops be numbered?
On whom does His light not shine? –Job 25:2–3

Job:

These are but glimpses of His rule,
The mere whisper that we perceive of Him;
Who can absorb the thunder of His mighty deeds? –Job 26:14

By God who has deprived me of justice!
By Shaddai who has embittered my life!
As long as there is life in me,
And God's breath is in my nostrils,
My lips will speak no wrong,
Nor my tongue utter deceit.
Far be it from me to say you are right;
Until I die I will maintain my integrity. –Job 27:2–5

Confusions about Job 25–27

Bildad offers his final speech in Job 25, and what is probably the last speech of one of Job's friends, as no other speech is attributed to Zophar, the third friend.

But among scholars there are serious disputes about who should be understood to be speaking in the text of Job 25–27.

What the reader sees in most English translations is that Bildad has a very short speech (25:1–6) and that Job 26–27 has Job replying at length.

Some scholars believe that Bildad does indeed have a short speech, with 26:1–27:6 recounting Job's reply, but then 27:7–23 being a final unattributed Zophar speech. The question is if those words would have come—could have come—from the character Job, as they are words rehashing just-world theology, which Job has continually and consistently rejected. And the text, if attributed to Job, seems out of place.

Robert Alter, in his translation, reconstructs the text more radically,[1] as follows:

Bildad's speech (25:1–6; 26:5–14)
Job's speech (26:1–4; 27:1–7)
Zophar's speech (27:8–23)

No one knows for sure, but based on consistency of arguments and word usage alone, I am inclined to follow the logic of Job, Bildad, and Zophar's words with the following segment attributions:

Bildad (25:1–6)
Job (26:1–27:6)
Zophar/unknown (27:7–23—another just-world theology repetition, which we will not treat here).

We Agree That God Is Supremely Powerful

Bildad's final remarks are puny indeed—just five verses. He makes two claims that in one way or another have been made several times earlier in the book:

God is sovereign ruler over the earth. He holds dominion/rule (Heb: *hamšel,* from *mašal*). His great power rightly inspires awe/fear/dread (Heb: *paḥad*). He rules in the heights and on earth, in realms visible and invisible to humans.

Human beings are therefore worms by comparison, who dare not claim innocence or purity in God's sight. The implication is that Job is way out of line in challenging God, especially on the matter of his innocence in God's sight. For that matter, Job has been consistently challenging the fairness of God's conduct toward him as well as God's overall rule of the world. Bildad is critiquing Job for this.

Job's response speech in chapters 26–27 begins with a derisive attack (26:1–4) on the unhelpfulness of Bildad's comments—and perhaps by extension, all the advice and commentary that Job's friends have been laying on him. The basic idea is that the friends have treated him as if he knows nothing and they know everything, and their comments have been worthless and unwelcome.

Job then goes on to offer a picturesque, highly mythology-tinged account of God's awesome power in creation, reflecting the ancient mythology of a vertically organized triple-decker world, and offering a picture of creation. Job's words here offer an interesting anticipation of God's speech from the whirlwind in chapters 38–41.

What Job brings to Job 26:5–14 is that God is the awesome creator of a world of grandeur that could only be functional for humans and creatures to live in through the creating, organizing, taming power that God demonstrated in creation. In Job's account of the creation, he references Rahab (v. 12) and the Elusive Serpent (v. 13); he refers to myths of creatures that had to be slain to bring order out of primeval chaos. The Babylonian-based mythology of creation he presents is not creation from nothing, but instead a divine taming of primeval chaos.

What rises from Job's response and account is that sense of amazement and awe at the grandeur of creation—that anything should exist at all—that it has great and terrifying power—think of the massive, terrifying creatures of land and sea—and the regular risk of catastrophic weather events. That God oversees all this makes God the ultimate source of the Powers on which we depend and by which we sometimes die. This is not creation as placid mountain streams and a gentle breeze on a cool evening, but instead creation as a mainly/barely tamed inferno. Who cannot feel fear, awe, and dread before such a world made by whatever kind of God makes such a world?

As the lawyers would say, Job is happy to "stipulate" to God's dominion over God's creation and also to stipulate to the fear and awe that humans feel before Powers far greater than our puny selves. While it is possible that the speech does not come from Job, or that if it does come from Job he is being ironic or sarcastic about God's great creative power, it looks most likely to me that Job is accepting and even deepening the picture of God's power over creation that Bildad had been weakly arguing.

We Do Not Agree That Humans Are Maggots

Implicitly, however, Job is unwilling to grant Bildad's other claim, that God's creative power somehow renders humans incapable of being right in God's sight, or that God's greatness means humans are maggots. Bildad uses two different words that apparently can be interchangeably translated as "worms" or "maggots" (25:6a—*rimmah*; 25:6b—*tole'ah*).

Bildad is trying to defend God's character by diminishing human worth to the level of earthworms. This is, unfortunately, a familiar move to anyone who has ever listened to a sermon in various hardline Christian traditions that derides humans as worthless, sinful maggots worthy only of damnation.

But Ps 8:4–6 does *not* accept that humans are worthless maggots:

> When I behold Your heavens, the work of Your fingers,
> the moon and stars that You set in place,
> what is man that You have been mindful of him,
> mortal man that You have taken note of him,
> that You have made him little less than divine,
> and adorned him with glory and majesty . . .

For Gen 1:26–27, humans are the pinnacle of creation, made in the image of God. For Psalm 8 we are just a little lower than Elohim, the divine or the heavenly beings. We are "adorned with glory and majesty"—all of us, as a species. The contrast with humans as maggots could hardly be starker.

We saw earlier that Job appeared to be riffing on Psalm 8 when he sardonically asked, "What is man that you pay so much attention to him, studying him so closely, looking for any flaw" (Job 7:17–21).

But that statement was not of the same spirit as what Bildad is offering here. Job was asking God for fair treatment considering the relative weakness and powerlessness of a human vis-à-vis God. Job was making a claim on God's justice, God's fairness. Bildad, by contrast, is saying that wormy, guilty humans have no claims on God at all.

Bildad's theology tries to clear God of moral blame by loading permanent existential guilt on all humans at all times and places without regard to any relative differences in their actual character, behavior, or piety—by declaring us to be loathsome worms.[2]

Of course, the incoherence of that view—even in the context of the book of Job—becomes quite clear when we recall that just-world theology is not in fact asserting that every human, wormy as we might be, deserves negative judgment in this life. The core assertion of just-world theology is that righteous humans deserve and receive divine rewards, and unrighteous humans deserve and receive divine punishment. It's not a matter of blanket wormy guiltiness. It's a matter of an attentive God making discriminating judgments based on real human behavior that can be evaluated as good or bad, right or wrong, blameworthy or blameless.

Curiously, as the "friends" spin out in their last presentations of their logic, now in attempting to protect God's good reputation by degrading all humans, Bildad undercuts the very theology he and his friends have been trying so hard to protect.

We Do Not Agree That I Have Done Something Wrong

If we suppose that Job's final response speech ends at 27:6, it is a quite striking way for Job to conclude. Job swears by the very God who has deprived him of justice that he has been a person of integrity throughout his life. He swears that until his final breath—"God's breath [that] is in my nostrils" (a reference to Gen 2:7)—he will never accept the accusations his friends have leveled at him. To do so would be to "utter deceit" and to "speak . . . wrong" (27:4), which is precisely what a person of integrity does not do.

As Kierkegaard's "young man" puts it in his classic work *Repetition*,

> Job continues to take the position that he is in the right. He does it in such a way that he thereby witnesses to the noble, human, bold confidence that knows what a human being is, knows that despite his being frail, despite his swift withering away like the

> flower, that in freedom he still has something of greatness, has a consciousness that even God cannot wrest from him even though he gave it to him.[3]

Job is here uttering a sacred vow—a key part of Hebrew Bible tradition, questioned by Jesus in the New Testament (Matt 5:33–37) but still sometimes practiced by Paul (Acts 18:18; 21:23–26; 2 Cor 1:23; Gal 1:20; Rom 9:1). To make a sacred vow by God or in the name of God is to cite the highest Authority in the universe—and, should the vow be a lie, to call the sacred name would be tantamount to calling down God's judgment.

The extraordinary irony, of course, is that Job swears by the God who has harmed him, the God who has "embittered [his] life" (27:2). He swears by this God that he has been a person of integrity and has lived beyond reproach. As a public act, an act in community, this swearing is an act of great and lonely courage. He is telling his ex-friends and his entire community that he will never, ever, accept their account of why he has been subjected to such suffering.

As a religious act, an act *coram Deo* (before God), Job demonstrates great and lonely courage. He is saying to God—the God who he is quite sure has harmed him gravely and unjustly—that he does not accept the justice of what God has done and that he will protest it until the last breath. But he can only offer such a vow within the terms of his tradition, swearing by the very God who has harmed him, using the very breath that God has breathed into him. Utterly dependent on God for life, utterly aware that he is calling on the justice of God to correct the injustice of God, he offers his vow.

Imagine that Job, swearing by God, in that act of bravery, then falls silent. Bracketing off 27:7–23 as displaced text, let us imagine that Job's friends then fall silent, too.

After a textual interlude (Job 28), Job will offer one final magnificent soliloquy in defense of his life and in lament of what has been lost (Job 29–31).

Kierkegaard writes, "Speak up, then unforgettable Job, repeat everything you said, you powerful spokesman who, fearless as a roaring lion, appears before the tribunal of the Most High!"[4]

V

Closing Moves of the Book of Job (Job 28–42)

30

Intermezzo: The Mysterious Wisdom Hymn (Job 28)

There is a mine for silver,
And a place where gold is refined.
Iron is taken out of the earth,
And copper smelted from rock.
He sets bounds for darkness;
To every limit man probes,
To rocks in deepest darkness . . .

But where can wisdom be found,
Where is the source of understanding?
No man can set a value on it;
It cannot be found in the land of the living . . .

God understands the way to it;
He knows its source;
For He sees to the ends of the earth,
Observes all that is beneath the heavens . . .

He said to man,
"See! Fear of the Lord is wisdom;
To shun evil is understanding."

—Job 28:1–3, 12–13, 23–24, 28

Who Is Speaking Here? Job or an Editor?

Within the book of Job, the last time a speaker—Job himself—has been named was in Job 26:1. If this is taken as definitive and the voice continuous, then his final discourse runs from Job 26 to 31.

This, however, does not seem likely. Job 27:7–23, which we did not review in the last chapter because it is probably displaced text, reads like classic just-world theology and is almost certainly not Job's words. Whereas, we come to 27:6 and readers know this killer last word is undeniably the voice and approach of Job: "My righteousness I hold fast, and will not let it go; My heart shall not reproach me so long as I live."

Here's a second reason: Job 29 opens differently from the other discourses: "Job *again* took up his theme and said" (29:1, italics added). This certainly sounds as if Job has been interrupted and is starting anew. Indeed, when we explore Job 29 in the next chapter, it will seem clear that Job is offering a new speech, amounting to a grand final lament and defense of his life.

So, then, what *is* Job 28? Often it is described by scholars as a hymn to wisdom, though without a speaker noted. Whoever is offering that hymn, it doesn't sound like Job, which is the third reason Job 26–31 should not be understood as a single continuous speech.

Who, then, wrote Job 28? Who are readers to imagine speaking to us here? It doesn't even sound like any of the three friends. And it isn't in the voice of God. It seems to reflect the broader thematics of the book of Proverbs or the pious conclusion to the book of Ecclesiastes.

Job 28, on its face, reads like a person or group representing the Wisdom tradition got hold of the electrifying, subversive book of Job and felt the need to interrupt with a "hold your horses" statement of the tradition before allowing the book to gallop forward to its end.

Scholars broadly (though not uniformly) argue that Job 28 really is an editorial interruption, presumably from a pious scribe or defender of the Wisdom tradition. Beyond the argument for the pious scribe, scholars do agree that the hymn is a beautiful piece of poetry.

In both Christianity and Judaism there are "protest" and "anti-protest" traditions, which Scott Davison and his colleagues document. It can be seen in biblical texts, nowhere more than in Job, and in interpretations of biblical texts, including Job.[1] Defending the honor of God and tamping down protest occurs throughout the tradition. And Job holds the quintessential honor of offering "protest," and "anti-protest," and commentary on both.

This seems to be the very thing happening here in the text of Job 28 as well, and maybe even the entire Elihu speech cycle that follows in Job 32–37. Many historical-critical biblical scholars consider both Job 28 and Job 32–37 to be later insertions by pious editors. Edward Greenstein is so dubious about the authorship of Job 28 as to leave it entirely out of his commentary. But, of course, everyday readers of the book of Job read it with the inclusion of this chapter, so that is what we will do as well.

I have concluded that if we think of Job as kind of like a musical score, we might consider Job 28 as something like an *intermezzo*.[2] Job 28 has all the weight of a late intermezzo linking all that has come before with the final climactic movement of the drama, of the book.

Job Reflects on Mining as a Metaphor (Job 28:1–11)

The book of Job is full of rich and picturesque observations, especially about the natural world but also about human behavior. The writer(s) of Job were close students of the world. We will see more evidence of that soon.

Here in Job 28, the author (whom we will call the wisdom poet) offers a striking description of metal and mineral excavations. The poet begins by naming silver, gold, iron, copper, and sapphires (the latter two derived from rock), all products that humans mine (vv. 1–2, 6).

And appropriately the focus of this first section of Job 28 (vv. 1–11) is the probing, relentless intensity of mining. Miners get under the earth, far beyond the boundary between light and darkness (v. 3), where they can dig very deep below and very far away from where people live, creating a kind of underground netherworld (vv. 3–4) of strenuous effort and—implicitly—great danger. Miners go to the deep places other creatures will never even see (vv. 7–8).

Through mighty labors, miners "overturn mountains," "carve out channels through rock," and "dam up the sources of the streams" (vv. 9–11) in order that "hidden things may be brought to light" (v. 11). The wisdom poet is vividly impressed by human power, ingenuity, and technology in ancient mining operations, which were able to surface valuable metals and stones for human benefit.

But Wisdom Is Much More Valuable than Gold (Job 28:12–19)

After the poetic and metaphorical opening about the riches from the depths, the last two sections of Job 28 begin with a nearly identical couplet:

> *But where can wisdom be found?*
> *Where is the source of understanding?* (28:12; cf. 28:20)

Job 28:12–19 addresses these questions mainly by describing how wisdom (Heb: *ḥokmah*) is much more valuable than anything that humans go to such effort to mine. As to what *ḥokmah* means here in Job 28, let's start by positing the idea that wisdom throughout the Hebrew Bible means something like the transcendent, cosmic, moral ordering principle of the universe or at least the ordering principle of the created order on earth. In turn, "understanding" (Heb: *binah*) means something like the human ability to discern this ordering principle and to order our lives accordingly. These terms are often understood as essentially synonymous, but each has been known to be parsed in these specific ways.

Wisdom, then, for Job 28, is more valuable than gold, silver, onyx, sapphire, glass, coral, crystal, rubies, or topaz. This is also a common theme in the book of Proverbs (Prov 3:13–15; 8:10–11, 19; 16:16). The materials that humans have decided are the most precious on earth are not nearly as precious as wisdom. Anthropologists remind us of how arbitrarily humans have decided to value so highly these bits of stone and rock.[3] Job 28 hints at that.

There is an interesting wrinkle in this second part of Job 28 when considering this line about wisdom: "No man can set a value on it" (v. 13). An ethicist's ear perks up here, for this reason: It is one thing to say that X is of very great value, or that X is of more value than Y. We know all about assigning relative monetary value to various objects.

It is altogether different to say that something is *beyond price*, that no value can be set for it. When I say that my grandchildren are priceless to me, I am saying that they are beyond any cash price or exchange value.

They are not commodities, not for sale, not available for exchange. It would be an obscenity to think of them in commodity terms.

Ethicists talk about how capitalism constantly threatens to turn everything into a commodity, including human bodies and human beings themselves. Indeed, this happens all the time—slavery, prostitution, child marriage, trafficking. The tendency to turn everything into a commodity is one of the main criticisms of capitalism.

Job 28 tries to mine, as it were, the metaphors, to push into meaning. The text says that wisdom is "better than rubies" (v. 18), that "gold or glass cannot match its value" (v. 17, exchange language), and that "no man can set a value on it" (v. 13) and "it cannot be bartered for gold" (v. 15). My sense is that the poet here is presenting some "commodity" language but really wants to land the latter meaning.

Think of part one and part two of Job 28 as saying something like this: *Hello, silly, ingenious human creatures! You have chosen to place immense value on objects you can dig from the ground at great risk and effort, while what you most need and so often ignore is wisdom, which is beyond all valuing!*

God Alone Knows Where Wisdom Is and What It Is (Job 28:20–28)

In the final movement of Job 28, the poet repeats the haunting question, "Whence does wisdom come?" He emphasizes its hiddenness from humans, from other creatures, and even from other Powers and Realms (vv. 21–22). God alone "understands the way to it" and "knows its source" (v. 23).

The book of Proverbs seems to emphasize the accessibility of wisdom to those who seek it. Lady Wisdom cries out in the streets, "Those who love me I love, and those who seek me will find me" (Prov 8:17). But for the wisdom poet of Job 28, wisdom is more elusive, mysterious, and transcendent than this: "It is hidden from the eyes of all living" (28:11). One wonders if this accent is offered by the wisdom poet specifically to address the agonized search for truth and wisdom going on throughout the discourses in the book of Job.

Carol Newsom considers Job 28 as the presentation of a paradox. Wisdom is "something that cannot be found because it is everywhere, a quest whose end is the same as its beginning. . . . Wisdom brings both profound peace and profound security. There is no one who does not yearn for that, and yet it seems so elusive."[4]

By the final section of Job 28, the wisdom poet claims that when God created and ordered the creation and its elements (vv. 25–26), God also "saw [wisdom] and gauged it; He measured it and probed it" (v. 27, NJPS). There are four verbs used here. The NJPS, our default text, handles these verbs somewhat differently than most translations. Here are the verbs and the semantic range:

- *ra'ah* NJPS: "saw"—little variation in translations here
- *sapar* NJPS: "gauged"—"declared," "recounted," "enumerated"
- *kun* NJPS: "measured"—"established," "prepared," "ordered," "framed"
- *ḥaqar* NJPS: "probed"—"searched it out," "investigated," "examined," "comprehended"

How interesting that God here is never described as simply creating wisdom. Just as the version of the creation narrative we are getting in Job seems to involve an awful lot of divine semiordering and semitaming of primeval powers like wind and water (Job 26:5–14; Job 38–41—thus, not *creatio ex nihilo*), so wisdom also seems to be something that preexists God, that God sees, declares, investigates, and orders but does not create out of nothing. We are told that God understands the way to wisdom, God knows the source of wisdom, but not simply that God is the creator of wisdom. This is different from the crucial related text in Prov 8:22–31.

Should this be taken to mean that, at least for the wisdom poet in Job, among the primeval elements that God orders in creation is a kind of already latent cosmic (moral) ordering power? But that like everything else in this creation-as-taming-primeval-elements story, that taming of wisdom is powerful but not complete, real but not tidy—not fully orderly, not fully fit to human need or preference?

We do not know but can only meet the question as the wisdom poet concludes (Job 28:28):

> *See! Fear of the Lord* (Heb: ʾ*adonai,* a term used only once in
> the book of Job) *is wisdom;*
> *To shun evil is understanding.*

This pious answer, familiar in Proverbs and in Ecclesiastes (Prov 1:7; 9:10; 15:33; Eccl 5:7; 7:18; 8:12–13; 12:13), seems, though, too neat and simple for the book of Job.

Is the poet saying to Job the character and to any readers who have been carried along by Job's questions over many chapters: *Stop your questioning and simply fear God and shun evil?*

The obvious problem is that this fearing of God and shunning of evil is *precisely* how Job was described in the very first line of the book (Job 1:1)! And look at what happened to him!

What then has the wisdom hymn, the mystic intermezzo before the great climax to the book of Job, really offered us?

If it is intended to get us back on track with a simple pious answer, it fails, like pretty much every explanation in the book of Job.

But perhaps the wisdom poet of Job 28 intends to *emphasize* that "wisdom," defined as cosmic order, is actually "hidden from the eyes of all living" (28:20), and only truly visible to the eyes of God (v. 24), a God who does not feel the need to share it with us humans.[5]

This would also suggest that "understanding," defined as humans coming to an accurate grasp of that cosmic order and living accordingly, is quite difficult, if not impossible. If *ḥokmah* (cosmic moral order) is inaccessible, so is *binah* (morally orderly choice-making).

Is the wisdom poet undercutting the simple clarity of any moral system based on humans responding appropriately to a discernible built-in moral order and reaping the positive consequences?

Could it be possible that such complex issues dealt with in the book require wisdom that is not easy to find? As Qohelet, the purported author of Ecclesiastes (Eccl 1:1, 12) advises, don't fall into the trap of thinking that being foolish or doing evil will somehow help (Eccl 7:15–18).[6] We do the best we can. Seeking wisdom, however elusive, is part of that. Job 28:28 may be taken to say: *Humans will never access wisdom and never understand the creation or its moral order. Fear God and shun evil, as best you can. That's all I've got for you.*

If that is what the wisdom poet of Job 28 is doing, consider this idea: that the sage on assignment from the Wise Elders to clean up the book of Job subverted the assignment by offering instead a constrained treatment of wisdom and human access to it.

O, the great wonderment of this extraordinary work of religious art!

31

The Good Old Days: Job's Final Lament (Job 29–30)

O that I were as in months gone by,
In the days when God watched over me . . .
When I was in my prime.

But now those younger than I deride me,
[Men] whose fathers I would have disdained to put among
my sheep dogs.

I cry out to You, but You do not answer me;
I wait, but You do [not] consider me.
You have become cruel to me.

—Job 29:2, 4a; 30:1, 20–22

After Everything, Job Speaks One Last Time

The intermezzo offered by the wisdom poet now gives way to the final movement of the Job symphony. It is quite a finish.

The first notes in this final movement have Job summoning himself to offer one last lament and defense of his life before that life was shattered by God.

As a quite young Christian ethicist in the 1990s, I was so impressed by the moral code Job offers in chapter 31, that I preached a chapel sermon on it called "Job 31: The Code of a Man of Honor." I saw it as an unambiguously powerful statement of a moral code that had relevance for today.

Others have also noted this "code." Karl Barth describes Job 31 as "a picture of pure and exalted piety for which there is hardly a parallel in the Old Testament . . . rivalled in intensity only by the Sermon on the Mount."[1]

Now, three decades later, I've been re-immersed in the book of Job, and I see Job 31 as part of Job 29–31, Job's final lament and defense, which needs to be considered in that wider context. No longer do I see his words here as morally unambiguous. Indeed, in his brokenness, Job offers an unfiltered expression both of the grandeur and of the limits of his former way of life and moral code.

Job 29: The Good Old Days

Job begins with a sad lament over "months gone by, in the days when God watched over me" (29:2). There was a time, he says, when God did indeed watch over him, when God's favor shone upon him like light (29:4). There was a time when "God's company graced my tent" (29:4), when his children were with him, when he was prosperous and comfortable, when blessings seemed to precede and surround him (29:5–6, via rich metaphorical language).

A big part of the good old days was Job's exalted social status (29:7–11). This section offers the clearest exposition in the book about our hero's former position in society and how very much he enjoyed it. "When I passed through the city gates to take my seat in the square, young men saw me and hid, elders rose and stood" (29:7–8).

Job's very physical presence was treated with respect. When he entered a social space, people visibly responded with expressions of fear, deference, and praise. Job was *somebody*. He was first among equals. Even "elders" and "nobles" and "princes" responded with deference. When Job entered social spaces, his was the most important voice. He was, after all, "the greatest man in the East."

A bit later Job again describes how "men would listen to me expectantly and wait for my counsel. After I spoke they had nothing to say" (29:31–32). Job had great social power: "I decided their course and presided over them; I lived like a king among his troops" (29:25).

Job tells the story of his "prime" (29:4; Heb: *ḥorep*, metaphorical use of a term that can mean "winter" or "harvest time"), when he was youthful, successful, vigorous (29:20), powerful, respected, and blessed. It was a peak he knew and experienced even as everyone else acknowledged it as well.

René Girard, referring to Job 29, writes, "He is a great leader who at first commands the respect of the people and is then abruptly scorned by them. . . . Before he became a scapegoat Job lived through a period of extraordinary popularity bordering on idolatry. . . . The contrast between past and present is not from riches to poverty, or from health to sickness, but from favour to disfavour with the very same people."[2]

Job hastens to add that the respect offered to him by his community had been based on his visible life of "righteousness" (29:14; Heb: *ṣedeq*) and "justice" (Heb: *mišpaṭ*), the two great words for justice and justice-making in the entire Jewish moral tradition. These words convey not only personal integrity but also a righteous commitment to justice in society, which in Jewish tradition focuses on acting on behalf of the vulnerable. Thus, Job names specific groups of highly vulnerable people he actively cared for that are also often mentioned in Torah: the poor, the orphan, the perishing, the widow, the blind, the lame, the needy, the stranger, and the victim (29:12–17).

It is quite striking how in 29:17 Job describes himself as one who "broke the jaws of the wrongdoer and . . . wrested prey from his teeth." This is highly evocative language of a lifestyle in which Job used his communal power to act on behalf of those at risk of being victimized. Job feared God and cared about people and thus functioned with a kind of judicial power on behalf of those at risk. Notice how this directly contradicts the spurious claims of Eliphaz in Job 22 about Job's indifference and harm to the poor.[3]

Job says that it was because of this justice-focused way of life that people honored and respected him. He also believes that it was because of this way of life that God had protected him and his family and blessed him so abundantly. It was why he once believed that "I would end my days with my family, and be as long-lived as the phoenix" (29:18).

Earlier in the book I borrowed a phrase from Tom Wolfe to describe the former Job as a "man in full." Here Job calls himself a man "in his prime."

Reading Job helps me to understand why I recoiled so deeply at the shock of lost respect almost overnight in the story I relayed earlier. I see more clearly how high levels of public social approval have been, for me at least, a huge intoxicant. Extreme honor paid by a large crowd to one person is a rare, coveted drug. I think of what a huge role this plays in sports and entertainment, where massive applause is offered to star performers first when they enter the arena of fifty thousand or eighty thousand fans and then again when they deliver the expected star performance. The rush of fans chanting your name!

I propose that Job grew not just to expect but to need the great deference and the high honor with which he was treated. He came to believe that he deserved it because of the genuinely laudable moral quality of his life. And he also came to believe that it was coming to him—all the good stuff, including wealth but also honor—as a reward from God.

Job's good-old-days lament in Job 29 illuminates the intermixing of privilege, pride, and power with justice and virtue in Job's former life. It also suggests that he was not quite as "innocent" or "blameless" as he thought he was. He was as innocent as a person can be who sits at the very pinnacle of a social order and who basks in social approval. But that caveat matters.

Job 30: Derided by Losers, Attacked by God

Job's discourse takes a further revelatory turn in chapter 30. His lament is that "men whose fathers I would have disdained to put among my sheep dogs . . . do not withhold spittle from my face" (30:1, 10).

This is a very specific kind of lament, and a not very attractive one. Job offers a dehumanizing dismissal of the people he is speaking of: Their fathers were so worthless he would not have valued them as much as his sheep dogs. Here, as Hebrew Bible scholar Suzanna Millar notes, Job sounds a note both of class prejudice and species prejudice.[4]

Now, a generation later, they are the hungry, homeless ruffians of his world, expelled from society (30:5), living in holes in the ground (30:6), "braying" like donkeys (30:7), "scoundrels, nobodies, stricken from the earth" (30:8).

Where did Job's compassion for the homeless, destitute ones go (cf. Job 24:1–12)? Is the difference that those were the "deserving" poor and these are the undeserving?[5] That appears to be the case, at least for Job.

This group in Job 30 appears to be the criminal class—"cried at like a thief" (30:5)—not the miserable abused poor of the land. In Job's eyes, they are deservedly outcasts. And yet it is these losers who now take the lead in mocking him, attacking him, and celebrating his downfall (30:9–13), "although it does them no good" (v. 13). After all, the one thing more satisfying than elevating superstars is bringing them down!

We see a connection with René Girard's theory that Job had been the idol of his community and now is the scapegoat. Girard views Job 30 as a key revelatory moment: "These people are not interesting in themselves; they are there only for Job to compare himself with them and define himself as the scapegoat of these scapegoats, persecuted by those who could least indulge in persecution, the victim of absolutely everyone."[6]

The mockery Job is experiencing from these "nobodies" is the most intense evidence Job can present of the loss of his social status (30:15). This is most clear in the translation decisions made in the NJPS:

> *Terror tumbles upon me;*
> *It sweeps away my honor like the wind;*
> *My dignity vanishes like a cloud.*

Job's contempt for those now treating him with contempt is not attractive, but it *is* illuminating. Sitting at the top of the social hierarchy, everyone below Job had been surveyed from the heights. The deserving poor he had treated with mercy and justice. The undeserving scoundrels he had dismissed as unworthy. The fact that this criminal class now spits in his face is the ultimate indignity. As Carol Newsom notes, "Despite the poignancy of Job's words, one cannot help being shocked by the way he expresses his contempt for the outcasts who now mock him."[7]

There was a lot of pride in the old Job, and there is a lot of pride in the new Job; the latter is wounded pride, an especially damaged and sometimes damaging form. The rage of those brought low from the heights is a unique kind of rage.

Toward the end of Job 30, Job renews his lament concerning not just God's absence, and God's silence, but also what he calls God's "cruel" attack on him (30:20–21). He reminds God again of the compassionate and just life he had once lived (v. 25), but all for naught. Now he is a miserable, lonely, sickened, dying, mournful man (vv. 23–31). He is now just "dust and ashes" (v. 19; Heb: *ʿapar waʾeper*), terms with a biblical resonance (Gen 2:7; 3:19; 18:27; 1 Sam 2:8 with a different Hebrew term for "ashes"; Job 2:8; 5:6; 7:21; 10:8–9; 42:6; Ps 103:14; 104:29; Eccl 3:20; 12:7; Esth 4:1; Isa 58:4) that becomes crucial at the end of the book (42:6). The good old days seem so very long ago.

32

The Code of a (Privileged) Man of Honor (Job 31)

Have I walked with worthless men,
Or my feet hurried to deceit?
Let Him weigh me on the scale of righteousness;
Let God ascertain my integrity.

O that I had someone to give me a hearing;
O that Shaddai would reply to my writ,
Or that my accuser draw up a true bill!
I would carry it on my shoulder;
Tie it around me for a wreath.
I would give him an account of my steps,
Offer it as to a commander.

—Job 31:5–6, 35–37

Job's Self-Imprecation as a Final Legal Argument

Finally, we reach Job 31, Job's last speech. At one level it is a life review, especially a life-moral-code review: *This was my moral path.* It is also a kind of vow: *If I have ever done X evil, let Y suffering happen to me/I would have deserved awful suffering.* (Scholars call this a "self-imprecation," "oath of innocence," or "oath of clearance."[1]) Ultimately, it is a defense summation for the trial with God that Job has sought and not been granted. But he at least addresses the jury.

Like the last speech of his ex-friend, Job's too feels a bit disarranged. Job 31:1, on Job's sexual ethic, would fit better with vv. 9–12. Job

31:38–40, on Job's treatment of his land and workers, would better fit earlier. Job 31:2–4 seems like the speech's opening, just like vv. 35–37 read like Job's final summation. Let's take the text, then, in its logical order to more clearly see his points.

Ten Commitments in Job's Moral Code

Within Job's moral code of chapter 31, I see ten discrete commitments. It is an impressive code, albeit deeply affected by the social and economic power he once enjoyed. As Newsom rightly says, it "provides an extended statement of the moral values of an aristocratic and patriarchal culture."[2]

1. Job 31:2–4: "Surely He observes my ways."

Job has been committed to living in a manner pleasing to God and to submit to God in accountability for his deeds.

Job opens his final defense by asserting that he has lived his life based on the belief that God observes human behavior and has observed Job's ways in the world. He has also believed that "calamity is surely for the iniquitous" (v. 3). In other words, Job has lived based on the idea that a just God expects just behavior from people and responds to people according to their deeds.

2. Job 31:5–8: "Have I walked with worthless men, or my feet hurried to deceit?"

Job has been careful in the company he keeps and has not strayed into temptation.

Job asks God to examine whether he has done either of two things: kept bad company or allowed his "feet" to stray into deceit because he has been tempted and succumbed to that temptation. These ideas are often linked in Proverbs (see Prov 11:1; 12:5, 17, 20; 14:8, 25; 20:23; 26:24). Keeping bad company—hanging out with and allowing oneself to be influenced by immoral and unjust companions—can lead one to stray from the path of right living, to place temptation before one's eyes, and to succumb to temptation with one's hands. Job says that if he has done this, he deserves to be punished. But he hasn't.

3. Job 31:1, 9–12: "I have covenanted with my eyes not to gaze on a maiden."

Job has been committed to sexual fidelity in marriage and to respecting the marriage of others.

Job deals with his sexual ethic in two moves. In 31:1, he says that he made a covenant (the classic Hebrew term *berit*) not to "gaze on a maiden," that is, a young unmarried woman ("virgin," in some translations). This is not just about a commitment not to succumb to the objectifying gaze known as lust; it is also about not taking advantage of a vulnerable young woman.

Then, in 31:9–12, Job makes clear that he also made a commitment not to open his heart to the appeals of a neighbor's wife or to "lay in wait at his door" (v. 9). Echoing the tenth commandment, Job is saying that he has been committed to not desiring his neighbor's wife. Job is also saying that he has not looked for opportunity to pursue a sexual relationship with a neighbor's wife, that is, adultery, framed in the patriarchal language of the Hebrew Bible in which it is mainly an offense against the male neighbor. The imprecation here that if he has done this, "may my wife grind for another, may others kneel over her!" (31:10). Both explicit and offensive, this may connote rape, as Job utters the most vile imprecation as a means of expressing his commitment not to act with sexual immorality.

4. Job 31:13–15: "Did I ever brush aside the case of my servants?"

Job has been committed to treating his servants/slaves with fairness and dignity and not ignoring their complaints.

Job describes his at-home business ethic here. Even though he (obviously) had great power over his servants, he says he did not ignore their complaints or abuse his power over them. Job knows that if he did that, he would be guilty before God and worthy of punishment. What Job then expresses is a beautifully egalitarian moral vision:

Did not He who made me in my mother's belly make him?
Did not One form us both in the womb?

All are equal in God's sight because God is equally the Maker of all. The words form perhaps the most impressive moral statement in the book. We do know, on the other hand, that at least some of Job's household workers were enslaved. Job treated enslaved people well, and yet they remained enslaved.

5. Job 31:16–23, 32: "Did I deny the poor their needs, Or let a widow pine away?"

Job has been committed to special care for the most vulnerable.

Job returns to the theme of his committed practice of caring for specific groups of vulnerable people. He names the poor, the widow, the orphan, and the "unclad wretch" (v. 19). Over in v. 32 he names his welcoming of the "sojourner" under his roof. Job also says explicitly that he never used his social, political, or judicial power "in the gate" to mistreat the "fatherless" (v. 21). Again, he says that the reason he did not do so was because of his proper "dread of God-sent calamity" (v. 23). Note that Job is placing himself here as part of the community whose order is vouchsafed through belief in God's close attention to human behavior, with rewards and punishments in this life.

6. Job 31:24–25: "Did I put my reliance on gold? Did I rejoice in my great wealth?"

Job has been committed to not overvaluing wealth.

In the next brief section, Job claims that, though he was the recipient of great wealth, he never relied on it or rejoiced in it. The delicate balance here is gratitude without excessive celebration, the use of wealth without idolatry.

Attitude toward wealth is a permanent issue in the biblical moral tradition. Where the tradition does not simply warn people off wealth or teach divestment (as in Jesus's teaching in several places; cf. Luke 18:18–25), it attempts to teach those blessed with wealth to maintain the proper moral and spiritual distance. It is interesting that nowhere in the book does Job explicitly lament losing his wealth.

7. Job 31:26–28: "If ever I saw the light shining . . . and I secretly succumbed. . . ."

Job has been committed to never practicing worship of anything or anyone other than God.

Probably the greatest offense against God in the Jewish tradition is idolatry, and that is what Job is saying that he has never practiced.

8. Job 31:29–31: "Did I rejoice over my enemy's misfortune?"

Job has been committed to moral restraint in relation to his enemies.

This is an elevated moral commitment. Job is not saying that he loved his enemies; but he is saying that he never wished for the death of his enemies, he never cursed them, and he never rejoiced when bad things happened to them. Job 31:31 seems to suggest that his restraint frustrated his men, who yearned for the chance to devour Job's foes. Consider the contrast between Job's commitment here and the lust for, and celebration of, harm to the enemy that one finds frequently in Scripture, notably in some of the imprecatory psalms (Pss 58, 59, 83).

9. Job 31:33–34: "Did I hide my transgressions like Adam/people/others?" (Heb: *ʾadam*)

Job has been committed to and has lived a life of integrity.

As Job's peroration nears its close, he begins summing up. Job has been accused by his friends of secret sins, for which God is punishing him. Job is explicitly denying any such secret life. Character is how we act when no one is looking. Integrity is oneness, wholeness, soundness of character, with no moral splitting. Job says he has been one person, without splitting or lying or deception. Thus, he does not deserve the threatening public rejection and "the contempt of families" that he has been receiving.

10. Job 31:38–40: "If my land cries out against me . . ."

Job has been committed to fair use of his land and fair treatment of those who work it.

Finally, in the obscurely stated last moral commitment, Job appears to be saying that he has not abused his land, has not taken produce from his workers or tenants without paying for it, and has not abused his power so as to ruin, perhaps even to kill, its owners, tenants, or workers.

Job Submits His Case to God

Those were Job's moral commitments. They were an expression of moral integrity, heartfelt, embodied, and comprehensive.[3] He believes that these commitments were laudable and in fact that they reflected God's will and his community's values. Yet still he has been attacked by God and rejected by his neighbors as a sinner.

In Job 31:35–37, Job submits his case to God. More precisely, he laments the fact that God has never given him the requested trial in which he could submit his case. God has never replied to his summons, nor has God ever offered a public bill of indictment (v. 35 NJPS: "true bill"). Once again, we see the two ways that Job has sought to engage God legally—through an indictment of God's mistreatment of him and/or through God writing up an indictment of Job, to which he could respond. Either way, Job would have had a chance to seek justice from God.

Job says with defiance, really, that if God should ever have written up a bill of indictment, Job would wear it with pride, like a "wreath" (v. 36). Then he would know exactly what he had been accused of and would be able to give a full "account of [his] steps," offering it "as to a commander" (v. 37). Job wants to look God in the eye and offer his defense. Biblical scholar Shalom Holtz calls this "an adjudicatory challenge to God," and identifies three examples of such in the Hebrew Bible (Josh 22:23; Job 31; Ps 44:21–22). It is a fierce form of protest, essentially *demanding* that God adjudicate Job's claims.[4]

We will see that God ultimately answers Job. But Job never gets God either to respond to his legal summons or to indict him. The trial never happens.

It turns out that this is Job's closing argument in defense of his life. His friends, his community, and we, his readers, are his audience. Perhaps we are also his jury? If so, how do we hear his defense of his life? Karl Barth says there are only two choices for those on the jury: "[It] can be understood only as the expression either of ungodly arrogance or of adamantine certainty of his practical commitment to God."[5]

From this point, only one other human being will enter the stage of this drama, a young man named Elihu.

33

Young Elihu Has His Say (Job 32–37)

Why do you complain against Him
That He does not reply to any of man's charges?
For God speaks time and again
—Though man does not perceive it—
In a dream, a night vision . . .
Then He opens men's understanding,
And by disciplining them leaves His signature
To turn man away from an action,
To suppress pride in man.

Surely it is false that God does not listen,
That Shaddai does not take note of it . . .
The case is before Him,
So wait for Him.

—Job 33:13–15a, 16–17, 35:13–14

"I Do Not Know How to Temper My Speech"

The text of Job 32–37 has always interested scholars because it is a completely unexpected break from Job's dialogue with his three friends. Various reconstructions of an editing process have been proposed. Most scholars dismiss Elihu's speech in Job 32–37 as a late editorial interruption—and a not very significant one at that. Carol Newsom documents the many textual reasons to believe that the Elihu speech is indeed a much later composition from a disgruntled scribe or editor who might even have been named Elihu. Her commentary sees it as reflecting the anxious concerns of someone who had access to the whole book and felt the need to clean it up.[1] Edward Greenstein is more dismissive when he says of the text that it is "Meant to educate Job and enrich the deity's presentation, Elihu's bombast and sense of self-importance have an almost ludicrous effect."[2]

My reading lands somewhere between the two. Elihu's speech is indeed long-winded, may indeed be a late addition from an editor, and *yet* there is also some new content here. Inherently interesting is that the authors and editors of Job give us this surprise appearance from a new character so very late in a long book. Instead of reaching the climax of the book, as a reader would expect with the last speeches made, Elihu's speech delays that climax of the book for six long chapters, which, depending on the reader's stance, can feel either effective (the plot thickens!) or enervating (will the God-response ever come?).

Chapter 32 opens with an editor shifting to prose and telling us that "these three men ceased replying to Job, for he considered himself right" (32:1). The conversation has ground to a standstill, even as everyone is still present. Into this void enters Elihu. The fact that Elihu is even there, and that he is described as having listened to everything so far, provides support for the idea suggested earlier that Job's dialogue with his friends has been a public event with an audience.

Three times in this brief introduction Elihu is described as angry. He is angry at Job, "because he thought himself right against God" (32:2), and he is angry at the friends, "because they found no reply" (32:3).

On this basis, Elihu finally feels compelled to speak. Out of respect for his elders, he has waited, but now, "The wind in my belly presses me. My belly is like wine not yet opened. . . . Let me speak, then, and get relief" (32:18–20). This is a comical way to describe the situation, leaving the impression of gas. Elihu goes on to say, "I do not know how to temper my speech" (32:22). In which ways, this will become apparent.

When put together with his self-description as "hav[ing] but few years" (32:6), Elihu strikes this seasoned professor as a very confident, cocky, seminary student. He thinks he knows a lot—but he knows less than he thinks he does. He has a lot to say—and he takes a long time to say it. He is filled with the fiery energy of the young, though he earns the ears of those around him and the respect of one of my student readers,

Mia Hong, who commented to me, "I have connected to Elihu in the past and admired his bravery in finally speaking to the older men. This is mostly because I know how intimidating it feels to speak my mind in spaces where everyone else is older and more experienced than me."[3] In a space where only the elders have spoken, we now hear a younger voice, one who has listened to both sides.

The Argument from Divine Discipline

It takes twenty-nine verses over two chapters for Elihu to even begin making his argument, an elaborate windup with little of note, given what's come before and what will come after.

Then he finally begins in 33:8–11. Elihu summarizes Job's claims before starting his long rebuke:

Indeed, you have stated in my hearing,
I heard the words spoken,
"I am guiltless, free from transgression;
I am innocent, without iniquity.
But He finds reasons to oppose me;
Considers me His enemy.
He puts my feet in stocks,
Watches all my ways."

Then Elihu adds this (33:13):

Why do you complain against Him
That He does not reply to any of man's charges?

This is an accurate, if abbreviated, summary of Job's protest: that he is innocent, that God has wronged him, and that God won't reply to his complaints.

Substantively, Elihu begins his critique on the last point. In 33:14, Elihu declares that "God speaks time and again, though man does not perceive it." In passing he points to dreams as one way God speaks to people. But his main move in the long section of 33:16–30 is to point to *divine discipline through suffering as both a major way that God instructs people and a major explanation of human suffering.*

Elihu warms to his theme through the rest of chapter 33 by telling a kind of story that he thinks should be familiar to Job. A person gets very sick: "He comes close to the Pit, his life verges on death" (33:22). But then an advocate (perhaps an angel, maybe just a righteous friend) intercedes for him with God, and God decides to show mercy (33:23–25). Through this near-death experience, the rescued one is drawn closer to God. He feels grateful for God's mercy, very much aware that he has sinned but has been spared (33:26–28). This kind of event is God's "signature" (33:16).

The upshot of this first move by Elihu is that if Job wants to know why he has suffered so and why God is silent, Elihu has an answer—God has brought suffering on him to discipline him, and the very suffering is a form of divine speech. Job's proper response would be to receive his suffering as discipline and divine communication, to be grateful to have survived, to repent of any sins, known or unknown, to express public gratitude to God rather than criticism, and to be restored to God.

While each of Job's three friends had suggested that Job's suffering might be a form of divine discipline, they were much harsher and emphasized Job's supposedly deserved punishment for his sins. Elihu is doing something more subtle here. His claim is that God can send suffering as a teaching tool, to deepen gratitude, knock down pride, and draw people closer to God. In other words, suffering can be a divine strategy, not a harsh punishment. The believer should listen for what God wants to teach through hard times, rather than complain about God being unjust.

As one who has sat by many a hospital bed, this resonates. There are things that can only be learned through grave suffering. The experience of weakness, vulnerability, and absolute dependence on God (and others) can be spiritually salutary in a way that ordinary times can't touch.

But Job hasn't just had a near-death experience. *He is still having it.* He has lost all his children. He has lost his wealth. He has lost his place in his community. Instructional divine discipline as an explanation is a nice try, but it is hard to imagine Job, or anyone similarly situated, feeling satisfied by such an explanation. And yet, we have seen evidence that Job has indeed learned some things through his suffering. There is truth to what Elihu is saying, not necessarily related to God sending instructional suffering, but of humans learning and growing through experiences with suffering, whatever their source.

The Argument from God's Character as Just and Sovereign

As the action moves to Job 34, Elihu again critiques Job for challenging God's justice and declaring his own innocence. He is outraged about this, in part because such a claim "makes common cause with evildoers" (34:8), undermining the basis of morality. Again, Job is treated as an enemy of piety and a threat to the moral cohesion of the community.

Elihu goes on to argue—or, really, to simply assert—that God is both just and sovereign. Elihu argues not only that "Shaddai does not pervert justice" (34:12) but also that God is the "Just Mighty One" (34:17). Elihu asks,

> *Who placed the earth in His charge?*
> *Who ordered the entire world?* (Job 34:13)

Elihu is essentially stipulating definitionally that God is both sovereign and just, indeed that God defines sovereignty and justice. God who creates sets all the relevant terms of creation, including whether anyone or anything survives on earth (34:14–15; cf. Eccl 12:7) and whether something that happens on earth is just or unjust.

It is a classic old argument from absolute divine sovereignty, and it has been made many times in the book of Job already. God is the potter; we are the clay (see Isa 29:16; 45:9; 64:8; Jer 18:1–6; Lam 4:2; Rom 9:20–21; cf. Job 10:8–9). If God should decide to bust up this piece of pottery, we have no basis on which to complain.

God the Creator and Judge is always at work in His creation, says Elihu. He brings the wicked down, no matter how powerful they are (34:19–27). He hears the cries of the poor and the needy and lifts them up (34:28). Just because God seems silent for a time (34:29), just because we cannot always be sure what God is doing, does not mean that God is not busily doing God-type things.

It is God's world, period. The only proper response of a puny human creature to the Just Mighty One is submission. That is Elihu's primary critique of Job:

Has he said to God,
"I will bear [my punishment] and offend no more.
What I cannot see You teach me.
If I have done iniquity, I shall not do so again"? (Job 34:31–32)

Instead, says Elihu, Job has demanded that God "requite as [Job sees] fit" (33:33), and this is simple impertinence and impiety. Elihu is so outraged that he utters an ominous threat, albeit in passing:

Would that Job were tried to the limit
For answers which befit sinful men.
He adds to his sin;
He increases his transgression among us;
He multiplies his statements against God. (Job 34:36–37)

Job should be "tried to the limit" (Heb: *ʿad neṣaḥ*). This at least means that Job's claims should be subject to rigorous scrutiny. The idea seems to be that the community must pressure Job to retract his claims until he does so or until he dies. Job's claims are simply intolerable to the community and must be suppressed or reversed.

This is not an argument. But it is an implication of the argument that humans do not have the right to challenge God.

The Argument for Patience

In Job 35, Elihu makes two moves that should be mentioned briefly.

In 35:4–8, Elihu makes an argument that Eliphaz had made earlier (chap. 22; cf. Job 7 for Job's brief attempt at this move as well). God is so transcendent that God is not affected by either human righteousness or wickedness. God is high up; we are down below. God is great; our affairs are small. "If you are righteous, what do you give Him?" (35:7). Conversely, "if your transgressions are many, how do you affect Him?" (35:6). Human actions affect other human beings, not God (35:8). One can see the point of this claim; it is a kind of argument against humans mattering all that much to God. But it undercuts the claims made in the prior chapter about God constantly watching and assessing human action (34:21), as well as God's very first claims about Job's piety and integrity.

Next, Elihu makes an unsympathetic argument about how humans who are suffering cry out to God (35:9–12). "Because of the multitude of oppressions people cry out" (35:9a, NRSVue). This is to be expected. But when they cry out, they don't properly address God, who is the Creator and giver of strength and knowledge (35:10–11). The idea seems to be that whining to God without a proper posture of piety and gratitude leaves God unimpressed. In a sense, an add-on to the prior claim, it doesn't hold as a new or impressive argument.

Job 35 offers only one significant argument, and it is found here:

Surely it is false that God does not listen,
That Shaddai does not take note of it.
Though you say, "You do not take note of it,"
The case is before Him;
So wait for Him. (Job 35:13–14)

Elihu is arguing that God does attend to human misery and does reply to human complaints about injustice. But God may not do so on our timetable. We know that the Israelites cried out to God for 430 years because of slavery. But the Bible says that God did hear and did respond (cf. Exod 3). Jews cried out under Hitler for twelve long years, but finally Hitler was dead, and liberation came. Each of these liberations arguably can be interpreted as God hearing and responding to the cries of the suffering, just not on their timetable.

It is true that humans are impatient, especially when we are suffering. It is true that we can mistake a long wait as a no or as sheer indifference. But it is also true that when we suffer greatly, we need help now, not 430 years from now. Individuals respond based on their suffering and with the urgency that their miseries naturally evoke. While pious counselors tell us to "wait," that God cares and that help is coming, after a while we will ask the natural question, "How long, O Lord?"—a question that recurs numerous times in the Bible itself.[4]

Sometimes, while we are forced to wait, the suffering that we endure goes beyond a place where it can be repaired. This can be true of individuals and certainly can be true of groups. Hitler's power only lasted twelve years, he was unsuccessful in destroying all the Jews he sought to kill, and yet Hitler killed six million Jews. There was no real recovery from that for the Jewish people. Every day that the Jewish people waited for deliverance at Auschwitz was a day too long.

This move by Elihu reminds me again of Jesus's parable of the unjust judge in Luke 18:1–8. Jesus concludes that parable this way: "Will not God grant justice to his chosen ones who cry to him day and night? Will he delay long in helping them? I tell you, he will quickly grant justice to them. And yet, when the Son of Man comes, will he find faith on earth?"

In the Gospel text we meet Jesus being much more realistic than Elihu about the limits of human endurance, as well as aware of the possibility that injustice so severe and so lengthy truly can grind faith to dust.

The Argument from Creation's Powers at God's Command

In Job 36:5–15, Elihu reaffirms God's just interventions in the world. But he highlights his claim that "He opens understanding by discipline, and orders them back from mischief" (36:10). The subtle argument Elihu is making is that God brings suffering upon those doing wrong, not merely as punishment but as goad to correction. This would explain why the wicked are not simply and quickly destroyed, and the needy not simply and quickly aided. God holds back to invite repentance and change. Elihu goes on to address Job directly in 36:16–21, suggesting that this is what is happening to Job. Job needs to trust that God is working a process that is aimed at his restoration, if only he will respond in humility rather than rebellion.

Finally, in Job 36:22–37:24, Elihu makes an argument from the grandeur of creation and the wonder of God's creating and governing power. The Creator and Governor of the universe is beyond human reproach (36:23), Elihu suggests. God's greatness is apparent in creation, in everything: rain, thunder, lightning, food, snow, storms, cold, ice, sun, heat, and so on. Elihu intimates that God even directs the majestic, sometimes terrifying power of creation, such as storms and high winds, as part of His sovereign manipulation of events on earth, "whether as a scourge or as a blessing" (37:13).

For Elihu, the end of the matter is this (37:23–24):

Shaddai—we cannot attain to Him;
He is great in power and justice
And abundant in righteousness; He does not torment.
Therefore, men are in awe of Him
Whom none of the wise can perceive.

Elihu understands God as combining greatness, power, justice, goodness, and mystery. "We cannot attain to Him" (Heb: *lo᾽ meṣa᾽nuhu*) means that God cannot be found by us and is beyond our reach. The best response of human beings is to stand "in awe of Him" (Heb: *yere᾽uhu*), a term connoting reverence, fear, humility, and submission. If Job 37:24 is translated as "He does not regard any who are wise in their own conceit" (NRSVue; note difference from NJPS above), it is a final rebuke of Job—and perhaps of those of us who have taken Job's claims to heart. The rebuke would be that anyone who is "wise in their own conceit" rather than bowing in reverent submission to God is a rebel who has not yet learned what God is trying to teach them.

There are lots of questions about Elihu's role in this conversation, and several different positions possible, ranging from dismissal to profound appreciation. There are many reasons to question the legitimacy of his speeches as a part of the book of Job, and yet in some ways he anticipates the divine speeches to come. He offers some arguments that are new, and his defense of God is, overall, more effective than that of the three friends. Elihu's speech is a reminder that the friends and the community around them are wrong about Job, but probably not wrong about everything they have said about God and the world.[5]

34

God Speaks to Job at Last (Job 38–41)

Then the Lord *replied to Job out of the tempest and said:*

Who is this who darkens counsel,
Speaking without knowledge?
Gird your loins like a man;
I will ask and you will inform Me . . .
Shall one who should be disciplined complain against Shaddai?
He who arraigns God must respond.

—Job 38:1–3; 40:2

The Manner of God's Response to Job

It might have been possible to end the book of Job at chapter 28, or chapter 31, or at chapter 37. After all, many have cried out to God; many have sought to hear God's voice, and have heard nothing. A significant theme in the book of Job is God's long silence in response to Job's cries for God to respond to his laments, his protests.

It would be easy to condemn God for this silence, and to link it with all the other times people have cried out to God, who has appeared to them to remain silent.

Perhaps, though, a different way to look at this text is that God has allowed Job to speak for days, weeks, and months. God has allowed Job to say all kinds of provocative things, to raise his defiant questions and speak his experiential truth until his final magnificent speech in Job 29–31 leads him finally to fall silent. He has said everything he had to say. Only after that does God speak. In that sense, God's silence can be seen as an expression of grace.

Finally, though, God does respond. And what do we make of that response, which has both bedeviled and delighted those who love Scripture and love this majestic book?

Some consider God's response deeply satisfying. More consider it deeply frustrating. William Safire says it is simply a browbeating: "[Job] predicts accurately that God will be a bully if and when confronted . . . his voice rings out of the whirlwind environed in wrath—sarcastic, capricious, intimidating."[1] Many readers agree that the voice of God here is solely an attempt at a display of intimidating divine power rather than an entry into a conversation.[2] But that is definitely not the only interpretation, as we shall soon see.

The divine discourse comes in two parts: Job 38:1–40:2, followed by a brief stunned comment from Job in 40:3–5, and then Job 40:6 to the end of chapter 41. Some scholars say it is two speeches, but I view it as one speech with a brief interruption.

The first three verses of Job 38 set the tone and manner of God's response.

The name of God that is offered is the unspeakably holy divine name, the tetragrammaton—transcribed as *adonai* in Hebrew, and traditionally as the Lord in English. It had appeared in the prose prologue, but not at all during the dialogues (except 12:9), and only reenters the book's vocabulary now (38:1; 40:1, 3, 6; 42:1, 7, 9–12). This has been seen by some scholars as an editorial issue. But the effect here, at least for a Hebrew reader, is to heighten both the drama and the authority of what follows.

God speaks out of a "tempest" (NRSVue: "whirlwind"). The Hebrew term is *se'arah*. Its meaning can extend to storm, windstorm, violent storm. Readers of the Hebrew Bible may be reminded of how God appeared at the top of Mount Sinai when giving the Ten Commandments (Exod 20). Others may think of the primordial chaos of the creation story. There are other times in the Bible in which God appears to people (a "theophany") out of a storm. That God would show up through a violent windstorm—a familiar and terrifying sight in the desert—or perhaps as a thundering voice amid lightning, rain, and hail, sets quite a mood: When God comes, it is in terrifying power.

An interesting question is whether this is a public or private theophany. Everything that has happened since Job 3 has occurred before an audience. If God speaks to Job out of a "tempest," is this public too? Unless it is metaphorical, I imagine the author of Job wants us to think of an actual violent whirlwind within which is the voice of God.

Perhaps the words of God are only heard by Job, but the storm is visible to all? That would be consonant with how God spoke to Moses in Exod 19:16–25. The people could hear the thunder, but only Moses could hear the words. The ending of this majestic book of Job only makes sense if this is how Job's experience of God in the whirlwind is pictured. Job is restored to his community in part because they have witnessed some part of this theophany.

When God speaks, God does so in a mood of angry rebuke. "Who is this who darkens counsel?" This line from 38:2 (Heb: *maḥšik ʿeṣah*) seems to signify a criticism of Job (and possibly of all the speakers) for uttering many words without adequate understanding, leaving everyone misdirected away from the truth.

So, "Gird up your loins like a man. I will ask and you will inform Me" (38:2–3). Whether in Hebrew (*ʾezar naʾ kegeber ḥalaṣeka*) or in English, these are words of confrontation. "Gird up your loins" meant tucking in one's tunic under the belt to free up the legs for a fight or physical labor. In English vernacular, it means something like *Let's get ready to rumble*.

The idea that God will now respond to Job's litany of questions with His own battery of questions is remarkable. It leaves the impression that perhaps God has no plan to respond to Job's questions and certainly not to submit to Job's arraignment. There will be no deposition, no contest before the bar.

This is also signaled when at the end of the first part of God's speech, the words are: "Shall one who should be disciplined complain against Shaddai? He who arraigns God must respond" (40:2). The NRSVue (better) renders the first part of 40:2, in this way: "Shall a faultfinder contend with the Almighty?"

So God will respond to Job. But God comes to Job in a fearful theophany, and with a tone that I, at least, consider to be an angry rebuke. This is the manner of God's response to Job.

James Parker puts it starkly:

> "Bind up your loins like a man," God warns Job, before stamping on the effects pedal and delivering perhaps the most shattering speech ever recorded. Question after question, power chord after power chord. . . . No explanation; no answer for Job; no moral or theoretical content whatsoever. It's the interrogation of consciousness by pure Being, by the Logos, by the unstopping, unmediated act of creation itself. . . . The human intellect shrinks before the onslaught. The language is incomparable. God, it turns out, is the greatest poet; no one can touch him.[3]

The Message of God's Response to Job

God's response to Job is not a direct response. Job has asked God why God has inflicted so much unjust suffering on him and his family. And God does not answer that question.

An outline of what God *does* offer in Job 38–41 suffices to reveal how vastly different God's answer is from Job's question.

1. "Who is this who darkens counsel?" (38:2–3).

God sets an aggressive tone.

Everything that follows will be in the form of rhetorical questions directed at Job.

2. "Where were you when I laid the earth's foundations?" (38:4–7)

God alone is the Creator.

God takes Job back to the day/week/time of creation.

3. "Who closed the sea behind doors?" (38:8–11)

God set the boundaries of the ocean.

This section continues the creation discussion with a special emphasis on the idea that an ordered creation required God to set limits on the sea and to protect dry land for human and other forms of land life.

4. "Have you ever commanded the day to break?" (38:12–15)

God creates the daily rhythms of nature.

This section emphasizes the awe-inspiring experience of daybreak. Verses 13 and 15, with their references to "the wicked," appear to reflect the idea that the wicked hide in the dark, so when dawn comes, they are exposed, unsettled, and deprived of their safety. This is one of only two places in God's speech where any form of God's engagement with human behavior is mentioned (the other is 40:10–14).

5. "Have you penetrated to the sources of the sea?" (38:16–18)

God alone knows what lives in the depths of the ocean.

This section gets at the amazing mystery of the ocean, its hidden depths, its extraordinary array of creatures mostly unknown to land creatures such as human beings. These verses go on to ask whether Job has experienced other "underneath" spaces such as "the gates of death" and "the gates of deep darkness."

6. "Which path leads to where light dwells?" (38:19–21)

God alone knows the source of light and darkness.

Here light and darkness are mythologized as having dwelling places; they live somewhere. God asks Job whether he has ever visited their address.

7. "Have you penetrated the vaults of snow?" (38:22–30)

God alone knows where the sky's deliveries upon earth are stored.

This longer section mentions not only snow but also hail, wind, thunderstorms, rain, and ice. A notable feature is the claim that God stores up hail "for a time of adversity, for a day of war and battle." This echoes a claim made by Elihu at 37:12. God uses the weather for divine purposes. Also notable is the reminder that rains fall on wilderness and "desolate wasteland," where no human lives. The meaning of this reminder will be considered below.

8. "Can you tie cords to Pleiades?" (38:31–33)

God created the heavens and established the movements of the stars.

This brief section points to the staggering grandeur of the starry skies and the constellations that humans have named there. A striking reference to "the laws" (Heb: *ḥuqqot*) of heaven probably refers to the rule (Heb: *mišṭar*) of natural laws over the celestial bodies, not to moral law or Torah.

9. "Who put wisdom in the hidden parts? Who gave understanding to the mind?" (38:34–38)

God alone inscribed wisdom in creation and creatures.

This mixed-content section includes further references to God directing rain and lightning. It also contains a reference to God putting wisdom in "hidden parts" or "inward parts" (Heb: *ṭuḥot* and *śekwi*), the latter an obscure term usually translated "mind" but open even to the translation "rooster." Edward Greenstein and Carol Newsom both read this couplet as about the "ibis bird" and the "rooster" or "cock."[4] Overall, this section probably refers to God's mysterious inscribing of wisdom in creation, perhaps including human consciousness. The meaning of this elliptical passage is uncertain.

10. "Can you hunt prey for the lion. . . . Who provides food for the raven when his young cry out to God?" (38:39–41)

God alone set up creation so that all animals can find food.

Notable here is the implicit assertion that God ordered the creation in such a way that lions and ravens get food. In both cases, humans have no role. The idea that all creatures cry out to God, regardless of the nature and extent of their "speech," has interesting implications.

11. "Do you know the season when the mountain goats give birth?" (39:1–4)

God alone knows the life cycles and behaviors of the wild animals.

The turn to Job 39 marks an emphasis on animals in the wild. It begins with a brief question about the calving process of mountain goats.

12. "Who sets the wild ass free?" (39:5–8)

God is the one who created and enjoys witnessing the freedom of the wild animals.

Here God contrasts the wild donkey with the domesticated kind. The wild one gets the better of the comparison: "He scoffs at the tumult of the city, does not hear the shout of the driver." Here the voice of God celebrates the wildness and untamability of certain creatures.

13. "Would the wild ox agree to serve you?" (39:9–12)

God reminds Job of the limits of human power over wild creatures.

The answer to God's rhetorical question is no. The wild ox, in contrast to the tamed ox, would have no interest in serving humans for agricultural work or any other purpose. God says, just try it!

14. "The wing of the ostrich beats joyously. . . . " (39:13–18)

God calls Job's attention to the odd behavior of the ostrich, which God created and of which Job knows nothing.

The only section not framed with a question, this discussion of the ostrich emphasizes its nonsensical (to us) childrearing practices. "Her young are cruelly abandoned as if they were not hers" (v. 16). Why? "For God deprived her of wisdom, gave her no share of understanding" (v. 17). This may well connect to 38:36, in this way: While much of the animal kingdom demonstrates behaviors that make rational sense—like protecting and feeding their young—the ostrich does not. This too is God's doing (v. 17).

15. "Do you give the horse his strength?" (39:19–25)

God loves seeing the physical power of animals such as horses.

This somewhat extended discussion reflects thrillingly on the strength, beauty, energy, and power of the horse—in this example, the warhorse. This animal has been "tamed" for human use, but its natural grandeur is the focus.

16. "Is it by your wisdom that the hawk grows pinions?" (39:26–30)

God knows and celebrates the details of the behavior of the wild birds of prey.

The birds of prey, especially living at mountain heights, draw God's attention. Their ability to fly, to build nests high in the rocks, and then to swoop down on their prey, draws commentary. "His young gulp blood; where the slain are, there is he" (v. 30). Yuck. But God seems to celebrate this.

There is a pause as God demands Job's response, which is the following (40:4–5):

See, I am of small worth; what can I answer You?
I clap my hand to my mouth.
I have spoken once, and will not reply.
Twice, and will do so no more.

If the goal of the voice of God was to overwhelm Job, that goal has been met. He is silenced. He will speak no more. But is that God's goal, simply to silence Job? Apparently not, as God continues.

17. "Would you impugn my justice? . . . Have you an arm like God's?" (40:8–14)

God appears to rebuke Job directly for challenging God's justice.

God's speech continues with God asking Job whether he would like to try to bring down proud men, humble them, and bury them in the earth. Notice that God never says that this is what He does, but it is certainly what the friends have been claiming of God throughout the dialogues, and it is an essential part of just-world theology. It may be implicit in this little passage, but it may not. More, it may be a challenge to Job, like this: *You complain of my unjust administration of this world. You try it.* Might it also imply the following idea? *You are asking for my engagement in the details of human behavior, either through vindication or condemnation; that I really do not do.* This assertion would challenge every speaker in the book of Job. We'll look more closely at this idea in the conclusion.

18. "Take now behemoth, whom I made as I made you." (40:15–24)

God calls Job's attention to behemoth, whose awesome power is to be a lesson to Job.

Now it really gets fun. In detail, God describes a creature called "behemoth." God says behemoth is "the first of God's works," which "I made as I made you." There is no sense of human superiority. The described creature resembles a hippopotamus or an elephant. It may describe another type of massive creature that is long gone from the earth. It may be symbolic and/or mythical, though it doesn't sound like it, and it would not fit with what the voice of God is doing elsewhere. The description is of a massive creature that dwarfs human beings; it cannot be domesticated, and it cannot be killed by anyone other than God, "its Maker" (40:19). It need not fear what humans fear. The majesty of Behemoth is its tremendous power and, again, its wildness and untamability.

19. "Can you draw out Leviathan with a fishhook?" (40:25–41:26 NJPS; 41:1–34 NRSV)

God describes Leviathan, the most terrifying creature in the world.

Here the chapter breaks differently in the Christian Bible than in the Hebrew Bible. The Christian Bible gives all of Job 41 to the Leviathan description, whereas in the Tanakh that awesome description starts at Job 40:25.

This climactic ending to God's speech in Job describes an utterly terrifying sea-creature. It makes one think of Godzilla or the Beast from Revelation or a hundred movies about fierce dragons. The description is of the wildest and most dangerous creature imaginable, who brings humans to absolute terror, who cannot be killed, trafficked, or tamed, whose skin is completely impenetrable to any human or animal weapons, who sneezes lightning, whose eyes are red, who blows out fire and smoke, who can smash through bronze and iron, who can wade through ocean water and make it boil. Whatever this creature is, it is the most terrifying thing imaginable.

God's speech ends this way (41:33–34; NJPS vv. 25–26):

There is no one on land who can dominate him,
Made as he is without fear.
He sees all that is haughty;
He is king over all proud beasts.

Maybe the implication is that Job is haughty and Leviathan is king. And that is how God ends His speech to Job. Wow.

Interpreting God's Reponse to Job

God has not discussed what has happened to Job, has not explained why, has not commiserated with him for his losses. God has not defended His actions in relation to Job and his family. God has not described the wager that He made with *ha-śaṭan* or offered any other explanation. God has not described how His treatment of Job could be assessed as just or good. God has not responded to Job's suit against him in any way. Jewish scholar Nahum Glatzer writes, "The Creator allows man to behold the vast panorama of the universe. One thing alone is missing in this majestic picture of heaven and earth: man."[5]

On the other hand, if what has happened to Job is because Job did something wrong that he can correct, God has not offered such information. If the friends had been right that God was punishing Job for his sins, those sins might have been enumerated by God, but God does not do this. We will see in the last chapter that the friends' position on Job is explicitly *not vindicated* by God. If the idea is that Job had been indicted by God for wrongdoing, and like so many other wicked people is paying the price for his sins (cf. 40:11–13), God has not spelled out the terms of His indictment. The legal metaphor that has been important to Job is not important to God.

Competing Interpretations

If all the commentaries about Job were weighed on a scale, it is this speech that would get the most metric tons of ink and page. Every commentary on the book of Job camps out here, and then onward to Job's pivotal words in chapter 42.

There appear to be three basic readings of this speech among informed readers.

The first is generally positive, arguing that even though Job does not get a direct answer to his anguished queries, it is the very fact that God speaks to Job, and perhaps also what God says to Job, that is meaningful. Another subtle category of positive readings, often existentialist, emphasize Job's experience of his encounter with God.

The second reading is generally negative, claiming that God simply or mainly tries to intimidate Job with bluster and rhetorical questions, leaving Job and the reader unsatisfied.

The third group sees the divine speech as a meaningful *reframing* of reality/morality that has value even if it does not answer Job.

Which reading is taken is very much tied to how the reader interprets Job's response in 42:1–6. The two go together. We will see this work itself out in the next chapter.

In general, traditionalist-apologetic Christian and Jewish readers find God's speaking to Job at all, and usually the content of God's speech, as meaningful and as a vindication of God after all Job's criticisms.

Negative readings tend to come from Jews, Christians, and other readers who find the speech disappointing and cannot muster a defense for it. This has been an increasingly significant trend.

What follows is a sampling of striking comments that exemplify the positive, reframing, and negative interpretations of God's speech from the whirlwind.

Positive Readings

Søren Kierkegaard: "How blessed it is to be rebuked by God! As a rule, a person very easily becomes defiant when censured; when God judges [though], then he subsides, and, surrounded by the love that wishes to educate him, he forgets the pain."[6]

Dylan Balfour: "[God's speech] is more than confrontational grandstanding. Contained within God's speech to Job about creation is a host of parental and second-personal language, in which God seems to have a caring, personal relationship with even the inanimate elements of creation. . . . Yes, these claims do demonstrate God's power. But, more significantly, they elucidate his *relationship* with creation. God presents himself not only as an all-powerful creator, but also as a loving parent and carer. . . . Job is awed by coming into direct second-personal contact with God. . . . Job seems to *learn* something in the Franciscan mode by experiencing God. . . . This does not mean that Job comes to understand his suffering. Instead, he comes to know that his suffering does not count as evidence against God's goodness by coming to know *directly* that God is good."[7]

G. K. Chesterton: "The refusal of God to explain His design is itself a burning hint of His design. The riddles of God are more satisfying than the solutions of man. . . . Job puts forward a note of interrogation; God answers with a note of exclamation. Instead of proving to Job that it is an explicable world, He insists that it is a much stranger world than Job ever thought it was."[8]

Richard Middleton: "The freedom God grants creatures includes their vulnerability, so that the strength, dignity, and beauty of various wild animals is intertwined with the realities of struggle and death—from which God does not automatically protect them. In this portrayal of the world, God is implicitly answering (and correcting) Job's assumptions of a tight act-consequence structure to the universe. . . . There is no good reason to maintain the traditional interpretation of God as an abusive tyrant attempting to silence Job. . . . It makes eminently better sense of the text to conclude that God comes not to bury Job but precisely to *praise* him."[9]

C. S. Lewis: "As long as a man is thinking of God as an examiner who has set him a sort of paper to do, or as the opposite party in a sort of bargain—as long as he is thinking of claims and counter-claims between himself and God—he is not yet in the right relation to Him. He is misunderstanding what he is and what God is. And he cannot get into the right relation until he has discovered the fact of [his] bankruptcy."[10]

Reframing Readings

Carol Newsom: "God's speeches, by beginning with the great structures of creation and speaking scarcely at all of the place of human beings in the cosmos, expose the limits of Job's anthropocentric categories. Similarly, Job's legal model for understanding divine-human relationships is also implicitly challenged . . . in God's speeches, the play between fundamental order and the restricted but still powerful forces of the chaotic is crucial for understanding the nature of reality."[11]

Gerald Janzen: "In [God's] speech nothing was said to thrust Job further into the mire. All that was done was to portray Yahweh as a cosmic creator who delights in a world sufficiently ordered to make life possible and worthwhile, but sufficiently free to allow for the possibility of bilateral participation. Humankind is not painted into the picture as one creature among many, but is addressed by the Creator in a series of questions, the response to which will disclose the human decision for self-understanding in such a world: solely as a creature; or as a creature (as "dust and ashes") challenged to take up the divine *image* through engagement with the partly determinate, partly indeterminate character of the world."[12]

William P. Brown: "In Genesis 1, creation is hierarchically defined with humanity receiving the 'blessing' of dominion. In Psalm 104 and Job, humanity assumes no such role. If one wants to find a royal figure in creation, Leviathan, the quintessential creature of chaos, is the only candidate that qualifies in Job. . . . In Job . . . the glory of God is a fully living creation, one that is biologically diverse. . . . What kind of world does YHWH present to Job? A world that is terrifyingly and wondrously vast and alien, teeming with life characterized by fierce strength, inalienable freedom, and wild beauty. Land, sea, and sky are host to myriad life-forms, all alien to the human eye and untamable to human hand but all affirmed and sustained by YHWH. YHWH's world is filled with scavengers and predators, even monsters (cf. Gen 1:21), all co-existing and thriving. This world is God's wild kingdom."[13]

Scott Davison et al.: "We should recognize human cognitive limitations that preclude us from making reasonable judgments about the nature of the universe. More specifically . . . we are not in a position to know whether our sample of good and evil things is representative of good and evil things in the universe on the whole, or whether our understanding of the relationships between good and evil things is representative of all such relationships."[14]

Georg Gasser: "The divine speeches call for a self-transcendence and redirection towards the worth of things in themselves, independent from their instrumental value for specific human purposes. They relativise our natural egocentric perspective and call us to complement it with one that assigns an intrinsic value to nature in its beautiful as well as dangerous and violent peculiarities. . . . The world as such is valuable to God independently of any ultimate moral order. God wants us to live a life immersed in such a world by accepting the beautiful as well as inexplicable tragic dimensions of creation and our existence in it. . . . God does not show himself closed to human longing but has a genuine interest that people are able to form an appropriate image of God—even if the grasp of this image entails a profound and painful transformation towards less anthropocentric categories of the divine."[15]

Jacqueline Lapsley: "However the human role is configured the desired result is the flourishing of all creation. To flourish for any creature is to live in a context in which the fulfillment of its God-given potential is made possible. . . . God's speech from the whirlwind evokes this flourishing well."[16]

Negative Readings

Maria Kardaun: "When it comes to power and knowledge, Job indeed wholeheartedly acknowledges God's superiority (42:2–3), but the question . . . was not who is the most powerful or who knows the most, but who should take responsibility for Job's undeserved misery."[17]

Nehama Verbin: "Having a first-person experience of God through God's revelations does not resolve the absurd for him. On the contrary, it enhances it. The divine revelations do not address the content of Job's moral complaints and accusations; they do not provide an answer that dissolves the contradiction. As such they do not provide him with an escape from the absurd. Rather, they consist in a display of unbounded and unreasonable power that enhances the contradiction."[18]

Sameer Yadav: "While vindicated, he remains more deeply disconsolate. . . . The whirlwind encounter therefore does not function to resolve the questions over Job's consolation . . . but rather to heighten and exacerbate them."[19]

Edward Greenstein: "The deity assumes a hostile persona—that of the storm god. . . . Instead of explaining to Job the circumstances of his suffering . . . the deity addresses Job aggressively, asserting his superiority by demonstrating Job's ignorance. . . . Job, acknowledged as a righteous person, is treated here in bullying fashion. God barely touches on anything connected to justice or to the providential care of humanity. . . . The exquisite imagery of the divine discourse portrays a fundamentally amoral world."[20]

I believe some meaningful reframing happens in God's speech, a reframing that should affect Christian theology and ethics. Without attempting any special insight into the voice of God offered in this speech, I will simply offer up a few considerations.

Job 38–41 offers a meaningful challenge to human knowledge of the created order and its origins. We know little and understand less. That should create humility, especially in our theological and moral claims about God and the world.

This passage is also an immensely picturesque series of depictions of striking dimensions of creation. The overall effect is to reinforce awe at the vastness, diversity, and grandeur of creation, and to decenter humanity. This, too, is valuable.

The voice of God emphasizes untamed, wild, and chaotic dimensions of creation. God makes a special point to contrast tamed animals with wild ones, safe animals with dangerous ones, elements of threat and not just elements that support human life.

Why this emphasis?

Maybe the voice of God is showing us that we tend to see creation from our narrow vantage point, for how it affects us, how we can use it, even dominate it. But God has a bigger agenda with creation. It is not for us. It is not all tamable. It is not all orderly. It is not all safe. But it does all belong to God and matter to God. Any God who can make Behemoth and Leviathan must have purposes, interests, and even aesthetic pleasures that are very different from our own. And God has a relationship with these other creatures. God made them, watches them, gives them some version of cognition, enjoys seeing them function as designed. This decenters humanity as the crown of creation and the sole object of God's attention. Millar writes, "For Job, the non-human was a source of derision; for God it is a source of delight."[21]

God offers a statement of having made provision for wisdom and for understanding, at least for almost all of the animals, maybe also for animals that are human (38:36–37). But it is "hidden" and thus mysterious. So while God has provided various kinds of cognition for the creatures, human cognition is only one type.

Only once does the voice of God even acknowledge the rounds of discussion over whether God is watching human affairs and punishing evildoers. In this speech, it is *pride* that God seems to disdain in humans (see 40:11–12, Heb: *geʾeh*), not *wickedness*. Perhaps this means that God is more offended by human pride than by human wrongdoing. In any case, the voice of God here *does* notice human pride and finds it absurd. But the way God deals with wickedness is not necessarily what we want or expect.

Job 38–41 teaches that God is not a tame God, and God has not created a tame world, that humans know very little and have very little power, and that pridefulness is a most inappropriate posture for puny creatures such as us.

And yes, it is meaningful that God speaks to Job after all the things that Job has said against Him.

Still, if I were forced to choose between the positive and negative reading of God's speeches to Job from the whirlwind, *I would take the negative.*

I read God's speech as avoiding Job's anguished grief and his questions about justice, as offering neither sympathy nor explanation to Job, as taking no responsibility for the brutal assault that God has inflicted upon Job. The positive approach seems more concerned with defending God's honor than assessing fairly whether God really responds to Job's legitimate questions, his grief, and his horrific trauma.

So, reframe, positive, or negative—is the character Job satisfied with God's answer from the whirlwind? We move to find out.

35

Job's Disputed Response (Job 42:1–6)

I know that You can do everything,
That nothing You propose is impossible for You.
"Who is this who obscures counsel without knowledge?"
Indeed, I spoke without understanding
Of things beyond me, which I did not know.
"Hear now, and I will speak;
I will ask, and you will inform me."
I had heard You with my ears,
But now I see You with my eyes;
Therefore, I recant and relent,
Being but dust and ashes.

—Job 42:2–6 (quotation marks added)

A Very Brief Response by Job

When one considers the sheer amount of verbiage that Job has offered throughout this long book in response to friends turned ex-friends, Job's response to God is surprisingly brief.

The response of Job is even shorter if we put quotation marks around the places Job is quoting (or very nearly quoting) what God has said to him. Oddly, NJPS does not do that, while NRSVue, NASB, and other translations do.

Job had been doing an awful lot of talking. Yet here, in his five-verse response, he devotes the equivalent of one full verse simply to repeating back to God what God had said to him.

What Does Job Say to God, Exactly?

The Jewish and Christian traditions have almost universally read Job 42:2–6 as a recantation of Job's inappropriate challenges to God. But that is *not* the only possible reading.

Job begins by acknowledging God's tremendous power—"I know that You can do everything." God's power has been one of the steady themes of the book. No one has really questioned it, and God's speech has certainly reinforced the theme.

Job moves on to acknowledge that he had spoken of things about which he did not have adequate understanding, that he was addressing matters that were beyond him (42:3). This is certainly true.

Job seems to be expressing gratitude in 42:5 that whereas once he had only "heard" God with his ears, now he had seen God with his eyes. God had appeared to him, albeit in a scary whirlwind, and this was at least something that had not happened before. God responded to Job at least insofar as God showed up for Job and spoke to him. Also meaningful is that this occurred in a public way, likely helping Job be restored to his community due to their perception of divine validation.

The Elusive Meaning of Job 42:6

But now we come to what many see as the most important verse of the book: Job 42:6.

Reading a host of biblical scholars on this verse, it is clear that how to translate the seven Hebrew words here is not definitively resolvable. At first, this seems quite a shame, given how much rides on this verse.

But it also turns out to be deeply instructive. As Carol Newsom points out, how one reads Job 42:6 will depend on how one has understood the divine speeches. It is also true that how one reads the epilogue (42:7–17) also depends on how one understands both the divine speeches and Job 42:6! Newsom writes, "Asking which possibility [for translating 42:6] is correct misses the interpretive significance of the ambiguity of Job's reply, which corresponds to the ambiguity that is also part of the divine speeches."[1]

Let's do a deep dive on the much-contested Hebrew of this verse. Here is all we have from the author of Job:

> *ʿal-ken ʾemʾas weniḥamti ʿal-ʿafar waʾeper*

And here are the root words and their basic range of meanings:

maʾas = "despise" [+ implicit object] / "recant" / "melt"
naḥam = "repent" / "relent" / "be comforted"
ʿal = "in/about/on/over/upon"
ʿapar + *ʾeper*
= *"dust/soil/ashes/plaster/realm of the dead" and "ashes/dust"* together to mean human mortality, humiliation, or mourning

Here is an extensive list of current translation options.[2] I first list the main idea of a given interpretation, then cite interpreters or Bible translation examples that convey this idea. In the last two instances, where there is only one idea, the interpreter is quoted as the main idea.

1a. Therefore I despise (myself) and repent in humiliation.

Therefore I abhor/reject/despise/loathe myself and repent upon dust and ashes. [Gordis 1978, KJV, ESV, (N)RSV(ue), NIV(all), ISV]

Therefore I reprehend myself, and do penance in dust and ashes. [Douay-Rheims]

So now I hate myself; I will change my heart and life. I will sit in the dust and ashes. [NCV]

Therefore I despise myself, and I repent in dust and ashes! [NET]

. . . and I loathe myself and repent in dust and ashes. [LB]

Therefore I despise (myself) and repent (of my words) in dust and ashes. [Rowley]

1b. Therefore I despise (myself) and consider my mortality.

Wherefore I demean myself and yield, reduced to dust and ashes. [Gray]

Therefore I disparaged myself and wasted away, and I regard myself as dust and ashes. [LXX in NETS]

2a. Therefore I retract (my words) and repent in humiliation.

Therefore I reject my words and am sorry for them. [CSB]

Therefore I disown what I have said, and repent in dust and ashes. [NAB/NABR]

Therefore I retract what I have said, and repent in dust and ashes. [NJB]

Therefore I retract, and I repent in dust and ashes. [NASB 1977, 1995]

Therefore I retract, and I repent sitting on dust and ashes. [NASB 2020]

Therefore I take back my words and repent in dust and ashes. [HCSB]

Therefore I yield, repenting in dust and ashes. [REB]

So I am ashamed of all I have said and repent in dust and ashes. [GNB]

So I recant and repent / In dust and ashes. [Pope]

I take back everything I said, and I sit in dust and ashes to show my repentance. [NLT]

2b. Therefore I retract (my words) and reject the symbols of mourning

Therefore I retract / And repent of dust and ashes. [Habel]

2c. Therefore I retract (my words) and have changed my mind to see the royal calling of humanity [Janzen]

2d. Therefore I retract (my words) and accept that I am mortal and vulnerable.

Therefore, I recant and relent, / Being but dust and ashes. [NJPS]

Wherefore I abhor my words, and repent, seeing I am dust and ashes. [JPS]

Therefore I reject (what I have said), and repent; because I am dust and ashes. [Isaac Leeser]

2e. Therefore I retract (my words) and am comforted concerning the human condition.

Therefore, I relent and find comfort on dust and ashes. [CEB]

Therefore do I spurn what I once said and take my solace in dust and ashes. [Saadiah]

3a. Therefore I submit and I accept consolation for my mourning.

Therefore I submit and I accept consolation for my dust and ashes. [Clines]

3b. Therefore I melt/submit and repent in dust and ashes.

Therefore I melt away; I repent in dust and ashes. [NEB]

That is why I sink down and repent, on dust and ashes! [Dhorme]

4. Therefore I reject (my former life of ease) and accept my mortality.

Therefore I revile (a good earthly life). Were my lot to be dust and ashes I would not mind! [Eisemann/Scherman]

5. Because of this I have loathed my wealth and I am comforted concerning my sons, who are dust and ashes. [Aramaic targum]

6. That is why I am fed up; I take pity on dust and ashes. [Greenstein]

If a reader takes either the positive or reframing views introduced in the last chapter, they are most likely to read Job 42:6 as a statement of repentance by Job, and/or a retraction of his various complaints against God, and/or a statement of submission to God. Job's reference to "dust and ashes" is variously taken to mean that Job accepts his humiliation, or his mortality, or a new view of the human condition, or acknowledges that it is time to accept God's comfort and end his mourning over his losses. Most Bible translations and interpretations of Job have understood him to be repenting and ending his protest based on God's appearance and/or words to him. That is normally how the book is taught in religious communities, as well.

The Defiant Job

Not so fast. Edward Greenstein electrified Job studies in 2019 when he rendered Job 42:6 as "*That is why I am fed up; I take pity on dust and ashes.*" Greenstein writes that Job "is expressing defiance, not capitulation. . . . If God is all about power and not morality and justice, Job will not condone it through acceptance."[3]

Since its rendering, this striking interpretation has found strong support from scholars and laypeople unsatisfied with the traditional take on Job. For James Parker, Greenstein's provocative reading offers "a Job unreconciled to the despotism of experience. He's been shattered by life-shocks; then God, like a wall of terrible noise, fills and overfills his mind. His response: *Thank you, but no.*[4]

Young biblical scholars Ilse Swart and Yasir Saleem agree: "In bringing God to court and refusing to remain silent, obedient, and to repent, Job resists power instead of obeying oppressive rule. Following this resistance, the book of Job disrupts the idea that God's power is absolute, or that the binary ideology of punishment and reward is sovereign."[5]

Some earlier interpreters were unsatisfied with the repentant/submissive Job, though they took for granted that this is what the book offers. William Safire, for example, rather starkly and unhappily saw Job as "letting down the side of Man—sheepishly express[ing] satisfaction with Authority's puzzling nonresponse, and in so accepting, Job loses the power struggle."[6]

Similarly, Elie Wiesel saw what was missing and ethically intuited Greenstein's reading of 42:6:

> Much as I admired Job's passionate rebellion, I am deeply troubled by his hasty abdication. . . . I prefer to think that the book's

> true ending was lost. That Job died without having repented, without having humiliated himself. . . . I was offended by his surrender in the text. . . . He should have said to God: Very well, I forgive you . . . but what about my dead children, do they forgive you? . . . . By accepting your inequities, do I not become your accomplice? . . . By repenting sins he did not commit, by justifying a sorrow he did not deserve, he communicates to us that he did not believe in his own confessions; they were nothing but decoys . . . we know that it is given to man to transform divine injustice into human justice and compassion.[7]

Nehama Verbin writes: "Job . . . merely refrains from voicing his moral protest, realizing that there is no point in doing so. . . . How may we understand Job's response? I maintain that it may be understood in terms of Job's forgiving God, while refusing to be reconciled with him."[8]

The traditional religious reading of the entire book of Job is that Job did suffer greatly, but he went too far in his complaints against God. Therefore, God rightly corrected him after listening patiently to Job's provocative protests. Job consequently repented and submitted and thus was restored to God's favor. This reading renders traditionalist-leaning readers satisfied but leaves others feeling that the ending of the book does not do justice to our hero's legitimate claims or provide an adequate theological response. This is especially true of those spiritual exiles and the suffering ones, like Wiesel, who may have started with a traditional lens, but also, in a sense, have found themselves on the dungheap, whether from community shunning or from the weight of loss, and need a model for responding to God other than silenced submission.

The Greenstein reading and its variants would say that Job suffered egregiously and unjustly, that his complaints against God and against his God-defending friends were fully legitimate, and that God offered an intimidating response that did not answer Job's protests. Job, in turn, does not repent or recant, but he does give up the pointless fight against God, recognize the defenseless vulnerability of the human condition, and decide to end his mourning and move forward with his life—with some evidence of being a man changed through his experience. One might say he now recognizes the moral tragedy rather than moral orderliness of creation, and he is ready to move on.

Both readings are plausible. I lean toward the latter.

Purposely Unfinalizable?

Or maybe theologian Trevor Williams is correct when, working with a concept introduced by Mikhail Bakhtin, he concludes that the "ambiguity in 42:6 creates an 'unfinalizable' quality that allows sufferers to be unsilenced and participate in the meaning-making process."[9]

Carol Newsom's proposal that Job is intentionally a "polyphonic text" and that the author intends for all voices to be taken seriously has been influential for my own understanding of Job. I believe that the reader of Job is being asked to take all the articulated perspectives seriously, to feel their weight, even if in the end the reader concludes that one, some, parts, or all must be rejected. It is certainly the case that by ending Job's verbal response with this enigmatic phrase, the author of Job makes a univocal reading impossible.[10]

The idea that Job 42:6 essentially ends the book on a deliberately ambiguous, "unfinalizable" note is a very appealing suggestion and fully appropriate to the extraordinary complexity of the book of Job. We will now see if the epilogue resolves our questions.

36

Job's Restoration, Vindication, and New Life (Job 42:7–17)

After the Lord *had spoken these words to Job, the* Lord *said to Eliphaz the Temanite, "I am incensed at you and your two friends, for you have not spoken the truth about Me as did My servant Job.*

—Job 42:7

All his brothers and sisters and all his former friends came to him and had a meal with him in his house. They consoled and comforted him for all the misfortune that the Lord *had brought upon him. . . . Thus the* Lord *blessed the latter years of Job's life more than the former.*

—Job 42:11–12a

Nowhere in the land were women as beautiful as Job's daughters to be found. Their father gave them estates together with their brothers. Afterward, Job lived one hundred and forty years to see four generations of sons and daughters. So Job died old and contented.

—Job 42:16–17

An Unloved Ending?

The last ten verses of Job offer a happy ending, in prose. There is much debate about who wrote this epilogue, whether it fits with the bulk of the book, and what it really adds—if anything. Safire speaks for many when he describes the epilogue as a "cornball conclusion . . . [a] pot of soothing syrup at the end of the suffering [that] negates the book's courageous and controversial point."[1]

Job 42:7–17 first has God rebuke the three friends, for "you have not spoken the truth about Me as did My servant Job" (42:7–8). The friends are instructed to provide Job with sacrificial animals to expiate their sins. Job does indeed pray in intercession for his friends, as instructed by God, and God blesses Job with a twofold restoration of his fortune (42:9–10). Job is also restored to his community, and everyone comes to his house for a celebratory dinner accompanied by gifts (42:11). In the end, "the Lord blessed the latter years of Job's life more than the former" (42:12). He is re-blessed with abundant prosperity and ten children, including three beautiful daughters (42:13). Job is given another 140 years to live and has the chance to see four generations of progeny (42:16). "So Job died old and contented" (42:17).

The ending is happy but still challenging. It certainly seems as if Job has just been rebuked by God for much that he has said throughout the dialogues. Thus, it does not seem easy to reconcile Job being simply lauded here for his truthful claims about God. Some, at least, of what the friends (and Elihu) have said tracks closely with what God says in the theophany, and in the divine speeches God had certainly seemed to be rebuking Job. Is Job being praised just for his last moment of repentance? If so, wouldn't that mean the friends were right all along? If so, why is God "incensed" at them for having "not spoken the truth about Me as did My servant Job" (42:7–8)?

The restoration of Job's fortune is great, though replacement children, no matter how beautiful, are problematic; children are among those "things" that cannot simply be "replaced." On this point, Jewish theologian Shai Held has written,

> When a parent looks at their child and thinks, "Nothing could possibly be more precious than you," they are not just expressing the depths of their own love; they are giving voice to the profound Jewish conviction that the child in front of them, like every child everywhere, is infinitely valuable. And when a grieving parent wails, insisting that "nothing can ever make up for the loss of this child," the unspeakable pain they convey actually discloses something that Judaism considers a foundational truth: Because each and every life is genuinely unique, each and every life is utterly irreplaceable.[2]

This feeling is not present in the epilogue to Job.[3]

Reading the Ending Differently

The most radical way to read the ending is not that Job's repentance has been blessed, but his questioning and protest have been. Biblical scholar Leo Perdue writes, "Eliphaz and the friends, not Job, are condemned for erroneous God-talk, while the language of the defiant, accusing, struggling Job is declared as right and true. For it is the struggle for justice, initiated by the caprice of an unjust judge, that is the proper way of being human in the world. And in the restoration of Job, there is the redemption of God."[4]

James Parker chimes in as follows:

> Consider what Greenstein's nonpenitent, polarity-reversing Job has done to the ending of the book. . . . As before, with the experiment over, Job is blandly restored to a state of health and wealth; as before, God upbraids the sententious friends. . . . The quality or valence of this honesty, however, has turned upside down. It has become a kind of white-knuckle existential tenacity, a refusal to disown oneself even in the teeth of the windstorm. Maybe that's what this God, faced with this Job, is telling us: Bring it all before him, the full grievance of your humanity. Bring him your condition, loudly. Let him have it.[5]

Biblical studies scholar Yitzhak Berger adds this note:

> Particularly on the assumption that Job, in his final speech, maintains an abidingly defiant posture toward God, his prayer [on behalf of his friends] constitutes a prerequisite for his restoration. Indeed, in subtle ways, the text emphasizes the prayer's pivotal role. The text's odd formulation, for its part, generates inner-biblical parallels that contribute to meaning. One parallel invokes a wider correlation to the Joseph story, implying that Job, in contrast to the victimized Joseph, must extend forbearance to his offenders before regaining wealth and stature.[6]

The epilogue does include several other interesting elements. For example, consider the fact that all kinds of kinfolk show up and throw Job a party (42:11). *Where have they been?* "Former friends" are mentioned also; this must mean that Job is now restored to his community, which had been rejecting him. This in turn must mean that the community is convinced that Job is (now) right with God. Was it the theophany that changed their minds? Notice that there is no mention of servants or slaves in Job's restoration. Does this mean that Job no longer owns slaves? And don't miss this: Whereas Job is affirmed by God for the truth of his words, the predictions of the friends that Job would be shown divine mercy and restored to blessing come true.[7] One other thing: We are not told whether Job is restored to physical health. It is generally assumed, but the text says nothing. It is interesting to think of Job as a man simultaneously weakened by illness, scarred by his wounds, and restored by God.

Consider also the way the text offers celebration of Job's daughters by naming them and giving each of them land along with their brothers. This is a trailblazing expression of gender equity. Job had not done that before; his daughters had gone to his sons' houses for those parties back in the good old days. Has Job perhaps learned some things from losing his daughters—and from his overall experience of suffering? Has he abandoned both patriarchy and slavery?

Gerald Janzen, in a lovely meditation, focuses on the very last verse: "So Job died old and contented" (Job 42:17). By the end, says Janzen, Job has found "satiation," blissful peace like that of a child at the breast, "a satiation that is the foundation of trust."[8]

Rather whimsically, Ellen Davis writes, "At the beginning of the book, Job is overscrupulous, fearful even of the possibility that his children may have sinned (1:5); at the end, he is freewheeling, his eyes and heart wide open to the reality of their beauty. Maybe Job has learned from the Creator to love pizzazz."[9]

And in a sweeping survey, Carol Newsom treats the epilogue as blocking any clean resolution to the story of the man Job and the drama of the book of Job. But, says Newsom, the effect is constructive: It keeps the questions raised by the book wide open. There will be no "closure." We are invited to continue our wrestling with God.[10]

CONCLUSION

On the Ethics of Job, Community, and God

Narrative, Character, Ethics

As we conclude our study of the book of Job, I want to offer reflections as an ethicist on what the story tells us about the three primary actors: Job, the friends (collectively), and God. Implicitly throughout the commentary, I've explored ethical themes, but here I'd like to fully engage that ethical lens and look at what the book of Job's depiction teaches us about the ethics of these three characters, and in turn, what believers can take away from studying them. I hope by doing so to address some notable gaps in studies on Job in which questions of theology and suffering have crowded out much attention to the rich ethical content of the book of Job.

Postliberal narrative theologian George Lindbeck signals something about my approach with these words:

> We now can make a distinction . . . between realistic narrative and historical or scientific descriptions. The Bible is often "history-like" even when it is not "likely history." It can therefore be taken seriously in the first respect as a delineator of the character of divine and human agents . . . the rendering of God's character is not in every instance logically dependent on the facticity of the story.[1]

This consideration of the book of Job as a realistic narrative rather than a historical account makes sense to me. It is a drama about a man who has everything—and then has everything taken away. It is a narrative about the interaction of that man with his community, which begins with his three friends but, as I have argued, extends beyond them. And it is an anguished account of this man's wrestling with God, with an extended account of God's response to his wrestling.

Lindbeck writes,

> The primary function of the canonical narrative . . . is "to render a character . . . , offer an identity description of an agent," namely God. It does this, not by telling what God is in and of himself, but by accounts of the interaction of his deeds and purposes with those of creatures in their ever-changing circumstances. . . . The primary focus is . . . on how life is to be lived and reality construed in light of God's character as an agent as this is depicted in the stories of Israel and Jesus.[2]

The book of Job "renders the character" of Job, of his friends, and, more mysteriously, of God, through the interactions between all of them and the words they speak to each other. If Lindbeck is right that the purpose of the canonical narratives is not just to tell a good story but to teach believers something about "how life is to be lived and reality construed in light of God's character," then this should be true of the book of Job as well. And the wonder of the book of Job is that what it seems to teach, or at least to suggest, in its narrative is a heterodox or at least dissenting account of the human relationship to God, the proper behavior of the human (religious) community,[3] and God's interaction with humans and the creation.

In what follows, I propose certain claims especially about the ethics of Job, the ethics of (religious) community, and the ethics of God derived from my reading of the book of Job. These claims have broader implications for reading Scripture and living life rather than "just" being plausible readings of what happens in this wondrous work of art. I do not claim that Job is the last word on any of these matters—nor my take on Job as the last word, but among the voices on Job, worthy of consideration.

Let's then turn to consider the ethics of Job, the ethics of (religious) community, and the ethics of God, as gleaned from the close reading we have done of the book of Job.

On the Ethics of the Character Named Job

The Legitimacy of Truthful Protest to Community and God

Already by Job 4, Job's friend Eliphaz expresses the worry that Job appears to be weakening in his long-standing commitment to the shared communal just-world theology. That comes after only one speech from Job! Eliphaz is indeed seeing something real; Job's commitment to just-world theology is not just weakening; it has been shattered. Apparently, that was a theology that made sense only from a place of privilege and eldership in society, not from the dunghill outside of town, scraping sores, mourning dead children. Especially given Job's erstwhile leadership position in his community, Eliphaz is concerned that Job is articulating views that will undercut communal religious beliefs and moral norms.

The moral issue for Job is whether he will swallow his doubts, suppress his questions, silence his protests under pressure from his community or in fear of God. We know, of course, that Job refuses to do so. The question for the reader of Job is whether the text is trying to tell us that Job is permitted to utter such stark challenges to the tradition. By Job 4, really, we have a new moral question emerge: Is protest against God a sin against God?

This particular concern is a question often addressed by commentators. In his theologically conservative monograph studying the entirety of the book of Job for its handling of Job's protest, Bible scholar William Pohl concludes, "The 'implied' author uses Job's verbal expression in protest prayer and in defense of protest prayer to shape the reader to see that this kind of God-talk is approved and encouraged for the innocent sufferer."[4]

Kathryn Lopez concurs, putting the matter this way:

> The book explores how we as believers can suffer with integrity. Suffering is inevitable; how we live through suffering is our choice. . . . Does Job maintain his integrity by refusing to curse God and die? Or does he lose his integrity by his passively patient acceptance of everything that happens to him? Does he

> lose his integrity by refusing to admit his sin, as his friends claim? Or does he maintain his integrity by refusing to submit to a theology that has no room for his lived experience?[5]

Another biblical scholar, Lance Hawley, writes,

> The multiple evaluations of Job's speech by the friends and Job himself reveal a development within the dialogue. The friends move from consolatory rebuke toward condemnation and blatant accusation not on the basis of secret sin that Job committed prior to his calamity but because of his words in chapter 3 and following. Job knows the rashness of his words, but he decidedly speaks them anyway, eschewing caution and proceeding with his accusation against God. Paradoxically, it is by means of his supposedly self-condemnatory speech that Job moves from hope for death to hope for vindication. YHWH also evaluates Job's words, assessing them both as ignorant (38:2) and right (42:7), thus rejecting the dialogue's assumed retributive relationship between accusatory protest and condemnation.[6]

Recall my rendering of Job 6:10:

Then this would be my consolation,
As I writhed in unsparing pains:
That I did not suppress my words against the Holy One.

As I wrote within the exegesis of that pivotal passage, many devout believers are reluctant to indulge in any protest against God. They have been taught silent submission along with various unpersuasive platitudes. But Job does not submit without protest to his horrific suffering. While he never does curse God, as the adversary said he would, Job does speak his truth, time and again, to ever greater communal anger and rejection. Job shows that in times of horror, suffering, and injustice, protest is precisely how the believer's dialogue with God remains open, even when that dialogue seems one-sided. In that exegesis, I conclude that the book of Job blesses his protest both by writing it/hosting it and by the way God vindicates Job in the prose epilogue (42:7–10).

Moral Agency, Moral Dignity, Moral Courage

Earlier in the book I noted something significant about Job 19:4:

If indeed I have erred,
My error remains with me.

Many commentators note that the book of Job appears to validate the legitimacy of protest as a form of communication with God. But few note that what the journey of the character Job also teaches is the prior value of moral agency, dignity, and courage. Job is protecting a space of moral self-direction that his friends and community are trying to annihilate because they consider it both threatening to the community and an affront to God. Job is telling his friends to back off, telling them that this is between himself and his soul and himself and God. Even though he stands utterly alone, he will not allow his loneliness to weaken his moral resolve.

In his appreciative treatment of Job, Enlightenment philosopher Immanuel Kant argues that Job's friends are speaking of things they don't understand and are trying to flatter God and stay on God's good side. Job alone "speaks as he thinks, and with the courage with which he . . . can well afford; his friends, on the contrary, speak as if they were being secretly listened to by the mighty one . . . as if gaining his favor through their judgment were closer to their heart than the truth."[7]

Kant goes on to write,

> Only sincerity of heart and not distinction of insight; honesty in openly admitting one's doubts; repugnance to pretending conviction where one feels none, especially before God (where the trick is pointless enough)—these are the attributes which, in the person of Job, have decided the preeminence of the honest man over the religious flatterer in the divine verdict.[8]

The book of Job offers the most extended treatment in the Bible of a human being wrestling honestly and publicly with what is true and what is real and what to say to God and neighbor about his unjust suffering. Job is a model of moral agency, moral dignity, and moral courage. Risking both human and divine condemnation, Job will not deny what he knows and will not silence what he must say. Even if both God and friends turn their face away from him, he will speak his truth to them.

From Privileged Blamelessness to Empathy at the Ash Heap

We have stipulated the book's description of Job as a man who was "blameless and upright," a man who "feared God and shunned evil" (Job 1:1). The prologue heightens this idea when it has God describing Job in precisely these terms and indeed as the best of all people on the earth (1:8). Of course, that language has a kind of epic, legendary quality that can be partially dismissed as an effort to heighten the drama of the story. But still, it seems right to establish as a baseline that Job merited praise for his faith and morality.

But there is a catch. We have seen in our close study of the text that Job's integrity was that of a man who lived within the very privileged upper end of his society. He was a kind of prince among people in his world. He had vast wealth. He commanded a large servantry, at least some of them enslaved. He had social and even juridical power in his community. He exercised religious and moral leadership. The impressive moral code by which he lived (Job 31) was closely tied to his high position in his social order, but it also had the blind spots associated with privilege, wealth, and power.

As seen in Job 19, the suffering that comes upon Job is of a particular type tied to his social location. He was *not* one of the wretched of the earth who was always beaten down. He was a leader, a wealthy, respected man with a large household and a dominant place in his community. It is this kind of man who has now lost all his privileges and status. He has even lost the power to command, and this astonishes him.

So, yes, Job, was a man of integrity and was honored as such by God and his community. The suffering that was visited upon him was capricious and unjust. But it is also true that *Job's suffering became an occasion for growth.* As early as Job 3, we see Job starting to notice and then to identify with the truly miserable ones of the earth. We see it again quite powerfully in Job 24, where he demonstrates a deep empathy for the suffering of the most destitute. He also offers realistic assessment of the grossly unjust actions creating such suffering.

Even though, at the beginning of the story, the narrator, Job, and God are all convinced of Job's blamelessness and integrity, there are some aspects of moral maturity that can only be learned through suffering.

And there are distinctive things to be learned when part of the suffering one experiences is the loss of social standing, privilege, wealth, and power.

There is more to morality than obeying moral rules, meeting moral expectations, and avoiding obvious wrongdoing. And there is more to religion than practicing heartfelt worship in the ways prescribed by one's faith tradition. As I said earlier, innocence and guilt are not the only way or the best way to understand the human moral condition. Human beings are shaped by their life experiences and deeply affected by their social location. Those who live at the very top of the social pyramid can blamelessly obey all the rules, meet all the expectations, avoid all the obvious sins, and practice all the prescribed worship forms, and still have things to learn and ways to grow.

The claim made by several of the friends and by Elihu (Job 33) that Job is being disciplined through suffering is, I contend, half-true. Since Job has done nothing "wrong" within the terms of his religious and social world, and again, even in God's sight (see 1:8), the suffering that comes upon him should not be viewed as discipline. But it should be viewed as a shattering experience that rocks him to his core and begins to work a change in his way of looking at the world. He now catches a glimpse of life from the ash heap, from the margins, from *below*. And in a moral sense this is good for him. He is a better, more compassionate, and more empathetic human being for it. No one wants to suffer like this, but many can attest that grave suffering is a school for growth—if it does not destroy us.

The interesting question morally for Job is, What's next after his restoration? Does he retain his identification with the poor? Does his ethic remain deepened by his suffering? Will the reborn, resurrected Job, with all his wealth restored, a bunch of beautiful new daughters and sons, now a happy old man, retain his identification with the poor?

Job's suffering had been inscribed on his scarred skin. Are its lessons inscribed on his heart, and practiced in his life, after the book ends in Job 42:17? We see some tantalizing signs of change in Job at the end of the epilogue; what comes next for him?

There is much to learn from examining the ethics of the character named Job in the book of Job. He teaches the permissibility and sometimes the necessity of protest as a form of communication with God. He teaches the sacredness of integrity, not understood as rule-following blamelessness but as protection of one's moral agency and dignity, and the courage to speak the hard truths that one has learned. And he teaches that while there is a kind of moral exemplarity available at every stratum of society, Job's descent from the richest man in the East to the ash heap outside of town shattered the complacent dimensions of his aristocratic moral vision and moved him into empathetic solidarity with the most destitute of the earth. This was growth, and it made a blameless man a better man. The challenge and question for us, as readers of Job, is whether we will choose to develop such empathetic solidarity or whether those of us who have privilege can only attain it through the shattering experience of dispossession.

On the Ethics of (Religious) Community

A rather underdeveloped aspect of Job scholarship is the role of, and implications for, community, especially religious community. Most readers are so dazzled by the theological argument between Job and his friends and his God that they overlook what is happening at the level of human community. In this section, we will seek to do better, and we will indeed be aided by observers who have not missed this crucial aspect of the book of Job.

The "Dilemmas and Demands of Consolation"

Sameer Yadav writes: "The book of Job is not so much about how to properly speak (or withhold speech) about God in the midst of innocent suffering. . . . It is instead a theological exploration of the dilemmas and demands of consolation imposed upon us as readers given the inexplicable enormities of innocent human suffering."[9]

Yadav, I think, is half-right here. He focuses the issue as a matter concerning the dilemmas and demands of consolation, especially during innocent suffering. When someone we know, a friend perhaps, undergoes terrible and unmerited suffering, how do we console them?

But at least for religious believers, a big part of the consolation we usually offer and the consolation we usually receive is God-talk. We do wrestle, as consolers of the suffering, with whether and how to speak or withhold speech about God. It is inevitable that we will ask: What do we say about where God is, what God is doing, what this suffering means for the sufferer in their relationship with God?

Most would agree that Job's friends are at their best when they sit silently with Job in his grief for that first week (Job 2). Job offers a terrible, anguished soliloquy, not directed to his friends (Job 3). The friends at this point had choices as to how to respond. They could remain silent. They could wait for Job to engage them with direct address. They could express sympathy and support. For that matter, they could have offered some practical help!

Unfortunately, they do none of this. Eliphaz feels threatened by the theological dimension of Job's speech, and he responds with theological backtalk in Job 4, and off we go into a sustained argument about how to think and talk about God in relation to Job's suffering and the world's injustice.

Yadav is especially acute in how he describes the nature of the friends' defensive theological speech to Job:

> When confronted with the grand narrative that purports to make theological sense out of the goodness of creation . . . we can begin to succumb to a temptation toward . . . the dangers of optimism. . . . Our capacity to listen to the suffering voices in Scripture can become dulled and our capacities to hear and attend to the sufferings of others can suffer from cultivated failures of compassion. . . . Even a correct notion of God's redemptive work can serve for us as a delusional attempt to avoid the realities of suffering that threaten us and afflict others around us. Christian theologies of flourishing can likewise become elaborate attempts at spiritual bypassing and toxic positivity that hide a thinly veiled form of terror-management—just so many self-protective religious games.[10]

Yadav is talking about how the Bible's positive themes such as the goodness of creation and God's redemptive love can lead us astray during times where our task is to offer consolation to suffering friends. More broadly, the relentless tendency toward "optimism" so often found in

Christian communities can become the default setting, making it difficult to offer anything but happy platitudes about how "God is in control," "God has a plan," "Everything happens for a reason," and so on.

At its worst, our efforts at religious consolation can become, in Yadav's pungent language, "spiritual bypassing," "toxic positivity," and "terror-management."

Spiritual bypassing happens when people use spiritual or theological concepts or practices to evade their unresolved emotional issues or challenging situations. This is a religiously laden defense mechanism that functions to bypass hard human problems. It is often what creates spiritual exiles, as those within religious communities fail to address suffering and emit toxic repetitions of theological party lines.

Those spiritual exiles who have been made aware of this problem—often by being cut off from community or by necessarily making a protective exit—try to leave the toxicity behind, for something more Job-like in suffering and honesty.

We noted in the exegesis that Job's friends are clearly trying to manage their own terror that something similar might happen to them. They feel a desperate need to offer words of "consolation" to Job that are little more than expressions of their own spiritual bypassing, their need for terror-management.

Clearly, one implication of the book of Job is that intentionality related to our approach in situations of religious consolation is essential. The book of Job can be a perennial tool for accessing the Bible's resources that speak to suffering people. The close reading we have done in this book might help us avoid letting spiritual bypassing or terror-management destroy the effectiveness of our consoling efforts with suffering friends.

Getting Beyond Defensiveness When Religious Tradition Is Challenged

One of the striking themes of the book of Job is the way that religious communities can close ranks to defend their traditions, even at the cost of scapegoating dissidents. Job was, at first, simply trying to articulate his own grief and his own questions, and very rapidly found himself in a spitting match with "friends" who heard his grief as an attack on sacred religious tradition. This also raises broader issues related to the tendency toward authoritarianism in at least some religious communities.

Safire writes,

> Challenging religion on moral grounds was shocking to established authority because it dared assert that tradition may not be rightly expressing God's design; in the same way, challenging authoritarian political leadership today on human-rights grounds is troubling to some powers that be because the challenge itself strikes at the basis of the regime's legitimacy.[11]

Note how Safire claims the right to protest even God's injustice, recognizing that when dissenters or sufferers assert moral agency, they often run into fierce resistance from the custodians of the religious tradition. The response of the custodians is often to attempt to crush dissent as well as crush dissenters. We saw this throughout the exegesis. For Safire, a great political commentator in his day, this connected with political authoritarianism's tendency to do the same thing.

Kathryn Lopez writes: "[Job] subverts theologically simplistic and harmful views of God that he saw around him. He holds up a mirror as if to say, 'Look at yourselves, and look at the God your words create!'"[12] During the exegesis of Job 19 we looked at our theories about what an invisible God is doing to us when we suffer as theological speculations, and what our community does to us as daily reality. Part of what they *do to us* might well be to inflict really bad theology on us.

Lopez maintains that religious traditions "create" (a version of) God through their teachings. This version of God may be better or worse, life-giving or destructive. Religious communities mediate and authorize visions and versions of God every day on every continent. The book of Job is about what happens when one such version crashed into the suffering reality of a human life. And it is also about the strenuous efforts that custodians of the tradition will take to suppress challenges.

Norman Gottwald asserts, "Probably the author would have been satisfied if his 'whistle blowing' on moralism and dogmatism managed to alert the custodians of wisdom to the price of cheapening and betraying its critical process of observation and reflection."[13]

This is an important point. The unreflective defense of tradition can become a betrayal of the tradition in the name of protecting it. Religious traditions develop over centuries. At their best, that development involves fine minds wrestling critically and creatively with crucial issues and doing so repeatedly as new challenges arise. But reflexive, unthinking defense of tradition represents its ossification and can be a step on the way to its demise rather than its survival. Many of the spiritually exiled have seen the signs of decay in the religious tradition we have left behind.

Ellen Davis offers a decisive word here: "The book of Job may have little to say (directly) about God's character and the nature of divine justice. However, it says much about human character as it is revealed and sometimes transformed under the pressure of the most extreme suffering and in relationship—even tortured relationship—with God. Job is the only person who learns and thus changes in the course of the book."[14]

Oh that last line! Job is indeed the only person who learns anything in the course of the book. Job does learn; we witness it. But the three friends simply dig in and defend their positions; it certainly seems like God does so as well. It is hard to learn anything while building a defensive wall around yourself and your tradition.

When God is Hiding, We Must Reveal Love

The idea that Job wants to put God on trial is one of the most shocking and audacious aspects of the book of Job.

Two responses from the Jewish community have struck me with great force. Abraham Joshua Heschel wrote this, in relation to Job:

> The Hebrew Bible records God's "mighty acts" in history. What is overlooked is that on every page of the Bible we come upon God's longing and waiting for *man's* mighty acts. This is the meaning of human existence. The world is unredeemed and deficient, and God is in need of man to be a partner in completing, in aiding, in redeeming. . . . The urgent issue is not personal salvation but the prevention of mankind's surrender to the demonic. The sanctuary has no walls; the opportunity to praise

> or to aid has no limits. When God is silent, man must speak in His place. When God is hiding His compassion, man must reveal His love in this name.[15]

This connects to some of what Rabbi Joshua Sperka says in his book about Job. Recall from an earlier chapter that Sperka is deeply opposed to the very idea that Job is putting God on trial—so opposed that he calls his book *Man on Trial*. The book is dedicated "to the Memory and Martyrdom of the Six Million Jews murdered by the Nazi Barbarians. This crime was resisted by few, assisted by many, with the indifferent silence of the entire civilized world."[16] Sperka reads God's answer in the whirlwind as "What are you, man, doing to avoid evil in the world?" He concludes, "It is man's task . . . to become a partner in creating a better world and ultimately hastening the messianic era."[17]

Both Heschel and Sperka read Job through the lens of Jewish tradition. Within both their responses, they bring the idea of *tikkun olam* (the healing of the world), and the distinctive (and original) Jewish messianism in which humans cooperate with God to repair the world and hasten the coming of the Messiah. In Job, the defenders of tradition mainly defend tradition and attack Job. There is no talk about how to assist Job in his need, or how to care for the poor and destitute, or how to prevent further violent crime such as has befallen Job, or how to make the world more just.

Heschel says, "When God is silent, man must speak in His place. When God is hiding His compassion, man must reveal His love in His place." Whatever we may want to say about why God is silent and why God seems to be hiding (6:24–30), we are always called to speak the words and do the deeds of justice that God has given us in Scripture and tradition, and to offer the love to which we are always called. In this sense, Sperka is spot on that the book of Job can be read to point to *us* being on trial, not God.

Whatever it is that God is doing, we are responsible for loving our neighbor and repairing the world as best we can. What we should not be doing is spending our time speculating about who sinned and why they are being punished by God. What the friends offer Job is speculative theology about what Job did wrong. What he *needs* is their solidarity, their practical help (never offered), and their partnership in making a better world. This is an agenda for spiritual exiles and for those heading in the direction of solidarity and acts of justice, not speculative theology.

On the Ethics of God in the Book of Job

The Question of Who Speaks Authoritatively about God in the Book of Job

Now, of course, we move to the most sensitive discussion of all: what we are to make of the ethics of God as depicted in the book of Job. It may help to think of "God" as a character in the play called "Book of Job," thus creating a little distance between that character's literary depiction here and the actual God of the universe. But the fact that this depiction of God has made it into the canon of Scripture certainly makes it relevant for any overall picture of God that believers develop.

As we think about how God is depicted in Job, remember that we have relatively little reliable information. We have lots of talk about God, but we only encounter God in the (much disputed) prologue and epilogue and in the speech from the whirlwind in Job 38–41. Besides that, we have lots of God-talk by Job, his friends, and Elihu, without a definitive declaration as to whether the reader is supposed to trust some, any, or all of what anyone in the book says. We clearly don't have a reliable theologian-narrator!

I propose that we allow Job's interpretation of God's treatment of him to carry a bit more weight, certainly more weight than the words of the friends. We can do that in view of the vindication of Job in 42:7–8, when God punishes the friends because "you have not spoken the truth about Me as did My servant Job." This is not at all unambiguous, but it does make it at least reasonable for us to attend closely to the words Job says about God in the book. We then must ask which of the things Job says qualify as true from God's perspective. We also, of course, must attend closely to the words about God's self in the divine speech in Job 38–41.

During the exegesis, we took stock of the horrifying nature of the prologue. It is easy to dismiss both the prologue and the epilogue in terms of both their theology and possible editorial history, but any final-form reading of the book of Job still demands we attend to both. And in both places God says and does things that are relevant to our task of considering the ethics of God in Job.

Job 1–2 offers a terrifying account of God. If read on its face, we are to believe that God twice allowed the *śaṭan* to attack an innocent and pious man as a kind of bet to see if he would curse God in response. The two unhappy interpretive options available dismiss the story as a fanciful setup, or as a way of granting that God tests innocent human beings this way sometimes—either with perfect justification or no justification depending on our view of such things. In general, though, we meet a terrible picture of a capricious God.

The epilogue, as we have seen, cleans up the story and gives us a happy ending. The God of the epilogue shows kindness to Job at last and offers clear vindication. God offers material restoration of Job and blesses him and his wife with new children. God's actions enable Job to be restored to his family and community. Presumably, Job's health is restored, as he is given many more years and then dies old and happy.

Job's Comprehensive Claims of God's Injustice against Him and in the World

As we review the speeches of Job once again, let's look specifically at Job's claims about (against) God:

Job 6:4: "The arrows of the Almighty are in me; My spirit absorbs their poison." In the rest of Job 6, Job accuses God of setting a watch over him, terrifying him, targeting him, and inspecting him every minute.

Job 9:17: "He wounds me much for no cause." In the rest of chapter 9, Job accuses God of crushing him, sating him with bitterness, destroying the blameless, mocking innocents as they fall, and handing over the earth to injustice. This continues in chapter 10, as Job goes on to accuse God of having created him only to destroy every part of him, hunting him like a lion, and drenching him in misery. Overall, Job depicts God as exercising arbitrary power over him.

Job 12:6: "Robbers live untroubled in their tents, and those who provoke God are secure." Also in this chapter, Job again says God allows injustice. He argues that God brings down leaders of various types, as well as nations. The implication is that God enjoys lifting people up just to be able to bring them down.

Job 16:7: "Now He has truly worn me out; You have destroyed my whole community." In this chapter, Job's most devastating attack on God's actions and (implicitly) God's character, Job also says God has shriveled him, torn and persecuted him, gnashed his teeth at him, handed him over to evil men, broken him into pieces, taken him by the neck and shattered him, set him up as a target for archers, pierced his kidneys with arrows, spilled his bile on the ground, breached (attacked) him again and again, and rushed at him like a warrior. And God has done so "for no injustice on my part" (16:17).

Note that in three places (9:32–33; 16:19–21; 19:25–27) Job had dreamed of a heavenly arbiter, mediator, or witness to act for him. He hoped for one in the heavens who would show compassion to his tear-stained face. In the book of Job, God neither serves in that role for Job nor provides someone else to do so.

Job 19:7: "I cry, 'Violence!' but am not answered; I shout, but can get no justice." Also in Job 19, Job accuses God of having wronged him, thrown up siege works around him, laid darkness on his path, stripped him of his glory, torn down every part of him, regarded him as an enemy, made war on him, alienated his immediate family, kinfolk and friends from him, made him an object of public derision, and sickened him so that he is but skin and bones.

Job 21:7: "Why do the wicked live on, prosper and grow wealthy?" Job 21 is a long attack by Job on the justice of God in the world. Quite contrary to just-world theology, Job doesn't just state but picturesquely describes the wicked prospering.

Job 24:1: "Why are times for judgment not reserved by Shaddai?" In Job 23, Job laments how God had been exercising unjust power against him and has chosen to hide from him. In Job 24, Job offers an intense, detailed description of specific injustices against vulnerable people that leave them hungry, naked, cold, thirsty, and dying. These poor ones are not helped, neither are their victimizers punished.

Job 30:11: "Because God has disarmed and humbled me, they have thrown off restraint in my presence." In Job 30, his final lament, Job accuses God of bringing him so low that the lowest of the low now deride him, of destroying his dignity, of making his life one long series of days of misery, of reducing him to dust and ashes, and of refusing to hear his cries for mercy and justice. His last words of lament are: "So my lyre is given over to mourning, my pipe, to accompany weepers" (Job 30:31). Job is a ruined man, and God has ruined him.

Job offers not an occasional lament or protest but a comprehensive indictment of God for injustice against him and for superintending a deeply unjust world. Is *this* what God is commending Job for in Job 42:7? What might that mean for our understanding of the character of God as depicted in this book? As we think about the character of God in the book of Job, do the whirlwind speech, Job's final words, and the happy epilogue negate the terrible significance of this indictment of God's actions?

The Moral Message of the God Who Speaks in the Whirlwind

A few chapters ago I explored the meaning and problems of the speech from the whirlwind; the general conclusion was that though the voice of God offers meaningful reframing of Job's thinking, including decentering humanity and emphasizing the value of wild creation and its most untamable creatures, there is very little in these chapters that addresses whether God is much or at all involved in the world as a justice-maker.

Carol Newsom does not agree. She sees in the whirlwind speech God establishing for Job "the fundamental reliability of the structures of creation."[18] This includes reminding Job that God has created a world full of valued creatures, most of which humans know nothing about. God also gives humans the capacity to freely "choose to perceive and embody . . . an order of rightness and respect in community." Newsom sees God in the book of Job reaffirming that God has given human beings the building blocks for the work of bringing justice. She writes, "A moral order is something that has to be created, or more properly, co-created. It comes into being and continues to exist through the actions of individual moral agents."[19]

Newsom goes on to say that God finds that Job must also be instructed "to recognize the presence of the chaotic as part of the design of creation,"[20] and to be satisfied with no real explanation for it. Despite its dangers to creatures including humans, Newsom also reads the grand tour of wild creation as "suggestive of the formation of a moral order" by God, characterized by "place, purpose, and limit." This "is a language of balance," not a fully developed ethic but a kind of framing for an ethic. She reads 38:12–15, related to the dawn "setting a limit to the wicked," as God's way of describing the temporary restraining of antisocial impulses rather than the violent crushing of God's enemies that had been envisioned, really, by all the speakers.[21]

This ingenious reading does a great deal of work. But, like all readings of Job, it can be challenged: If one is accused of something in court and refuses to answer but shouts about something else, it is usually taken to mean that the accused is unable or unwilling to answer the charges. Is this how we should read God's nonresponse to Job's specific charges about injustice, both in his situation and in the world?

This was a moment where God could have offered a direct explanation of what has happened to Job and for that matter what happens to so many other sufferers. This was a moment where God could offer an account of his providential superintending of justice in the world God has made. Perhaps God could have said explicitly that the unexplained chaotic dimension of creation just claims its casualties from time to time. Or God could have said that He made a bet with the accuser and regrets it very much.

It would have been helpful if God had clarified what role He plays in bringing justice on the earth. There are so many biblical texts in and beyond Job that suggest that role is profound and active. God's defenders have said as much for many chapters. For that matter, Job has believed in it as well and wants to hold God to account for the justice that He has declared to be central to His character and demands on humans.

God could say that, in fact, the design of creation is that there will be no justice on earth unless it is co-created by humans. Co-creation would mean that humans do it together. God's role—weak claim—is having equipped us to do it in the ways Newsom suggests. Or God's role—stronger claim—is in mysterious co-participation, motivating and empowering and aiding and capping off human efforts to do the work of justice and righteousness once we get the ball rolling. We might call that the work of God's Spirit. But no such account is offered in God's speech.

One plausible reading of the theological-ethical message of the book of Job is that there is, in fact, no humanly discernible, thus no humanly accessible, moral order to the universe. We live in a tragic world, and in terms of what happens here, we are responsible. I suggest that Job comes to accept that and is able to make peace and rebuild his life within this less-illusory reality. We are all instructed to do the best we can because this world's well-being is entirely in our hands.

If we are to be honest in our assessment of the character of God in Job we must take seriously once again the manner of God's speech to Job. Where is the welcoming invitation to co-create justice, if that is God's intent? Theologian David Burrell argues that Job as a book does not attempt to offer a theodicy but to show that an encounter between creator and creature *just is the consolation, the sole consolation.* He writes,

> Job is commended in the end because he dared to address the creator-God; his interlocutors are castigated for purporting to speak knowingly about that One. Speaking *about* something veers toward explaining, while speaking *to* someone can engage both in a relationship of exchange open to yet other forms of understanding. . . . The creator-God does answer Job's extended complaints . . . what is most startling of all: *that* God responded to him.[22]

For Burrell, the very fact that God responds to Job means that God cares about a relationship with Job. God is Creator, and God is in covenant with creatures, including Job, including us.

To this claim, I am not so sanguine. The manner of God's speaking to Job is more imperious than tender, by far. Job is not invited into a discussion of the nature of his covenant with his creator. A straightforward reading is that Job attempted to speak to God for a very long time, and God remained silent. Then, when God finally spoke to Job, God did not address the content of Job's complaints at all. Instead, God forcefully directed Job's attention to the wild frontiers of creation, indicating their great interest and value, and challenged Job's ignorance and powerlessness relative to Himself. In its distinct nonanswer, God's speech showed no markers of covenant love.

* * *

Within the whole of the Bible, Job is but one single book. But overall, this majestic book is quite destabilizing of a major theme of the Bible—that God is a God of active justice-making who superintends the world. That the book of Job made it into the Bible continues to stun me.

Even stunned, I end this study with a deep sense of gratitude that the ingenious book of Job did indeed find its place in the Hebrew Bible and then the Christian canon. Written to address a crisis for the Jewish people 2,500 years ago, the book seems very much up to the minute.

We live in an era in which we can daily find out exactly how wicked people behave and how unjust the world is through our social media feeds. We can look through our GPS satellites at the battered landscape of war-ravaged lands all over the world. We can watch people get killed on TikTok. We can buy pornography where children and women are abused. We can study books that describe the mass killings that have taken place just in the last century. Where shall we start? Armenia? Russia? Nazi Europe? China?

The idea that God actively superintends this world and brings justice in this world is less plausible than it has ever been. Weaker accounts of God's role risk a kind of abstract wispiness. No one really knows what it might mean to co-create a just world with God, even as we do know what it means to get up on Monday and join the group marching for human rights.

Where God is hidden, Rabbi Heschel wrote, we must show up. Where hatred rules, we must bring love.

Perhaps the book of Job helps us to see God as Creator. And as the One who puts the sense of justice in our hearts. And as the One who gave moral commands long ago that still orient us today. And then, as the One who left the rest to us.

The moral order of the world is what we create in response to the travail of our neighbors.

It is up to us.

Acknowledgments

In addition to being a professor and writer, throughout my adult life I have had the privilege of serving as a Christian pastor, preacher, and Bible study teacher. In my tradition, that involves daily scriptural immersion and weekly biblical exposition in church community.

My idea to write a complete work on Job emerged from the delight of working through the book verse by verse in 2019 with my immensely patient and deeply engaged Seeking the Kingdom class of First Baptist Church in Decatur, Georgia. This book is dedicated to them.

Leslie Madden provided invaluable research on the extensive literature about Job. Jeremy Hall provided detailed exegetical notes on the first twelve chapters of Job, dialogued with me throughout this book's composition, and provided the study questions. I am grateful to Mia Hong, Douglas Miller, Ken Wilson, and Jeremy Hall (again), who have carefully engaged the manuscript in development. Special thanks go to Douglas Miller, who provided advanced technical assistance on both interpretive issues and Hebrew usage for this volume.

Restore Church, in Austin, Texas, hosted my first sermon on this material. I am also grateful for the eager audience at the January 2026 Jones Lectures, at Austin Presbyterian Theological Seminary, who heard the first lectures based on the submitted manuscript.

I also wish to express my gratitude and joy to be working with my patient and wonderful friend, the legendary editor of Orbis Books, Robert Ellsberg, on this long-delayed project, as well as my editor, Lil Copan, and my agent, David Morris. As always, I am grateful to my wife, Jeanie, for dialoguing with me about the ideas in this book.

And of course, full responsibility for the work rests with the author.

Notes

Introduction

1. Martin Buber, *The Prophetic Faith* (Harper & Brothers, 1960), 188.

2. Robert Gordis, *The Book of God and Man: A Study of Job* (University of Chicago Press, 1965), v.

3. Not to mention Elie Wiesel, René Girard, G. K. Chesterton, William Safire, Karl Barth, John Calvin, Thomas Aquinas, Peter Rollins, and a cast of thousands. See the Bibliography.

4. Older scholarship, and the very arrangement of most Christian Bibles, has long treated "Wisdom Literature" as a distinct theological and literary category. For two examples, consider Kathleen M. O'Connor, *The Wisdom Literature* (Abingdon Press, 1990), esp. 11–15; and William P. Brown, *Character in Crisis: A Fresh Approach to the Wisdom Literature of the Old Testament* (Eerdmans, 1996). But some recent scholarship—led by Mark R. Sneed and Will Kynes—has suggested that the category is a modern scholarly construction without validity. See Mark R. Sneed, "Is There a Wisdom Tradition? Yes, No, Maybe So," *Currents in Biblical Research* 13, no. 1 (2014): 44–64; Will Kynes, *An Obituary for "Wisdom Literature": The Birth, Death, and Intertextual Reintegration of a Biblical Corpus* (Oxford University Press, 2019). For an edited work with essays taking various positions, see Mark R. Sneed, ed., *Was There a Wisdom Tradition? New Prospects in Israelite Wisdom Studies*, Ancient Israel and Its Literature 23 (SBL Press, 2015).

5. Carol A. Newsom, "The Book of Job: Introduction, Commentary, and Reflections," in *The New Interpreter's Bible: A Commentary in Twelve Volumes*, ed. Leander E. Keck (Abingdon Press, 1996), 4:318–637, here 323.

6. Note that I will follow scholarly practice in treating the book of Job as a literary work, not inappropriately considered a drama (at least in part), with a primary author. Sometimes this unnamed author is called the Job-poet, especially when discussing the dialogue section of the book. This author constructs characters. We as readers are constantly challenged to consider what we make of these characters, mainly Job, the friends, and God. Just because the author depicts them in a certain way doesn't mean we are supposed to approve their words or deeds uncritically. We never are informed as to the author's perspective but can only infer it.

7. Newsom also dates the book in the early postexilic period ("Book of Job," 323).

8. Gustavo Gutiérrez, *On Job: God-Talk and the Suffering of the Innocent*, trans. Matthew J. O'Connell (Orbis Books, 1987), 14.

9. Buber, *Prophetic Faith*, 189.

10. Alexander E. Breitkopf, *Job: From Lament to Penitence* (Sheffield Phoenix Press, 2020), 1.

11. John Bright, *A History of Israel*, 2nd ed. (Westminster Press, 1972), 452.

12. Ellen F. Davis, *Opening Israel's Scriptures* (Oxford University Press, 2019), 349–50.

13. Davis, *Opening Israel's Scriptures*, 351.

14. J. Richard Middleton, *Abraham's Silence: The Binding of Isaac, the Suffering of Job, and How to Talk Back to God* (Baker Academic, 2021), 128.

15. Gordis, *Book of God and Man*, 18.

Chapter One

1. Robert Gordis, *The Book of Job: Commentary, New Translation, and Special Studies* (Jewish Theological Seminary, 1978), 10.

2. J. Gerald Janzen, *Job*, Interpretation (John Knox Press, 1985), 34.

3. C. L. Seow, *Job 1–21: Interpretation and Commentary* (Eerdmans, 2013), 253.

4. Marvin H. Pope, *Job*, Anchor Bible 15 (Doubleday, 1973), 6.

5. Edouard Dhorme, *A Commentary on the Book of Job*, trans. Harold Knight (1926; repr., Nelson, 1967), 2.

6. Gutiérrez, *On Job*, 4.

7. Dhorme, *Commentary on the Book of Job*, 2; Samuel E. Balentine, *Job*, Smith & Helwys Bible Commentary (Smith & Helwys, 2006), 47.

8. Seow, *Job 1–21*, 254.

9. John Goldingay, *The First Testament: A New Translation* (IVP Academic, 2018).

10. Edward L. Greenstein, *Job: A New Translation* (Yale University Press, 2019), 4. Of the most used translations, only the NJPS identifies Job as possessing "slaves" beginning in Job 1:3. Most others use the term "servants."

11. Janzen, *Job*, 36.

12. Dhorme, *Commentary on the Book of Job*, 4.

13. Leonard S. Kravitz and Kerry M. Olitzky, *The Book of Job: A Modern Translation and Commentary* (Wipf & Stock, 2017), 4.

14. William Safire, *The First Dissident: The Book of Job in Today's Politics* (Random House, 1992), 33.

15. Reference is to Tom Wolfe, *A Man in Full: A Novel* (Farrar, Straus & Giroux, 1998).

Chapter Two

1. A helpful introduction to the divine council idea in the ancient Near East and how it was adapted in the Hebrew Bible is offered by John H. Walton, *Job: NIV Application Commentary* (Zondervan, 2012), 63–64.

2. H. H. Rowley, *The Book of Job*, New Century Bible Commentary (Eerdmans, 1970), 31.

3. Balentine, *Job*, 48–49.

4. Gordis, *Book of Job*, 13.

5. Seow, *Job 1–21*, 256.

6. Pope, *Job*, 9–10.

7. N. H. Tur-Sinai, *The Book of Job: A New Commentary* (Kiryath Sepher, 1967), 42.

8. Francis I. Andersen, *Job*, Tyndale Old Testament Commentaries (Intervarsity Press, 1976), 90.

9. Gordis, *Book of Job*, 15; Seow, *Job 1–21*, 256.

10. Gutiérrez, *On Job*, 4.

11. Davis, *Opening Israel's Scriptures*, 348.

12. Norman Gottwald, *The Hebrew Bible* (Fortress Press, 1985), 575.

13. David J. A. Clines, *Job 1–20*, Word Biblical Commentary 17 (Zondervan, 1989), 29.

14. Rowley, *Book of Job*, 32.

15. Pope, *Job*, 12.

16. Kathryn Lopez, "A Capricious, Insecure God," *Christian Century*, May 4, 2022, 12–13, here 12. Katharine J. Dell is known for her extended proposal that Job should be seen as a parody (*Job: Where Shall Wisdom Be Found?* [Bloomsbury T&T Clark, 2017]; see ch. 3).

17. Tod Linafelt, "Why Is There Poetry in the Book of Job?" *Journal of Biblical Literature* 140, no. 4 (2021): 681–701, here 701.

18. Gutiérrez, *On Job*, 22. In the scholarly literature on Job, this central idea is also sometimes called "the deed-consequence nexus," and the "doctrine of reward and punishment." See Ilse Swart and Yasir Saleem, "Taking God to Court: Job's Deconstruction and Resistance of Dominant Ideology," *International Journal of Philosophy and Theology* 84, nos. 3–4 (August 2023): 181–98, here 181.

19. The "just-world hypothesis" is a concept developed in the 1960s by social psychologist Melvin J. Lerner. Lerner developed it to explain his observation that people often rationalize injustice by assuming that victims somehow deserve their fate—a cognitive bias that helps people maintain the belief that the world is fundamentally fair and just. Later scholars evolved the concept to call it "just-world fallacy." In this book, I adapt it further to "just-world theology," while sharing Lerner's conviction that it is a rationalization and the clarification that it is a fallacy. See Melvin J. Lerner, *The Belief in a Just World: A Fundamental Delusion* (Plenum Press, 1980).

20. For direct divine intervention in the Wisdom literature, see Prov 3:12, 33; 15:25; Eccl 2:26; 3:14. Despite the prevalence of just-world theology in Proverbs, several texts acknowledge that the poor and righteous are not always given what they deserve (Prov 11:10; 13:23; 16:8, 19; 19:1, 22; 28:6; 29:7). Ecclesiastes also sees the inequities yet refuses to relinquish confidence in God's ultimate justice (Eccl 2:16; 3:16–17; 7:15–18; 8:10–15; 11:9). One could also cite the psalms of lament. In the prophets, there is the entire book of Habakkuk as well as parts of Jeremiah. A minor

note elsewhere becomes the major motif of Job, which sets the book apart. My thanks to Douglas Miller, private correspondence.

21. A considerable body of literature engages Job from a post-Holocaust perspective—or challenges such engagement. For two overviews, see Isabel Wollaston, "Post-Holocaust Jewish Interpretations of Job," in *The Oxford Bible Handbook of the Reception History of the Bible*, ed. Michael Lieb, Emma Mason, and Jonathan Roberts (Oxford University Press, 2011), 488–501; and David C. Tollerton, *The Book of Job in Post-Holocaust Thought* (Sheffield Phoenix Press, 2012). For three works focused on the overall reception history of Job, see Nahum N. Glatzer, *The Dimensions of Job: A Study and Selected Readings* (Schocken Books, 1969); Mark Larrimore, *The Book of Job: A Biography* (Princeton University Press, 2013); and Stephen J. Vicchio, *The Book of Job: A History of Interpretation and a Commentary* (Wipf & Stock, 2020).

22. Ariel Burger, *Witness: Lessons from Elie Wiesel's Classroom* (Houghton Mifflin Harcourt, 2018), 90.

Chapter Three

1. Rowley, *Book of Job*, 32.

2. Tremper Longman III, *Job*, Baker Commentary on the Old Testament Wisdom and Psalms (Baker, 2012), 85.

3. Brian R. Doak offers a focused study on the role of competing claims about and from nature throughout the book of Job (*Consider Leviathan: Narratives of Nature and Self in Job* [Fortress Press, 2014]). We will want to pay attention to every time one of the speakers makes a claim about creation/nature. Such statements are abundant.

4. Gordis, *Book of Job*, 16.

5. John E. Hartley, *The Book of Job*, New International Commentary on the Old Testament (Eerdmans, 1988), 74.

6. Norman C. Habel, *The Book of Job: A Commentary* (Westminster Press, 1985), 92.

7. This is the first but definitely not the last use of the crucial Hebrew term *ruaḥ* in the book of Job. Joel A. J. Atwood devotes an entire monograph to the use of that term and finds that it has a broad semantic range, including uses related to nature (here, as directed destructively against Job), but also related to God's agency, the human spirit, feelings, vitality, and more. See Joel A. J. Atwood, *Semantics and "Spirit": [Ruaḥ] and Humanity in Proverbs, Ecclesiastes, and Job* (Brill, 2023). A reader/hearer of the Hebrew in Job would sense the complex interplay/overlay whenever the term *ruaḥ* is used.

8. Dhorme, *Commentary on the Book of Job*, 12.

9. Rowley, *Book of Job*, 33.

10. Dhorme, *Commentary on the Book of Job*, 12.

11. Gordis, *Book of Job*, 77.

12. An exception is Kravitz and Olitzky, *Book of Job*, 5.

13. Dhorme, *Commentary on the Book of Job*, 14.

14. Goldingay, *First Testament,* at Job 1:22.
15. Greenstein, *Job,* 8.
16. Quoted in Janzen, *Job,* 43.
17. During the composition of this book I discovered "The Testament of Job," a composition from the first-century BCE, which retells the Job story in a way that has Job remain undoubting and submissive to God throughout his experience. It is, according to Nahum Glatzer, "a reading that does not admit the communion between God and man to be disturbed by the sad and sorry state of this world" (Nahum N. Glatzer, *The Rest Is Commentary: A Source Book of Literature from the Second Temple through the Talmudic Age* [Beacon Press, 1961], 99).

Chapter Four

1. Dhorme, *Commentary on the Book of Job,* 16.
2. Habel, *Book of Job,* 94.
3. Hartley, *Book of Job,* 80.
4. Andersen, *Job,* 96.
5. Hartley, *Book of Job,* 80.
6. Quoted in Balentine, *Job,* 59.
7. Seow, *Job 1–21,* 294. Detailed also in Middleton, *Abraham's Silence,* 73.
8. Pope, *Job,* 21.
9. Rowley, *Book of Job,* 36.
10. Pope, *Job,* 21.
11. Laura Quick, "'Like a Garment Eaten by Moths' (Job 13:28): Clothing, Nudity and Illness in the Book of Job," *Biblical Interpretation* 30 (2022): 46–65, here 46.
12. Seow, *Job 1–21,* 293.
13. Balentine, *Job,* 62.

Chapter Fve

1. Janzen, *Job,* 49.
2. Goldingay, *First Testament,* at Job 2:10; Robert Alter, *The Wisdom Books: Job, Proverbs, and Ecclesiastes* (Norton, 2011), 16; Raymond P. Scheindlin, *The Book of Job* (Norton, 1998), 57.
3. For a scholarly study of the Septuagint translation of both Job and Proverbs, see Bryan Beeckman, *One or Two Translators? Translation Technique and Theology of LXX Proverbs and Its Relation to LXX Job* (De Gruyter, 2024).
4. Quoted from Albert Pietersma and Benjamin G. Wright, eds., *A New English Translation of the Septuagint and the Other Greek Translations Traditionally Included under That Title* [NETS] (Oxford University Press, 2007).
5. Samuel Terrien and Paul Scherer, "The Book of Job," in *The Interpreter's Bible,* ed. George A. Buttrick et al., 3:877–1198, here 921, 12 vols. (Abingdon Press, 1954).

6. Clines, *Job 1–20*, 51.
7. Janzen, *Job*, 50.
8. Consideration of Job through the lens of trauma, or trauma theory, is on the rise. For one example, see the recent work by esteemed Holocaust scholar Norman C. Habel, *God Trauma and Wisdom Therapy* (Fortress Press, 2024). After a lifetime of Job scholarship, Habel recasts the entire book of Job as "Wisdom therapy" addressing trauma. See also Michelle Keener, *A Trauma Theory Reading of the Book of Job* (T&T Clark, 2025).

Chapter Six

1. Rowley, *Book of Job*, 37.
2. Dhorme, *Commentary on the Book of Job*, 22; Pope, *Job*, 24–25.
3. Habel, *Book of Job*, 97.
4. Clines, *Job 1–20*, 64; confirmed by Kravitz and Olitzky, *Book of Job*, 12.
5. Elie Wiesel, *Memoirs: All Rivers Run to the Sea* (Alfred A. Knopf, 1995), 151: "I decided to wait, to make a kind of vow: Ten years would pass before I would speak, before I would come forward with my deposition." See Wiesel, *Night* (Hill & Wang, 1960).

Chapter Seven

1. Pope, *Job*, 27.
2. Seow, *Job 1–21*, 320.
3. Dhorme, *Commentary on the Book of Job*, 24.
4. Greenstein, *Job*, 13.
5. James Parker, "Sorry, Not Sorry," *The Atlantic*, September 2019, 28–30.
6. Dhorme, *Commentary on the Book of Job*, 32.
7. Pope, *Job*, 31; Tur-Sinai, *Book of Job*, 61.
8. Andersen, *Job*, 42.

Chapter Eight

1. Pope, *Job*, 27.
2. Terrien and Scherer, "Book of Job," 927.
3. Scheindlin, *Book of Job*, 60.
4. Kravitz and Olitzky, *Book of Job*, 16.
5. Alter, *Wisdom Books*, 20.
6. Seow, *Job 1–21*, 359.
7. Balentine, *Job*, 89.
8. Balentine, *Job*, 90. Though compare Jeremiah (ch. 20) and Qohelet (Eccl 4:1–3). David wishes he had died instead of Absalom (2 Sam 18:33).
9. Gutiérrez, *On Job*, 16.

10. I credit the following article with helping me to focus on the issue of slavery in Job: Imhotep Newsome, "Job's Silence on Slavery: Theodicy and Retribution in Tension (Job 31:13)," *Journal of Black Religious Thought* 1, no. 2 (2022): 140–51.

11. Balentine, *Job*, 90. The same point is made by Gutiérrez, *On Job*, ch. 5.

12. Rabbi Moshe Eisemann and Nossen Scherman, *Iyov/Job: A New Translation with a Commentary Anthologized from Talmudic, Midrashic, and Rabbinic Sources* (Mesorah Publications, 1994), xx.

13. Dietrich Bonhoeffer, *"After Ten Years": Dietrich Bonhoeffer and Our Times*, ed. Victoria J. Barnett (Fortress Press, 2017), 30.

Chapter Nine

1. Alter, *Wisdom Books*, 16.

2. Hartley, *Book of Job*, 105.

3. David John Atkinson, *The Message of Job: Suffering and Grace*, rev. ed. (InterVarsity Press, 2022).

4. A. Cohen, Victor E. Reichert, and A. J. Rosenberg, *Job: Hebrew Text and English Translation* (Soncino Press, 1985), 13.

5. Cf. Victoria Adams, *Redefining Job and the Conundrum of Suffering* (Wipf & Stock, 2020), 112–15.

6. Newsom, "Book of Job," 335.

Chapter Ten

1. Rowley, *Book of Job*, 47.

2. John D. Burnight, "Is Eliphaz a False Prophet? The Vision in Job 4.12–21," *Journal for the Study of the Old Testament* 46, no. 1 (September 2021), 96–116, here 96.

3. My thanks to Douglas Miller.

4. Yasir Saleem, "'For a Man Is Born to Suffer': Intertextuality between Job 4–5 and Gen. 2.4b–3.24," *Journal for the Study of the Old Testament* 46, no. 3 (March 2022), 388–407, here 388. Saleem sees Job 4:9 as an allusion to Gen 2:7, Job 4:19 as alluding to Gen 2:7a and 3:19b, and Job 5:6–7a as alluding to Gen 3:17–19.

5. Saleem, "'For a Man Is Born to Suffer,'" 397.

6. My thanks to Douglas Miller.

7. David P. Gushee, *The Moral Teachings of Jesus: Radical Instruction in the Will of God* (Wipf & Stock, 2024), 25–28.

Chapter Eleven

1. Cohen, Reichert, and Rosenberg, *Job: Hebrew Text*, 18.

2. Alter, *Wisdom Books*, 27.

3. Seow, *Job 1–21,* 417. See also Saleem, "'For a Man Is Born to Suffer,'" 397–98.

4. Saleem, "'For a Man Is Born to Suffer,'" 399.

5. Greenstein, *Job*, 22.

Chapter Twelve

1. Newsom, "Book of Job," 464.

2. N. (Nehama) Verbin, "Faith and the Absurd: Kierkegaard, Camus and Job's Religious Protest," *Harvard Theological Review* 117, no. 2 (2024), 293–316, here 297.

3. Quoted in Richard L. Rubenstein and John K. Roth, *Approaches to Auschwitz: The Holocaust and Its Legacy*, rev. ed. (Westminster John Knox Press, 2003), 330.

Chapter Thirteen

1. Greenstein, *Job*, 68.

2. Greenstein, *Job*, 27; cf. Scheindlin, *Book of Job*, 65.

3. Doak, *Consider Leviathan*, xviii.

4. Kravitz and Olitzky, *Book of Job*, 36.

5. My thanks to Douglas Miller.

Chapter Fourteen

1. Sameer Yadav, "A Joban Theology of Consolation," *Harvard Theological Review* 117, no. 2 (2024): 181–203, here 193.

2. Yadav, "Joban Theology of Consolation," 194.

Chapter Fifteen

1. My thanks to Jeremy Hall.

2. My thanks to Ken Wilson.

3. This is a Jewish idiom ultimately coming from the Hebrew. The verb *satar* means "to hide," and in the *hiphil binyan* adds "*h*," e.g., *histir*. The word *Hester* may be connected to the word *Esther* (but not linguistically), and so that book is said to challenge the reader to find the face (*panim*) of God in the book though God's name is not mentioned. The phrase *histir panim* is found several times in the Bible, for example, of Moses before God in Exod 3:6. And God hides the divine face due to people's sin (see Deut 31:17–18).

4. Verbin, "Faith and the Absurd," 295.

Chapter Sixteen

1. Alter, *Wisdom Books*, 35.

2. Seow, *Job 1–21*, 492.

3. Pope, *Job*, 60.

4. Alter, *Wisdom Books*, 35.

5. Seow suggests that the phrase communicates both fragility and tedium, but not speed (*Job 1–21*, 494).

6. "Savage parody" is Newsom's language ("Book of Job," 397). Doak says, "The irony of Job's cry comes from the fact that, as most [scholars] agree, Job cites an earlier use of a nearly identical phrase in Psalm 8" (*Consider Leviathan*, xv–xvi). For an extensive study of the Job 7/Psalm 8 connection that affirms that Job 7 is indeed parodying Psalm 8, see Israel McGrew, "'What Is Enosh?' The Anthropological Contributions of Job 7:17–18 through Allusion and Intertextuality," *Catholic Biblical Quarterly* 84 (2022): 404–23. McGrew argues that, while the parody is real, the author of Job does not want us to give the character Job the final word, especially with regard to this parody.

7. Abraham Joshua Heschel, *Moral Grandeur and Spiritual Audacity: Essays*, ed. Susannah Heschel (Farrar, Straus & Giroux, 1996), 69.

8. Will Kynes, "Morality and Mortality: The Dialogical Interpretation of Psalm 90 in the Book of Job," *Journal for the Study of the Old Testament* 44, no. 4 (June 2020): 624–41, here 624. "Aggadic" means having to do with a nonlegal or narrative bit of the Hebrew Bible. Note that this claim is based on the belief, which I affirmed earlier, that Job was written late, and that the Job author(s) had most if not all of what became the Hebrew Bible available for reflection and citation.

9. Peter Rollins selects Job 7:12–21 as a principal example for his claim that challenging God, including God's justice, is a central through-line in the Bible (*The Orthodox Heretic and Other Impossible Tales* [Paraclete Press, 2010], 91–94).

Chapter Seventeen

1. Dhorme, *Commentary on the Book of Job*, 201.
2. Alter, *Wisdom Books*, 40.
3. Kravitz and Olitzky, *Book of Job*, 51.
4. David P. Gushee, *Changing Our Mind*, 3rd ed. (Read the Spirit Books, 2017).
5. David P. Gushee, *Introducing Christian Ethics: Core Convictions for Christians Today* (Front Edge Publishing, 2022), ch. 1.
6. G. K. Chesterton, *Orthodoxy: The Romance of Faith* (1908; repr., Doubleday, 1990), 48.
7. Roland E. Murphy, *The Book of Job: A Short Reading* (Paulist Press, 1999), 29.
8. Newsom, "Book of Job," 405.
9. Gutiérrez, *On Job*, 27.

Chapter Eighteen

1. Alter, *Wisdom Books*, 42.
2. Balentine, *Job*, 163.

3. Newsom, "Book of Job," 415–16.

4. Safire, *First Dissident*, 8–9.

5. Rabbi Joshua S. Sperka, *The Book of Job: Mankind on Trial* (Bloch Publishing, 1979), 12. I will return to Rabbi Sperka's argument later. Note that Jewish rabbis Eisemann and Scherman quite straightforwardly acknowledge that the text contemplates litigation initiated by Job against God (Eisemann and Scherman, *Iyov/Job*, 92–93). So do most Job scholars.

6. Alter, *Wisdom Books*, 42.

7. Cited in Safire, *First Dissident*, 21.

8. Safire, *First Dissident*, xi–xv.

Chapter Nineteen

1. Janice A. Thompson, "'O That My Words Were Written Down!': Contested Bodies and Unwelcome Words in the Book of Job and Modern Poetry of Disability," *Horizons* 49, no. 2 (2022), 277–304, here 277. Thompson reviews several recent works in the field of disability theology that address the book of Job, revealing once again the endless relevance and fecundity of the book.

2. Balentine, *Job*, 185.

3. Janzen, *Job*, 97.

4. Gordis, *Book of Job*, 117.

5. Balentine, *Job*, 200.

6. Søren Kierkegaard, "The Lord Gave and the Lord Hath Taken Away," in Nahum N. Glatzer, *The Dimensions of Job: A Study and Selected Readings* (Wipf & Stock, 2002), 267. For a thoughtful treatment of Kierkegaard on Job, see Timothy Polk, "Kierkegaard and the Book of Job," *Word & World* 31, no. 4 (2011): 405–13.

7. Thomas Wagner, "Job as the Sufferer: Self-Knowledge under the Influence of Permanent Pain," *Hebrew Bible and Ancient Israel* 12, no. 3 (2023): 309–22, here 309.

8. Thompson, "'O That My Words Were Written Down!,'" 277.

9. Longman, *Job*, 203.

10. Habel, *Book of Job*, 216.

11. Seow, *Job 1–21*, 626.

12. Gordis, *Book of Job*, 127.

Chapter Twenty

1. Habel, *Book of Job*, 223.

2. Janzen, *Job*, 107.

3. Habel, *Book of Job*, 225; Balentine, *Job*, 211. Greenstein renders the line: "Though he slay me, I will no longer wait" (*Job*, 57).

4. Habel, *Book of Job*, 226.

5. Janzen, *Job*, 107,

6. Kravitz and Olitzky, *Book of Job*, 81.

7. For more on Wiesel as "witness," see Burger, *Witness.*
8. Balentine, *Job*, 209.
9. Abraham Joshua Heschel, *A Passion for Truth* (Jewish Lights, 2013), 279.
10. Janzen, *Job*, 106.
11. Newsom, "Book of Job," 436.
12. Buber, *Prophetic Faith*, 189.
13. Janzen, *Job*, 106.
14. Gordis, *Book of Job*, 127.
15. Balentine, *Job*, 220.
16. Gordis, *Book of Job*, 127.
17. Habel, *Book of Job*, 226.
18. Habel, *Book of Job*, 227.

Chapter Twenty-One

1. Stephen Mitchell, *The Book of Job* (HarperPerennial, 1992), 41.

2. Katharine J. Dell, "Representing Tradition: Exploring the Epistemology of the Friends in the Book of Job," *Hebrew Bible and Ancient Israel* 12, no. 3 (2023): 282–94. Dell comments, "They fall back on the sources of their knowledge from inherited tradition, notably from generational wisdom from within circles of the wise" (282).

Chapter Twenty-Two

1. René Girard, *Job: The Victim of His People* (Stanford University Press, 1987), 6.

2. Karl Barth, *Church Dogmatics IV.3.1: The Doctrine of Reconciliation*, ed. G. W. Bromiley and T. F. Torrance, trans. G. W. Bromiley (T&T Clark, 1961), 388.

3. Competitors for the honor include Jer 20:7, where Jeremiah calls God a liar (cf. Moses in Exod 5:22–23; Eccl 1:13; 7:14). His community is also empowered to attack him. Later in that chapter there are expressions of hope, but then reversion to despair (cf. Job 3). In a number of the lament psalms, God is actually part of the problem being lamented (e.g., Psalm 88). There is more raw honesty in the Bible than most of us were taught to see. My thanks to Douglas Miller.

Chapter Twenty-Four

1. David P. Gushee and Glen H. Stassen, *Kingdom Ethics: Following Jesus in Contemporary Context*, 2nd ed. (Eerdmans, 2016), 72.

2. Douglas Miller, private correspondence: "Of course, Job might still accept this but now refuses to accept some of the entailments embraced by his culture, viz., that someone suffering is necessarily guilty of sin. So he appears to be rejecting the entire core conviction but may not be."

3. Girard, *Job*, 4.

Chapter Twenty-Five

1. Greenstein reads this as "young-hooligans" (*Job*, 85).

2. Quick, "'Like a Garment Eaten by Moths,'" 49.

3. This should be noticed much more than it is by readers of Job. One who does notice is Katherine E. Southwood, *Job's Body and the Dramatised Comedy of Moralising* (Routledge, 2021); see ch. 4.

4. My thanks to Douglas Miller.

5. Newsom, "Book of Job," 480.

Chapter Twenty-Six

1. Regarding vv. 30–33, Qohelet has a similar complaint about the wicked (7:15; 8:10, 14). Ecclesiastes 8:10 provides a similar interesting comparison between NASB and NJPS (and other translations, because the Hebrew is difficult). One of the challenges in Job 21:28–30 is to know where the quotation ends that Job attributes to his friends in v. 28. Does it continue through v. 30? Unfortunately, there are no ancient quotation marks to help us. My thanks to Douglas Miller for this insight.

2. To try to identify moral exemplars from history for our terribly divided age, I co-wrote this book with Colin Holtz: *Moral Leadership for a Divided Age: Fourteen People Who Dared to Change the World* (Baker, 2018).

Chapter Twenty-Seven

1. Continue to keep in mind that none of these persons is Israelite. The audience, however, is Israelite.

2. Gutiérrez, *On Job*, 35–37. From what we know from Hammurabi and others, there is much similarity among legal codes in the ancient Near East. Although we should not assume complete agreement, for issues of basic social justice such as care of the poor there is evidence of similarity. My thanks to Douglas Miller.

Chapter Twenty-Eight

1. Davis Hankins argues, "The friends counsel Job to assume a pious posture of *fear*, which is unavailable to him because of his experience of anxiety" ("What Does Job Want? Desire, Fear, Anxiety, and God in and beyond Job 23," *Biblical Interpretation* 31, no. 3 [2023]: 311–31, here 311). In other words, Job cannot return to the default pious posture of respectful, awe-filled reverence toward God; his experience has driven him to a place of terror and anxiety.

2. Gutiérrez, *On Job*, 32–33.

3. Newsom, "Book of Job," 513.

4. Some scholars believe that this section is a missing portion of a speech by either Bildad or Zophar and was not originally connected to Job. Others think that this is an independent poem. I think that, translated correctly, it sounds like Job.

Chapter Twenty-Nine

1. Alter, *Wisdom Books*, 106–14.

2. In Ps 22:6, the wretched psalmist declares himself a worm, but in context it appears he is reflecting the negative judgment of others. In Isa 41:14, exiled/broken Israel is described as a worm/maggot, but mainly by contrast to the great redemption God is soon to bring. These are the only two other references to humans as worms or maggots in the Bible.

3. Søren Kierkegaard, *Repetition*, trans. and ed. Howard V. Hong and Edna H. Hong (Princeton University Press, 1983), 208.

4. Kierkegaard, *Repetition*, 198.

Chapter Thirty

1. Scott A. Davison, Shira Weiss, and Sajjad Rizvi, *The Protests of Job: An Interfaith Dialogue* (Palgrave Macmillan, 2022), 11.

2. An intermezzo is a short piece of music played between the movements of a major musical composition.

3. Yuval Noah Harari, *Sapiens: A Brief History of Humankind* (Harper, 2015), ch. 10.

4. Newsom, "Book of Job," 534.

5. This is reminiscent of Genesis 3, where God forbids the man and woman from eating from the tree of the knowledge of good and evil (Heb: *tov/ra'*). Recall that "the tree was desirable as a source of wisdom" (Gen 3:6). The Hebrew word there derives from *sakal* rather than *hokmah*, but it is quite interesting that in this story God did not feel the need to share wisdom with humans and indeed banned their access to it. My thanks to Mia Hong.

6. My thanks to Douglas Miller.

Chapter Thirty-One

1. Barth, *Church Dogmatics IV.3.1*, 385.

2. Girard, *Job*, 11.

3. Gutiérrez, *On Job*, 35–36.

4. Suzanna R. Millar, "Dehumanization as Derision or Delight? Overcoming Class-Prejudice and Species-Prejudice in Job," *Biblical Interpretation* 30, no. 2 (2022): 150–70, here 150.

5. Newsom, "Book of Job," 548.

6. Girard, *Job*, 6.

7. Newsom, "Book of Job," 547.

Chapter Thirty-Two

1. Job 31 reminds one of the "Egyptian Book of the Dead," ch. 125, in which the person declares they have not committed various moral offenses, "I have not . . . ," e.g.,

robbed the poor, maligned a servant to his master, killed, made anyone suffer, etc. My thanks to Douglas Miller.

2. Newsom, "Book of Job," 327.

3. Cf. Patricia Vesely, "The Physicality of Virtue in Job 31: The Use of Bodily Terms in Job's Depiction of Moral Integrity," *Journal of Theological Studies* 73, no. 1 (April 2022): 1–21.

4. Shalom E. Holtz, "The Truncated Oath of Innocence and the Adjudicatory Challenge to God: Three Examples (Job 31:5–6; Ps 44:21–22; Josh 22:23)," *Vetus Testamentum* 73, nos. 4–5 (2023): 607–21.

5. Barth, *Church Dogmatics IV.3.1*, 386.

Chapter Thirty-Three

1. Newsom, "Book of Job," 321–22, 558–94.

2. Greenstein, *Job*, 134.

3. My thanks to Mia Hong.

4. Psalms 6; 13; 35; 62; 74; 79; 80; 82; 89; 90; 94; 119. God asks it in Exod 16:28; Num 14:11, 27. Then Wisdom asks a similar question of mortals: Prov 1:22; 6:9. Jeremiah asks this question several times in various aspects. Sounding like the Psalms are Hab 1:2; 2:6; Zech 1:12; Rev 6:10.

5. My thanks to Douglas Miller.

Chapter Thirty-Four

1. Safire, *First Dissident*, xix, xxi.

2. Swart and Saleem write: "From the reader's perspective, the boastful response of God's creative power in front of a downtrodden miserable man appears to be distasteful" ("Taking God to Court," 192). But then, following Michel Foucault, they say, "one could thus wonder whether God's display of power in the answer to Job testifies to the limits of God's power."

3. Parker, "Sorry, Not Sorry," 30.

4. Greenstein, *Job*, 170; Newsom, "Book of Job," 605.

5. Glatzer, *Rest Is Commentary*, 98.

6. Kierkegaard, *Repetition*, 212.

7. Dylan Balfour, "Second-Personal Theodicy: Coming to Know Why God Permits Suffering by Coming to Know God Himself," *International Journal for Philosophy of Religion* 88, no. 3 (2020): 287–305, here 293. Balfour is commenting on the work of Eleonore Stump on Job, *Wandering in Darkness: Narrative and the Problem of Suffering* (Oxford University Press, 2012).

8. G. K. Chesterton, "Introduction to the Book of Job," https://www.chesterton.org/introduction-to-job (accessed August 16, 2025), 10–11.

9. Middleton, *Abraham's Silence*, 120, 128.

10. C. S. Lewis, *Mere Christianity* (1952; repr., New York: Harper, 2001), 145.

11. Newsom, "Book of Job," 336–37.

12. Janzen, *Job*, 257.

13. William P. Brown, "Biophilia, Biodiversity, and the Bible," *Religions* 12, no. 11 (November 2021): 1–12, here 9.

14. Davison, Weiss, and Rizvi, *Protests of Job*, 6–7.

15. Georg Gasser, "Animal Suffering, God and Lessons from the Book of Job," *Religions* 12, no. 12 (December 2021): 1–14, here 12–13.

16. Jacqueline E. Lapsley, "A Theology of Creation—Critical and Christian." In *Theology of the Hebrew Bible, Volume 1: Methodological Studies*, ed. Marvin A. Sweeney (SBL Press, 2019), 141–52, here 149.

17. M. (Maria) Kardaun, "God's Own Guinea Pig. The Book of Job and Secularization," *PsyArt* 27 (2022): 74–87, here 74.

18. Verbin, "Faith and the Absurd," 311.

19. Yadav, *Joban Theology of Consolation*, 195.

20. Greenstein, *Job*, 165–66.

21. Millar, "Dehumanization as Derision or Delight?," 150.

Chapter Thirty-Five

1. Newsom, "Book of Job," 629.

2. My deepest thanks to Douglas Miller for organizing most of these translation options.

3. Greenstein, *Job*, xx–xxi.

4. Parker, "Sorry, Not Sorry," 30.

5. Swart and Saleem, "Taking God to Court," 193.

6. Safire, *First Dissident*, xxv.

7. Safire, *First Dissident*, 29.

8. Verbin, "Faith and the Absurd," 312–13.

9. Trevor B. Williams, "Job's Unfinalizable Voice: An Addendum to David Burrell's Deconstructing Theodicy," *New Blackfriars* 101, no. 1096 (November 2020): 681–97, here 681.

10. See Carol A. Newsom, *The Book of Job: A Contest of Moral Imaginations* (Oxford University Press, 2003), especially 21–31.

Chapter Thirty-Six

1. Safire, *First Dissident*, 26.

2. Shai Held, *Judaism Is about Love: Recovering the Heart of Jewish Life* (New York: Farrar, Straus & Giroux, 2024), 29.

3. But this may be a modern view. Nicholas J. Campbell argues that, in context, "The focus upon progeny as heirs to continue the house of Job explains why the replacement of children in the epilogue is not presented as problematic in the text. . . . Progeny is the sign of divine favor, not specific children" ("God and Heirs: The Theme of Progeny in Job," *Scandinavian Journal of the Old Testament* 36, no. 1 (2022): 150–62, here 150.

4. Leo G. Perdue, *Wisdom in Revolt: Metaphorical Theology in the Book of Job*, Library of Hebrew Bible/Old Testament Studies (Sheffield Academic Press, 1991), 272.

5. Parker, "Sorry, Not Sorry," 30.

6. Yitzhak Berger, "On the Restoration of Job: Poetics and Meaning in Job 42," *Vetus Testamentum* 74, no. 1 (2024): 1–27, here 1.

7. Newsom, "Book of Job," 337–38.

8. J. Gerald Janzen, "Trust Is Job One: My Last Take on Job," *Encounter* 81, no. 1 (2021): 23–37, here 37.

9. Davis, *Opening Israel's Scriptures*, 358.

10. Newsom, "Book of Job," 636–37.

Conclusion

1. George A. Lindbeck, *The Nature of Doctrine: Religion and Theology in a Postliberal Age*. 25th Anniversary Edition. (Westminster John Knox Press, 2009), 108.

2. Lindbeck, *Nature of Doctrine*, 107.

3. I have been reading the friends as a collective standing in for Job's community; in addition, due to the religion-drenched nature of their communications with Job, I think it fair to read them as functioning as Job's *religious* community. Thus, I will work with the idea that the friends can illuminate ethical issues related to human community in general and religious community, including church community, in particular.

4. William C. Pohl IV, *Ethical God-Talk in the Book of Job: Speaking to the Almighty*. Library of the Hebrew Bible/Old Testament Studies (T&T Clark, 2020), 249.

5. Lopez, "Capricious, Insecure God," 13.

6. Lance Hawley, "The Rhetoric of Condemnation in the Book of Job," *Journal of Biblical Literature* 139, no. 3 (2020): 459–78, here 459.

7. Immanuel Kant, *Religion with the Boundaries of Mere Reason*, ed. Allen Wood and George di Giovanni (Cambridge University Press, 1998), 25.

8. Kant, *Religion with the Boundaries of Mere Reason*, 26.

9. Yadav, *Joban Theology of Consolation*, 188.

10. Yadav, *Joban Theology of Consolation*, 202.

11. Safire, *First Dissident*, xiv–xv.

12. Lopez, "Capricious, Insecure God," 13.

13. Gottwald, *Hebrew Bible*, 579.

14. Davis, *Opening Israel's Scriptures*, 353.

15. Heschel, *Moral Grandeur and Spiritual Audacity*, 278.

16. Sperka, *Book of Job*, 6.

17. Sperka, *Book of Job*, 12.

18. Newsom, "Book of Job," 614.

19. Newsom, "Book of Job," 495.

20. Newsom, "Book of Job," 614.

21. Newsom, "Book of Job," 626.

22. David B. Burrell, *Deconstructing Theodicy: Why Job Has Nothing to Say to the Puzzle of Human Suffering* (Brazos, 2008), 124.

Bibliography

Adams, Victoria. *Redefining Job and the Conundrum of Suffering*. Wipf & Stock, 2020.

Alter, Robert. *The Wisdom Books: Job, Proverbs, and Ecclesiastes*. W. W. Norton, 2011.

Andersen, Francis I. *Job*. Tyndale Old Testament Commentaries. Intervarsity Press, 1976.

Anderson, Bernhard W. *Understanding the Old Testament*. 3rd ed. Prentice-Hall, 1975.

Atkinson, David John. *The Message of Job: Suffering and Grace*. Rev. ed. Inter-Varsity Press, 2022.

Atwood, Joel A. J. *Semantics and "Spirit": [Ruaḥ] and Humanity in Proverbs, Ecclesiastes, and Job*. Brill, 2023.

Balentine, Samuel E. *Job*. Smith & Helwys Bible Commentary. Smith & Helwys, 2006.

Balfour, Dylan. "Second-Personal Theodicy: Coming to Know Why God Permits Suffering by Coming to Know God Himself." *International Journal for Philosophy of Religion* 88, no. 3 (2020): 287–305.

Barth, Karl. *Church Dogmatics IV.3.1: The Doctrine of Reconciliation*. Edited by G. W. Bromiley and T. F. Torrance. Translated by G. W. Bromiley. T&T Clark, 1961.

Beeckman, Bryan. *One or Two Translators?: Translation Technique and Theology of LXX Proverbs and Its Relation to LXX Job*. De Gruyter, 2024.

Berger, Yitzhak. "On the Restoration of Job: Poetics and Meaning in Job 42." *Vetus Testamentum* 74, no. 1 (2024): 1–27.

Bonhoeffer, Dietrich. *"After Ten Years": Dietrich Bonhoeffer and Our Times*. Edited by Victoria J. Barnett. Fortress Press, 2017.

Boone, Benson. *Beautiful Things*, performed by Benson Boone, released January 18, 2024, on Night Street/Warner Records, streaming audio, Spotify, https://open.spotify.com/track/6tNQ70jh40wmPGpYy6R2o9.

Breitkopf, Alexander E. *Job: From Lament to Penitence*. Sheffield Phoenix Press, 2020.

Bright, John. *A History of Israel*. 2nd ed. Westminster Press, 1972.

Brown, William P. "Biophilia, Biodiversity, and the Bible." *Religions* 12, no. 11 (November 2021): 1–12.

———. *Character in Crisis: A Fresh Approach to the Wisdom Literature of the Old Testament*. Eerdmans, 1996.

Buber, Martin. *The Prophetic Faith*. Harper & Brothers, 1960.

———. *Two Types of Faith*. Translated by Norman P. Goldhawk. Syracuse University Press, 2003.

Burger, Ariel. *Witness: Lessons from Elie Wiesel's Classroom*. Houghton Mifflin Harcourt, 2018.

Burnight, John D. "Is Eliphaz a False Prophet? The Vision in Job 4.12–21." *Journal for the Study of the Old Testament* 46, no. 1 (September 2021): 96–116.

Burrell, David B. *Deconstructing Theodicy: Why Job Has Nothing to Say to the Puzzle of Human Suffering*. Brazos, 2008.

Campbell, Nicholas J. "God and Heirs: The Theme of Progeny in Job." *Scandinavian Journal of the Old Testament* 36, no. 1 (2022): 150–62.

Chesterton, G. K. "Introduction to the Book of Job." https://www.chesterton.org/introduction-to-job. Accessed August 16, 2025.

———. *Orthodoxy: The Romance of Faith*. 1908. Reprint, Doubleday, 1990.

Clines, David J. A. *Job 1–20*. Word Biblical Commentary. Zondervan, 1989.

Cohen, A., Victor E. Reichert, and A. J. Rosenberg. *Job: Hebrew Text and English Translation*. Soncino Press, 1985.

Coogan, Michael D. *The Old Testament: A Historical and Literary Introduction to the Hebrew Scriptures*. Oxford University Press, 2006.

Davis, Ellen F. *Opening Israel's Scriptures*. Oxford University Press, 2019.

Davison, Scott A., Shira Weiss, and Sajjad Rizvi. *The Protests of Job: An Interfaith Dialogue*. Palgrave Macmillan, 2022.

Dell, Katharine J. *Job: Where Shall Wisdom Be Found?* Bloomsbury T&T Clark, 2017.

———. "Representing Tradition: Exploring the Epistemology of the Friends in the Book of Job." *Hebrew Bible and Ancient Israel* 12, no. 3 (2023): 282–94.

Dhorme, Edouard. *A Commentary on the Book of Job*. Translated by Harold Knight. 1926. Reprint, Thomas Nelson, 1967.

Doak, Brian R. *Consider Leviathan: Narratives of Nature and Self in Job*. Fortress Press, 2014.

Eisemann, Rabbi Moshe, and Nosson Scherman. *Iyov/Job: A New Translation with a Commentary Anthologized from Talmudic, Midrashic, and Rabbinic Sources*. Mesorah Publications, 1994.

Gasser, Georg. "Animal Suffering, God and Lessons from the Book of Job." *Religions* 12, no. 12 (December 2021): 1–14.

Girard, René. *Job: The Victim of His People*. Stanford University Press, 1987.

Glatzer, Nahum N. *The Dimensions of Job: A Study and Selected Readings*. Schocken Books, 1969.

———. *The Rest Is Commentary: A Source Book of Literature from the Second Temple through the Talmudic Age*. Beacon Press, 1961.

Goldingay, John. *The First Testament: A New Translation*. IVP Academic, 2018.

Gordis, Robert. *The Book of God and Man: A Study of Job*. University of Chicago Press, 1965.

———. *The Book of Job: Commentary, New Translation, and Special Studies*. Jewish Theological Seminary of America, 1978.

Gottwald, Norman. *The Hebrew Bible*. Fortress Press, 1985.

Gray, John. *The Book of Job*. Sheffield Phoenix Press, 2010.

Greenstein, Edward L. *Job: A New Translation*. Yale University Press, 2019.

Gushee, David P. *Changing Our Mind*. 3rd ed. Read the Spirit Books, 2017.

———. *Introducing Christian Ethics: Core Convictions for Christians Today*. Front Edge Publishing, 2022.

———. *The Moral Teachings of Jesus: Radical Instruction in the Will of God*. Wipf & Stock, 2024.

———, and Colin Holtz. *Moral Leadership for a Divided Age: Fourteen People Who Dared to Change the World*. Baker, 2018.

———, and Glen H. Stassen. *Kingdom Ethics: Following Jesus in Contemporary Context*. 2nd ed. Eerdmans, 2016.

Gutiérrez, Gustavo. *On Job: God-Talk and the Suffering of the Innocent*. Translated by Matthew J. O'Connell. Orbis Books, 1987.

Habel, Norman C. *The Book of Job: A Commentary*. Westminster Press, 1985.

———. *God Trauma and Wisdom Therapy*. Fortress Press, 2024.

Hankins, Davis. "What Does Job Want? Desire, Fear, Anxiety, and God in and beyond Job 23." *Biblical Interpretation* 31, no. 3 (2023): 311–31.

Harari, Yuval Noah. *Sapiens: A Brief History of Humankind*. Harper, 2015.

Hartley, John E. *The Book of Job*. New International Commentary on the Old Testament. Eerdmans, 1988.

Harvey, Warren Zev. "Questions on the Book of Job." *Religious Studies* 59, no. S1 (December 2023): 7–16.

Hawley, Lance. "The Rhetoric of Condemnation in the Book of Job." *Journal of Biblical Literature* 139, no. 3 (2020): 459–78.

Held, Shai. *Judaism Is about Love: Recovering the Heart of Jewish Life*. Farrar, Straus & Giroux, 2024.

Heschel, Abraham Joshua. *Moral Grandeur and Spiritual Audacity: Essays*. Edited by Susannah Heschel. Farrar, Straus & Giroux, 1996.

———. *A Passion for Truth*. Jewish Lights, 2013.

Holtz, Shalom E. "The Truncated Oath of Innocence and the Adjudicatory Challenge to God: Three Examples (Job 31:5–6; Ps 44:21–22; Josh 22:23)." *Vetus Testamentum* 73, nos. 4–5 (2023): 607–21.

Janzen, J. Gerald. *Job*. Interpretation: A Bible Commentary for Teaching and Preaching. John Knox Press, 1985.

———. "Trust Is Job One: My Last Take on Job." *Encounter* 81, no. 1 (2021): 23–37.

Jung, C. G. *Answer to Job*. In *The Collected Works of C. G. Jung*. Volume 11. Translated by R. F. C. Hull. Princeton University Press, 1958.

Kant, Immanuel. *Religion within the Boundaries of Mere Reason*. Edited by Allen Wood and George di Giovanni. Cambridge University Press, 1998.

Kardaun, M. (Maria). "God's Own Guinea Pig. The Book of Job and Secularization." *PsyArt* 27 (2022): 74–87.

Keener, Michelle. *A Trauma Theory Reading of the Book of Job*. T&T Clark, 2025.

Kierkegaard, Søren. "The Lord Gave and the Lord Hath Taken Away." In Nahum N. Glatzer, *The Dimensions of Job: A Study and Selected Readings*. Wipf & Stock, 2002.

———. *Repetition*. Translated and edited by Howard V. Hong and Edna H. Hong. Princeton University Press, 1983.

Kravitz, Leonard S., and Kerry M. Olitzky. *The Book of Job: A Modern Translation and Commentary*. Wipf & Stock, 2017.

Kynes, Will. "Morality and Mortality: The Dialogical Interpretation of Psalm 90 in the Book of Job." *Journal for the Study of the Old Testament* 44, no. 4 (June 2020): 624–41.

———. *An Obituary for "Wisdom Literature": The Birth, Death, and Intertextual Reintegration of a Biblical Corpus*. Oxford University Press, 2019.

Kynes, Bill, and Will Kynes. *Wrestling with Job: Defiant Faith in the Face of Suffering*. Intervarsity Press, 2022.

Lapsley, Jacqueline E. "A Theology of Creation—Critical and Christian." In *Theology of the Hebrew Bible, Volume 1: Methodological Studies*, edited by Marvin A. Sweeney, 141–52. SBL Press, 2019.

Larrimore, Mark. *The Book of Job: A Biography*. Princeton University Press, 2013.

Leeser, Isaac, trans. *The Twenty-Four Books of the Holy Scriptures: Carefully Translated according to the Massoretic Text, on the Basis of the English Version, after the Best Jewish Authorities; and Supplied with Short Explanatory Notes*. 4th ed. Bloch, 1891.

Lerner, Melvin J. *The Belief in a Just World: A Fundamental Delusion*. Plenum Press, 1980.

Lewis, C. S. *Mere Christianity*. 1952. Reprint, HarperSanFrancisco, 2001.

Lieb, Michael, Emma Mason, and Jonathan Roberts, eds. *The Oxford Handbook of the Reception History of the Bible*. Oxford University Press, 2011.

Linafelt, Todd. "Why Is There Poetry in the Book of Job?" *Journal of Biblical Literature* 140, no. 4 (2021): 681–701.

Lindbeck, George A. *The Nature of Doctrine: Religion and Theology in a Postliberal Age*. 25th Anniversary Edition. Westminster John Knox Press, 2009.

Longman, Tremper, III. *Job*. Baker Commentary on the Old Testament Wisdom and Psalms. Baker, 2012.

Lopez, Kathryn. "A Capricious, Insecure God." *Christian Century*, May 4, 2022, 12–13.

MacLeish, Archibald. *J.B.: A Play in Verse*. Houghton Mifflin, 1958.

Mangan, Céline, John F. Healey, and Peter S. Knobel. *The Aramaic Bible: The Targum of Job and The Targum of Proverbs and The Targum of Qohelet*. Edited by Kevin Cathcart, Michael Maher, and Martin McNamara. Aramaic Bible 15. Liturgical Press, 1991.

McGrew, Israel. "'What Is Enosh?' The Anthropological Contributions of Job 7:17–18 through Allusion and Intertextuality." *Catholic Biblical Quarterly* 84 (2022): 404–23.

Middleton, J. Richard. *Abraham's Silence: The Binding of Isaac, the Suffering of Job, and How to Talk Back to God*. Baker Academic, 2021.

Millar, Suzanna R. "Dehumanization as Derision or Delight? Overcoming Class-Prejudice and Species-Prejudice in Job." *Biblical Interpretation* 30, no. 2 (2022): 150–70.

Mitchell, Stephen. *The Book of Job*. HarperPerennial, 1992.

Murphy, Roland E. *The Book of Job: A Short Reading*. Paulist Press, 1999.

Newsom, Carol A. "The Book of Job: Introduction, Commentary, and Reflections." In *The New Interpreter's Bible: A Commentary in Twelve Volumes*, edited by Leander E. Keck, 4:318–637. Abingdon Press, 1996.

———. *Job: A Contest of Moral Imaginations*. Oxford University Press, 2003.

Newsome, Imhotep. "Job's Silence on Slavery: Theodicy and Retribution in Tension (Job 31:13)." *Journal of Black Religious Thought* 1, no. 2 (2022): 140–51.

O'Connor, Kathleen M. *The Wisdom Literature*. Abingdon Press, 1990.

Ortlund, Eric. *Piercing Leviathan: God's Defeat of Evil in the Book of Job*. Intervarsity Press, 2021.

Parker, James. "Sorry, Not Sorry." *The Atlantic*, September 2019, 28–30.

Perdue, Leo G. *Wisdom in Revolt: Metaphorical Theology in the Book of Job*. Library of Hebrew Bible/Old Testament Studies. Sheffield Academic Press, 1991.

Pietersma, Albert, and Benjamin G. Wright, eds. *A New English Translation of the Septuagint and the Other Greek Translations Traditionally Included under That Title* (NETS). Oxford University Press, 2007.

Pohl, William C., IV. *Ethical God-Talk in the Book of Job: Speaking to the Almighty*. Library of the Hebrew Bible/Old Testament Studies. T&T Clark, 2020.

Polk, Timothy. "Kierkegaard and the Book of Job." *Word & World* 31, no. 4 (2011): 405–13.

Pope, Marvin H. *Job*. Anchor Bible 15. Doubleday, 1973.

Quick, Laura. "'Like a Garment Eaten by Moths' (Job 13:28): Clothing, Nudity and Illness in the Book of Job." *Biblical Interpretation* 30 (2022): 46–65.

Rollins, Peter. *The Orthodox Heretic and Other Impossible Tales*. Paraclete Press, 2010.

Rowley, H. H. *The Book of Job*. New Century Bible Commentary. Eerdmans, 1980.

Rubenstein, Richard L., and John K. Roth. *Approaches to Auschwitz: The Holocaust and Its Legacy*. Rev. ed. Westminster John Knox Press, 2003.

Saadiah Ben Joseph al-Fayyūmī. *The Book of Theodicy: Translation and Commentary on the Book of Job*. Translated from the Arabic with a Philosophic Commentary by L. E. Goodman. Yale Judaica Series 25. Yale University Press, 1988.

Safire, William. *The First Dissident: The Book of Job in Today's Politics*. Random House, 1992.

Saleem, Yasir. "'For a Man Is Born to Suffer': Intertextuality between Job 4–5 and Gen. 2.4b–3.24." *Journal for the Study of the Old Testament* 46, no. 3 (March 2022): 388–407.

Scheindlin, Raymond P. *The Book of Job*. W. W. Norton, 1998.

Seow, C. L. *Job 1–21: Interpretation and Commentary*. Eerdmans, 2013.

Sneed, Mark R. "Is There a Wisdom Tradition? Yes, No, Maybe So." *Currents in Biblical Research* 13, no. 1 (2014): 44–64.

———, ed. *Was There a Wisdom Tradition? New Prospects in Israelite Wisdom Studies*. Ancient Israel and Its Literature 23. SBL Press, 2015.

Southwood, Katherine E. *Job's Body and the Dramatised Comedy of Moralising*. Routledge, 2021.

Sperka, Rabbi Joshua S. *The Book of Job: Mankind on Trial*. Bloch Publishing, 1979.

Stump, Eleonore. *Wandering in Darkness: Narrative and the Problem of Suffering* (Oxford University Press, 2012).

Swart, Ilse, and Yasir Saleem. "Taking God to Court: Job's Deconstruction and Resistance of Dominant Ideology." *International Journal of Philosophy and Theology* 84, nos. 3–4 (August 2023): 181–98.

Sweeney, Marvin A. *Theology of the Hebrew Bible, Volume 1: Methodological Studies*. SBL Press, 2019.

Terrien, Samuel, and Paul Scherer. "The Book of Job." In *The Interpreter's Bible*, edited by George A. Buttrick et al., 3:877–1198. 12 vols. Abingdon Press, 1954.

Thompson, Janice A. "'O That My Words Were Written Down!': Contested Bodies and Unwelcome Words in the Book of Job and Modern Poetry of Disability." *Horizons* 49, no. 2 (December 2022): 277–304.

Tollerton, David C. *The Book of Job in Post-Holocaust Thought*. Sheffield Phoenix Press, 2012.

Tur-Sinai, N. H. *The Book of Job: A New Commentary*. Kiryath Sepher, 1967.

Verbin, N. (Nehama). "Faith and the Absurd: Kierkegaard, Camus, and Job's Religious Protest." *Harvard Theological Review* 117, no. 2 (2024): 293–316.

Vesely, Patricia. "The Physicality of Virtue in Job 31: The Use of Bodily Terms in Job's Depiction of Moral Integrity." *Journal of Theological Studies* 73, Issue 1 (April 2022): 1–21.

Vicchio, Stephen J. *The Book of Job: A History of Interpretation and a Commentary*. Wipf & Stock, 2020.

Wagner, Thomas. "Job as the Sufferer: Self-Knowledge under the Influence of Permanent Pain." *Hebrew Bible and Ancient Israel* 12, no. 3 (2023): 309–22.

Walton, John H. *Job*. NIV Application Commentary. Zondervan, 2012.

Wiesel, Elie. *Memoirs: All Rivers Run to the Sea*. Alfred A. Knopf, 1995.

———. *Messengers of God: Biblical Portraits and Legends*. Summit Books, 1976.

———. *Night*. Hill & Wang, 1960.

Williams, Trevor B. "Job's Unfinalizable Voice: An Addendum to David Burrell's Deconstructing Theodicy. *New Blackfriars* 101, no. 1096 (November 2020): 681–97.

Wolfe, Tom. *A Man in Full: A Novel*. Farrar, Straus & Giroux, 1998.

Wollaston, Isabel. "Post-Holocaust Jewish Interpretations of Job." In *The Oxford Bible Handbook of the Reception History of the Bible*, edited by Michael Lieb, Emma Mason, and Jonathan Roberts, 488–501. Oxford University Press, 2011.

Yadav, Sameer. "A Joban Theology of Consolation." *Harvard Theological Review* 117, no. 2 (2024): 181–203.

Žižek, Slavoj, and John Milbank. *The Monstrosity of Christ: Paradox or Dialectic?* Edited by Creston Davis. MIT Press, 2011.

Index of Passages

Index of Topics

Study Guide for Reading Groups and Individuals

By Jeremy Hall

Chapter 1

Have you encountered the book of Job before in your faith life or studies? What impressions or discomforts have stayed with you from that first reading?

How have you seen Job's story used by others, either to comfort or to explain suffering? What assumptions do people commonly bring to his character?

David frames Job as a fable rather than history. How does that shift your expectations for the book? Does it free you to read differently, or does it complicate things?

We meet Job as virtuous, devout, and upright, yet he is about to lose everything. How do you hold goodness and tragedy together in one story? What questions rise when virtue does not protect someone from disaster?

Chapter 2

How does exploring the identity of the adversary reshape or expand the way you read Job's story? What shifts when we consider who or what this figure might be?

How do you feel about the heavenly throne room scene? How does David's interpretation challenge or deepen your understanding of what unfolds in the divine council?

Where does this scene of divine deliberation fit within the larger question that haunts us: Why does God allow suffering? Does it answer anything, or does it complicate everything?

David suggests this scene dismantles "just world theology," the belief that good is rewarded and evil punished. What rises in you when you sit with that claim? How does it press against your assumptions about who God is and how God acts?

Chapter 3

What makes the sequence of Job's losses so overwhelming? Is it the speed, the totality, the particular order, or how personal each blow feels?

How does Job respond in the immediate aftermath? What does his response reveal about the theology he has carried quietly inside him? How have you heard others interpret his posture?

What rituals or traditions of grief have you seen among sufferers in your own community? What practices have struck you as especially meaningful?

David ends with a pop song reference about loss. Where have you seen pain turned into art, and what does that instinct reveal about the human spirit?

Chapter 4

Here Job says bluntly that God has caused his suffering. What are your thoughts about God's relationship to pain in the world? How have you wrestled with that tension in your own life?

David explores different readings of Job sitting in ashes or on a dung heap. Which interpretation resonates with you? Who are the people in your own city who sit on its margins, and what forces keep them there?

Where have you absorbed the idea that bodies are corrupt while souls are pure? How has that shaped your view of suffering, health, or embodiment?

How have churches or faith groups you've known talked about suffering? Where have they spoken truthfully, and where have they fallen short?

Chapter 5

What assumptions did you have about Job's wife before reading this chapter? How has tradition shaped her image for you?

The Septuagint gives her a voice; the Hebrew text does not. How does hearing her grief change the meaning of her words? Do you see her differently now?

Job's wife raises a difficult question: Is unquestioning piety truly integrity, or can it be denial of one's own moral sense? When have you felt torn between honesty and expected religious composure?

David suggests she may simply be further along in processing her trauma. What does it mean that embodied grief can reach truth before formal theology does?

Chapter 6

What strikes you most about the friends' initial response? What does their silence communicate before they ever speak?

David names how friendships built on shared theology can become conditional. Have you experienced relationships that depended on doctrinal agreement? What happened when that agreement changed?

When have you witnessed the healing power of silent presence? What makes silence sacred in some moments and painful in others?

David compares Job's silence to moments when speech feels like desecration. What does it mean that some suffering resists language?

Chapter 7

Job breaks his silence by cursing the day of his birth. Have you ever encountered suffering so deep that nonexistence seemed easier to imagine than endurance?

Job reverses the creation story, calling for darkness where God called for light. When has your experience felt like an argument against the goodness of existence?

Job doesn't speak to God directly here, yet his lament challenges the One who created him. What does it mean to critique God without addressing God? Is this avoidance, or a kind of sideways prayer?

David describes Job as a critic of Scripture within Scripture. How does this model give you permission to wrestle more honestly with your own faith?

Chapter 8

Job imagines kings, nobles, and the powerful ending in the same dust as everyone else. How does that picture speak to seasons of loss or endings in your own life?

Job sees in death a justice that life lacks. What does it say about the world that he finds equality only in the grave? How is this similar or different from your beliefs about the afterlife?

David notes that Job's suffering expands his moral vision. When has your own pain opened your eyes to the hurting in ways privilege never could?

Bonhoeffer says suffering, not happiness, is the key to understanding the world. How does that challenge or affirm your spiritual journey?

Job speaks into a void, asking questions he cannot yet aim anywhere. When have you lived in that space?

Chapter 9

Eliphaz remembers Job as a source of strength for others. Can you picture Job as that respected, stabilizing figure? How does that deepen the tragedy of his collapse?

Eliphaz gently rebukes Job for unraveling under suffering. When have you received "comfort" that felt like a subtle correction instead? When have you seen comforting words function more for the speaker's reassurance than for the sufferer's healing?

David writes that suffering shatters our certainties. When have your own certainties been challenged by your experience?

Eliphaz insists the innocent do not perish. What world is he living in? How does clinging to this belief protect him from reality?

Chapter 10

Why might Eliphaz rely on a supernatural visitation to strengthen his argument? What does this reveal about fear and authority? Where do you see similar appeals to outside authority in the world today?

What if the divine voice asked an honest question and Eliphaz missed it? When have people failed to see truth in front of them because their theology would not permit it?

How do you hold the tension between Job's blamelessness and the idea that no one is righteous? What is the difference between integrity and perfection?

David explores how suffering expands moral vision. When have loss or vulnerability revealed what you could not see before?

Chapter 11

Why does Eliphaz need just-world theology to be true? What happens if it collapses?

Eliphaz paints a comforting picture of God. Why might such beauty feel cold to someone in deep pain?

What does seeking God look like when old certainties no longer hold?

When have previously comforting truths become impossible for you to return to?

Chapter 12

Where have you encountered the belief that suffering is divine discipline? How did it shape the way you interpreted your own trials?

When has someone offered you theological "comfort" that only deepened the wound?

Eliphaz promises blessings already lost forever. Can promised restoration ever undo injustice? How do you sit with that tension?

When have you been asked to accept a theological consensus your experience could not support? How did you handle that tension?

Chapter 13

Job describes his suffering like poison in his bones. When has your own pain felt like something eating you from the inside?

Job does not speak to Eliphaz directly, as if the offered comfort is too shallow to answer. When have you felt isolated because others could not meet you where you were?

Many Christians are taught that protest is faithlessness. How were you taught to respond to suffering? When did you first challenge that teaching?

How does seeing biblical figures protest God reshape what faithful engagement can look like?

Chapter 14

Job says his friends see his suffering and are afraid. What are they afraid of losing? Their theology? Their security? Their sense of control? How does suffering in the world affect your sense of security?

When have you seen people cling to a belief not because it is true but because letting go feels too dangerous?

Job says he never asked his friends for anything but compassion, and they still failed him. When have you been hurt by the people who came to help?

Job claims friendship means loyalty even when belief falters. How does that challenge the way communities often practice relationship?

Chapter 15

Job begs for an explanation that would allow him to return to what he once believed. When have you prayed for that kind of clarity?

When have your difficult questions been dismissed as immaturity or rebellion?

Job asks his friends to look him in the eyes. When have people turned away from you and offered doctrine instead of presence?

David reflects on divine and human hiddenness. When have you felt abandoned by both God and community?

What does it mean to turn toward someone when their world is collapsing?

Chapter 16

Job describes time stretching and collapsing under the weight of grief. When has suffering distorted your experience of time?

Job twists beloved Scripture into accusation. How does this challenge your assumptions about how we can engage holy texts?

Job begs God to look away and his friends to look toward him. When has divine or religious attention felt like scrutiny instead of care?

When has human presence been more bearable than divine presence?

Chapter 17

Bildad claims Job's children died because they sinned. What kind of theology creates such cruelty? When do you see theological cruelty in the church today?

How do you navigate conflict between tradition and experience when both claim authority?

Have you been accused of abandoning right theology because your experience changed? Have you ever accused someone else?

Why do some communities fear honest questions more than devastating loss?

Chapter 18

Job imagines God as his legal opponent. What does it mean to picture God in the defendant's seat?

When have you experienced systems where power was absolute and beyond question?

What does it mean to stay in relationship with God through anger and protest? Is this allowed in your faith tradition?

Where have you seen theological frameworks used to justify unconstrained authority?

Chapter 19

Zophar tells Job he deserves worse than he has received. When have you heard suffering dismissed as less than deserved?

David notes how rigid systems react to honest questions with fear and disgust. When has your honesty threatened someone else's certainty?

Kierkegaard says there is no hiding place from trouble. What false securities have you held, and what happened when they collapsed? How has suffering reshaped your understanding of God or yourself?

When have theological explanations been used against you or someone you love?

Chapter 20

Have you been misrepresented, slandered, or dismissed in the name of God? Explain.

Job insists that divine standards of justice must apply even when God is the accused. What does that boldness stir in you? Does your faith background allow you to challenge God like this?

Job needs God to change, not just himself. Have you ever prayed that kind of prayer?

Job moves between accusation and longing. When have you felt that same tension of wanting God's face even as you fear what that encounter may reveal?

Chapter 21

Eliphaz accuses Job of undermining faith itself. When have your honest questions been treated as dangerous?

How have your tears or the tears of others changed what you can see? How has your worldview been challenged by human suffering?

How do you navigate tension between the needs of tradition and the needs of vulnerable people?

Chapter 22

Job says he would comfort his friends with kindness rather than judgment. When have you been on either side of that contrast? When have you shown unexpected kindness, what was the outcome?

Job describes pain that is not eased by speaking or silence. When have you felt trapped in that same tension?

Job's ruined body becomes evidence against him in a just-world system. When have people interpreted your suffering as guilt?

Where have you witnessed scapegoating in religious communities, and what makes it so powerful? How can we defuse the scapegoating instinct?

Chapter 23

Job appeals to a God he hopes is better than the God he has been taught. When have you longed for a God beyond the versions handed to you?

When have you experienced a community weaponizing its idea of God? How were people victimized by this theology?

When have you glimpsed a God of compassion that neither your accusations nor your community's doctrines could fully name?

When have you asked God to stand with you against the religious voices that claimed to speak for God? Did you find God in that space, or divine absence?

Chapter 24

Bildad fears that Job's questions could unravel the whole moral universe. When have your questions felt threatening to others?

When have you been pressured to recant, not because you were wrong, but because your truth was destabilizing?

How do you hold the need for moral order alongside the reality of innocent suffering?

When have you seen someone as guilty so others could preserve their worldview?

Chapter 25

When have others used suffering as proof that someone deserved it or lacked faith?

When has someone claimed authority over your spiritual life without your consent? How did you respond?

When have you lost social standing or communal respect? What did that fall teach you? Where have you seen this type of behavior in the church?

Job appeals to God as redeemer even while believing God harmed him. What does it mean to seek vindication from the One you accuse?

Chapter 26

When did you first notice that Scripture does not speak with one voice? How did that realization shape your faith?

Job says the wicked prosper and die in peace. Who are the people in our world who embody that reality? How have you made sense of it?

What does it mean when we cannot agree on who is righteous or wicked?

How do we form community in a world without shared moral vocabulary? What does that mean for the church?

Chapter 27

Eliphaz abandons coherence and aims to wound. When have arguments turned from truth-seeking to harm-seeking in your life?

When have contradictory accusations revealed someone's underlying fear or agenda?

When have you been accused of violating the very values you cherish most? How did you respond?

When have your questions been reframed as denial rather than wrestling?

Chapter 28

Job experiences God as hidden rather than absent. How do you understand that difference?

When have others pressured you to accept guilt you did not carry?

Job's suffering expands his awareness of the systemic oppression around him. How has your own pain opened your eyes to injustice? Whose suffering is invisible to your community?

When have you shifted from seeing poverty as personal failure to seeing it as manufactured?

Chapter 29

While Bildad and Job agree God is powerful, they disagree on what that power *means* for humanity. Have you ever been told that God's power removes God's—or our—obligation for justice or accountability?

Have you encountered a theology like Bildad's that erases moral distinctions by declaring everyone equally guilty—or that assumes some are righteous?

Job refuses to surrender his convictions or his sense of self, despite what others claim about him. How do you hold onto your integrity when others attempt to redefine you?

When have you held onto your integrity when pressured to say what was not true?

Chapter 30

There remains a question about the authorship of Job 28. Who do you think wrote this chapter? And what do you think they were trying to accomplish?

Name some things/people/experiences that you consider "beyond price." Have you ever thought of wisdom as among those precious things? Given its high value, why is it wisdom is rarely a part of religious instruction in most congregations?

Consider Carol Newsom's words about wisdom as "something that cannot be found because it is everywhere, a quest whose end is the same as its beginning. . . . Wisdom brings both profound peace and profound security. There is no one who does not yearn for that, and yet it seems so elusive." How can wisdom be both everywhere and yet so hard to find?

Chapter 31

Job remembers being honored and respected. When have you tasted that kind of approval, and what did it do to you?

Job's virtue was real, but privilege shaped it. Where has privilege shaped your own moral blind spots?

Job despises those who now despise him. What does this reveal about the limits of empathy in all of us? When has your empathy run dry? How did you deal with this experience?

How has wounded pride exposed things in you that comfort never revealed?

Chapter 32

Job's moral commitments assumed stability, power, and resources. How does your own moral framework depend on the same?

Job saw his servants as equals in God's sight yet kept them enslaved. Where have you noticed gaps between belief in equality and lived practice?

Job refused to curse his enemies. When has loving your enemies cost you something real?

Job demands God answer him. When have you demanded the same?

Chapter 33

Elihu bursts onto the scene with confidence and limited wisdom. When have you been that young and certain voice? What have you learned since?

Elihu frames suffering as divine teaching. When has this framing helped, and when has it wounded?

When have communities treated your questions as intolerable rather than honest?

When has "wait on God's timing" become more harmful than helpful?

Chapter 34

God responds from the whirlwind without addressing Job's questions. Which reading of God's speech resonates with you and why?

God delights in the wildness of creation. How does that reshape what you expect from a creator?

Is divine presence enough when explanations are withheld? What do you need from God in suffering?

When have you felt God sidestep your cries rather than meet them?

What does it cost to name dissatisfaction with God out loud? How would your faith community respond to such dissatisfaction?

Chapter 35

Does Job repent or resist in chapter 42? Which reading feels truer to your own faith experience, and what does that preference reveal?

Can you forgive God without reconciling with God?

What happens to faith when justice does not apply to God in the ways we expect?

Is Scripture's ambiguity here a burden or a gift? How do you live with a story that refuses to resolve?

Chapter 36

God says Job spoke rightly. What truth did Job speak that the friends did not?

Restoration gives Job new children, but David reminds us nothing replaces the ones he lost. How does this ending sit with you?

In the epilogue of Job, his daughters are named, and his household shows hints of change. What signs of moral growth do you see? What remains unresolved?

James Parker suggests God needs Job's protest to be redeemed. How does that idea reshape how you see the role of human honesty in faith?

Conclusion

David says Job teaches three lessons: protest as faith, moral courage in suffering, and empathy born of loss. Which speaks most to you?

When have you seen religious community choose certainty over compassion? What alternative does Job suggest?

Abraham Joshua Heschel calls us to reveal God's compassion when God seems hidden. How does that shift what faithfulness looks like in suffering?

Does God's refusal to answer Job's charges feel like admission, mystery, or something else? What do you make of that silence? How do you handle God's silence in your own life?

David ends by suggesting God gave moral commands and entrusted the world to us. Does that feel liberating or terrifying? What becomes possible when justice is in human hands?